International Experiences A Comprehensive Guide

Empowering Your Journey Aborad

Brandon Arroues, M.Ed.

Brilliant Consulting

Dedication

This book is dedicated to the courageous and adventurous individuals who dare to step out of their comfort zones to explore the world and our global communities. Your journeys inspire and pave the way for future explorers.

This comprehensive guide is designed to help internationals navigate the complexities of studying, working, and living abroad. Covering everything from preparation and planning to cultural adaptation and academic success, this book provides essential information, practical advice, and valuable insights to ensure a rewarding and enriching experience.

Contents

Contents

Acknowledgements

Acknowledgements

Author's Note

Thank you to all the international students and educational professionals who shared their experiences and insights, making this guide a valuable resource for future generations of embarking on their own global adventures. Drawing on my own diverse global experiences, and the thought-provoking wisdom shared by others, I began the arduous task of writing this comprehensive guide. I hope it may encourage, support, and guide you through your amazing journey as you prepare to embark on your next international adventure.

Forward

Forward

Forward

Welcome Message

Welcome to **International Experiences: A Comprehensive Guide**! We are thrilled to have you join the global community of learners, explorers, and cultural ambassadors. Embarking on an international program is a remarkable adventure, filled with opportunities for personal growth, academic achievement, and cross-cultural understanding. This guide is crafted to be your trusted companion throughout this journey, offering you the essential information, practical tips, and supportive advice you need to make the most of your experience.

Imagine stepping into a new world, where every day brings fresh discoveries, new friendships, and profound learning moments. As an international student, you have the unique chance to immerse yourself in a different culture, gain valuable academic experience, and build lifelong connections. This guide aims to make your transition smoother, your experiences richer, and your journey more rewarding.

How to Use This Guide

Navigating through an international experience can be both exciting and overwhelming. This guide is designed to provide a structured yet flexible roadmap to help you at every stage of your journey. Here is how you can make the most of it:

- **Structured Navigation**: The guide is divided into chapters that align with the various phases of your international journey—from preparation to cultural integration, academic life, and returning home. Whether you are just starting or already in your host country, you can find relevant information tailored to your current needs.
- **Actionable Insights**: Each chapter is packed with practical advice, real-life anecdotes from former international students, and expert insights to help you navigate common challenges and make informed decisions. Look for highlighted tips, checklists, and step-by-step guides, such as Carlos's story:

Anecdotes and Insights
Navigating Transportation in Italy- Carlos's Story

Student Perspective: Carlos, a student from Mexico, was studying architecture in Rome, Italy. While he loved the historical architecture and vibrant street life, he found navigating the public transportation system to be quite challenging.

"The first few weeks in Rome were chaotic. The bus schedules were confusing, and I often found myself getting lost. One day, I missed an important class because I couldn't figure out the tram route. I felt frustrated and stressed. However, after talking to some local students and using a few travel apps, I started to get the hang of it. They showed me how to use the city's transportation efficiently and gave me tips on the best routes to take."

Expert Insight: Carlos's experience underscores the importance of mastering local transportation early in your stay. Efficient navigation of public transport can significantly reduce stress and improve your overall experience. Leveraging technology and seeking advice from locals are effective strategies for overcoming initial challenges.

Actionable Tip: Familiarize yourself with the public transportation system as soon as possible. Use travel apps to help navigate routes and schedules. Do not hesitate to ask local students or residents for tips on the best ways to get around. Practicing your routes and using real-time updates can make your daily commute smoother and more predictable.

- Bookmarking and Highlights: Consider bookmarking key sections that you find particularly useful. Highlight tips and create a personalized checklist of important tasks to ensure you do not miss any critical steps.
- Interactive Engagement: Engage with the reflective exercises and questions at the end of each chapter. These activities are designed to help you internalize the content, apply it to your personal situation, and deepen your learning experience.
- Community Connection: Connect with fellow international students through recommended online forums, social media groups, and alumni networks. Sharing experiences and advice with peers can provide additional support and enhance your journey.

Purpose and Goals

The primary goal of this guide is to empower you with the knowledge and tools needed to have a successful and enriching international experience. Here is what you can expect to achieve with this guide:

1. **Thorough Preparation**: From understanding the intricacies of the application process to packing essentials, we provide comprehensive steps to ensure you are well-prepared for your departure. Our aim is to alleviate the stress of preparation and instill confidence as you embark on this new adventure.

2. **Smooth Transitions**: Adjusting to a new country, culture, and academic system can be challenging. This guide offers strategies to help you adapt smoothly and thrive in your new environment, ensuring you make the most of your time abroad.

3. **Academic and Personal Growth**: We emphasize the importance of maximizing your academic opportunities and personal development. This guide encourages you to set achievable goals, embrace new learning experiences, and reflect on your progress throughout your journey.

4. **Cultural Understanding**: By providing insights into cultural differences and offering tips for effective communication, we aim to help you build meaningful connections and appreciate the diversity of your host country. This section is designed to foster empathy and intercultural competence.

5. **Well-being Support**: Your health and safety are paramount. This guide includes comprehensive advice on maintaining your physical and mental well-being, managing homesickness, and accessing support services. We prioritize your holistic well-being, ensuring you feel supported every step of the way.

6. **Preparation for Re-entry**: Returning home can be as challenging as adjusting to a new country. We offer guidance on dealing with reverse culture shock, reintegrating into your home culture, and leveraging your international experience for future academic and career opportunities.

Importance of This Guide

The experiences and challenges faced by international students are unique and multifaceted. This guide was created with the understanding that each student's journey is personal and diverse. By combining practical advice with real-world insights, we aim to provide a resource that is not only informative but also empathetic and encouraging. Here is why this guide is indispensable:

- **Empowerment**: We believe in empowering you to take charge of your international experience. This guide provides you with the tools, knowledge, and confidence to navigate every aspect of your journey.
- **Holistic Approach**: Our approach is holistic, addressing not just the logistical aspects of your international journey but also your emotional, social, and academic well-being. We aim to support you in every dimension of your experience.
- **Community and Connection**: This guide fosters a sense of community and connection among international students. By sharing stories, tips, and resources, we create a network of support that extends beyond borders.
- **Inspiration and Encouragement**: We aim to inspire and encourage you to embrace the transformative potential of your international experience. This guide is filled with motivational insights and stories that highlight the incredible opportunities that await you.

We wish you an incredible journey filled with learning, growth, and unforgettable memories. Welcome to the global community of international students, and may this guide serve you well along your path. Let the adventure begin!

{ 1 }

Preparing for Your Journey

Embarking on an international program is a thrilling adventure filled with the promise of new experiences, academic enrichment, and personal growth. However, the journey begins long before you step onto the plane. Proper preparation is crucial to ensure a smooth transition and a successful international experience. This chapter is designed to guide you through the essential steps of preparing for your journey, from understanding the different types of international programs and navigating the application process to managing your finances and obtaining the necessary visas.

Preparing for an international program is like setting the foundation for a building. Each step you take now will support your experiences abroad, helping you to avoid common pitfalls and maximize the opportunities that lie ahead. This chapter aims to equip you with practical advice, detailed insights, and actionable steps to ensure you are well-prepared for the exciting journey ahead.

1.1 Understanding the International Program

The first step in preparing for your journey is to understand the different types of international programs available and what each entail. Whether you are participating in an academic exchange, a cultural immersion program, or a work exchange, each type offers unique benefits and challenges.

Academic Programs: These programs are typically organized between universities and involve studying at a partner institution for a semester or an academic year. They provide a structured environment for academic growth and often include credit transfer agreements that ensure your studies abroad contribute to your degree.

Cultural Exchange Programs: Focused on cultural immersion, these programs may include homestays, language learning, and cultural activities. They are designed to provide a deep understanding of the host culture and are ideal for those looking to enhance their cultural competence and language skills.

Work Exchange Programs: These involve internships or work placements abroad, offering hands-on experience in a professional setting. Work exchange programs are perfect for gaining international work experience and building a global network of professional contacts.

Understanding the specific requirements, benefits, and challenges of your chosen program will help you set realistic expectations and prepare effectively.

1.2 Application Process

Once you have chosen the right international program, the next step is navigating the application process. This can be a daunting task but breaking it down into manageable steps can make it more approachable.

Step-by-Step Guide to Applying for an International Program:

1. **Research Programs**: Identify international programs that align with your academic and personal goals. Pay attention to eligibility criteria, application deadlines, and program details.
2. **Meet with Advisors**: Schedule meetings with academic advisors and study abroad coordinators to discuss your options and receive guidance on the application process.
3. **Prepare Required Documents**:
   a. **Transcripts**: Obtain official transcripts from your home institution. These documents showcase your academic history and performance.
   b. **Letters of Recommendation**: Request letters of recommendation from professors or mentors who know you well and can speak to your strengths, character, and suitability for the program. Give them ample time and provide any necessary background information to help them write a comprehensive letter.
   c. **Statement of Purpose**: Write a compelling statement of purpose that clearly articulates your motivations for participating in the international program, your academic and personal goals, and how the program aligns with your future aspirations. Be specific about why you chose this particular program and what you hope to gain from the experience.
   d. **Language Proficiency Test Scores**: If required, take a language proficiency test (e.g., TOEFL, IELTS) and include your scores in your application. Ensure you meet the minimum score requirements of the host institution.
   e. **Passport Copy**: Provide a copy of your passport. Ensure your passport is valid for at least six months beyond the end of your planned stay.

European Union: Schengen Student Visa

- **Purpose**: The Schengen student visa allows students to study in any of the 26 Schengen Area countries for up to 90 days within a 180-day period. For longer stays, a national visa from the specific country is required.
- **Requirements**: Students must have an acceptance letter from a recognized educational institution, proof of sufficient financial means, and valid health insurance covering at least €30,000 in medical expenses.
- **Application Process**:
  - Determine which consulate to apply to based on your main destination.
  - Complete the visa application form specific to the country.
  - Schedule an appointment at the consulate or visa application center.
  - Submit required documents, including proof of accommodation, travel itinerary, and financial means.
  - Attend a visa interview if necessary.

Australia: Student Visa (Subclass 500)

- **Purpose**: The Student Visa (Subclass 500) allows international students to study full-time at an accredited educational institution in Australia.
- **Requirements**: Applicants need a Confirmation of Enrolment (CoE) from their host institution, proof of English language proficiency, evidence of sufficient funds to cover tuition and living expenses, and health insurance under the Overseas Student Health Cover (OSHC) scheme.
- **Application Process**:
  - Obtain a CoE from your host institution.
  - Create an account and apply online through the ImmiAccount portal.
  - Pay the visa application fee.
  - Provide required documentation and undergo a health examination if requested.
  - Submit biometrics and attend an interview if necessary.

Canada: Study Permit

- **Purpose**: The Canadian study permit is for students enrolled in designated learning institutions (DLIs) in Canada for courses longer than six months.
- **Requirements**: Applicants need a letter of acceptance from a DLI, proof of sufficient funds to cover tuition and living expenses, and a police certificate if required. Some may also need to provide a medical exam result.
- **Application Process**:
  - Apply online or on paper and pay the application fee.

- Provide a letter of acceptance from a DLI.
- Submit proof of financial support and other required documents.
- Provide biometrics and attend an interview if necessary.

China: X1 and X2 Visas

- **Purpose**: China offers two types of student visas: the X1 visa for students studying in China for more than six months, and the X2 visa for short-term studies (less than six months).
- **Requirements**: Applicants must have an admission letter from a Chinese educational institution and a completed JW201 or JW202 form issued by the Chinese Ministry of Education.
- **Application Process**:
  - Obtain an admission letter and a JW201 or JW202 form from your host institution.
  - Complete the visa application form and gather required documents, including passport-sized photos and proof of financial means.
  - Submit your application at the nearest Chinese embassy or consulate.
  - Attend an interview if requested and undergo a medical examination if required.
  - Upon arrival in China, X1 visa holders must apply for a residence permit within 30 days.

Japan: Student Visa

- **Purpose**: The student visa for Japan is intended for students enrolled in Japanese educational institutions, including universities, junior colleges, professional training colleges, and Japanese language schools.
- **Requirements**: Applicants need a Certificate of Eligibility (CoE) issued by the Japanese Ministry of Justice and an acceptance letter from their host institution.
- **Application Process**:
  - Obtain a CoE from your host institution.
  - Submit the visa application form, along with the CoE and other required documents, to the nearest Japanese embassy or consulate.
  - Provide a valid passport, recent photographs, and proof of financial means.
  - Attend an interview if required.
  - Once in Japan, register your address at the local municipal office and obtain a residence card.

South Korea: D-2 Student Visa

- **Purpose**: The D-2 student visa is for students enrolled in regular education programs at universities, graduate schools, and colleges in South Korea.

- **Requirements**: Applicants need an admission letter from a South Korean educational institution, proof of financial means, and a completed visa application form.
- **Application Process**:
  - Obtain an admission letter from your host institution.
  - Complete the visa application form and gather necessary documents, including passport-sized photos and proof of financial means.
  - Submit your application at the nearest South Korean embassy or consulate.
  - Provide additional documents if requested, such as a medical report or police clearance certificate.
  - Upon arrival in South Korea, register at the local immigration office to obtain an Alien Registration Card (ARC).

By understanding the specific visa types and their requirements, you can ensure a smooth application process and avoid potential delays. Each country has its own set of rules and procedures, so it is essential to stay informed and follow the guidelines closely. Preparing thoroughly for the visa application process will not only help you secure your visa but also give you peace of mind as you embark on your international exchange journey.

1.3 Common Visa Requirements and Application Procedures

Despite the differences among visa types and countries, there are common requirements and procedures that most student visa applications will involve. Understanding these can help you prepare effectively for your visa application process.

Common Visa Requirements:

1. **Acceptance Letter**:
   - **Purpose**: This letter confirms that you have been accepted into an educational institution in the host country.
   - **Documentation**: Ensure you have an official acceptance letter from your host institution. This document is crucial for all visa types.
2. **Proof of Financial Support**:
   - **Purpose**: To demonstrate that you have sufficient funds to cover tuition fees, living expenses, and other costs during your stay.
   - **Documentation**: This may include bank statements, scholarship award letters, sponsor letters, or financial affidavits.
3. **Valid Passport**:
   - **Purpose**: Your passport must be valid for at least six months beyond your intended stay.

■ **Documentation**: Ensure your passport is up-to-date and has enough blank pages for visa stamps.

4. **Health Insurance**:
   - ■ **Purpose**: Proof of health insurance ensures that you have coverage for medical expenses while abroad.
   - ■ **Documentation**: Provide insurance documents that meet the host country's requirements. Some countries, like the UK, require an Immigration Health Surcharge (IHS).

5. **Language Proficiency**:
   - ■ **Purpose**: To demonstrate your ability to understand and participate in academic programs conducted in the host country's language.
   - ■ **Documentation**: This may include test scores from standardized language proficiency tests like TOEFL, IELTS, or others specified by the host country.

6. **Tuberculosis Test (if applicable)**:
   - ■ **Purpose**: Required by some countries to ensure you do not have active TB.
   - ■ **Documentation**: Test results from an approved clinic, if required by your host country

Application Procedures:

1. **Complete the Visa Application Form**:
   - ■ **Process**: Most countries require you to complete an online or paper visa application form. Ensure all information is accurate and matches your supporting documents.
   - ■ **Example**: The DS-160 for the US, the online application for the UK, or the Schengen visa form for EU countries.

2. **Pay the Visa Application Fee**:
   - ■ **Process**: Pay the required fee as specified by the host country. Keep the receipt as proof of payment.
   - ■ **Example**: SEVIS fee for the US, application fee for the UK Tier 4 visa.

3. **Schedule and Attend a Visa Interview (if required)**:
   - ■ **Process**: Schedule an interview at the embassy or consulate. Be prepared to discuss your study plans, financial situation, and ties to your home country.
   - ■ **Example**: US F-1 visa interviews are mandatory, whereas some countries like Australia may only require an interview in certain cases.

4. **Submit Biometrics and Other Supporting Documents**:
   - ■ **Process**: Provide fingerprints and a photograph as part of your application. Submit all required documents, including financial proof, health insurance, and test results.
   - ■ **Example**: Biometric appointments for the UK, Canada, and Australia.

5. **Receive Visa Decision and Prepare for Travel**:
   - **Process**: After submitting your application and attending any required interviews, wait for the decision. Once approved, you will receive your visa, which allows you to travel to the host country.
   - **Example**: Collect your passport with the visa stamp from the embassy or consulate.

Tips for Preparing for Visa Interviews

Preparing for a visa interview can be nerve-wracking, but with the right preparation, you can approach it with confidence. Here are some tips to help you succeed:

Understand the Purpose of the Interview:

- **Goal**: The interview is to assess your genuine intent to study, financial stability, and likelihood to return to your home country after your studies.
- **Mindset**: Approach the interview with honesty and clarity about your intentions.

Gather All Required Documents:

- **Checklist**: Ensure you have all necessary documents, including your acceptance letter, financial proof, passport, health insurance, and any additional forms.
- **Organization**: Arrange your documents in a logical order for easy access during the interview.

Prepare for Common Questions:

- **Study Plans**: Be ready to explain why you chose the specific program and institution, and how it fits into your academic and career goals.
- **Financial Stability**: Demonstrate your ability to cover tuition and living expenses without relying on illegal work.
- **Ties to Home Country**: Provide evidence of your intention to return home after completing your studies, such as family connections, job offers, or property ownership.

Practice Your Responses:

- **Mock Interviews**: Conduct mock interviews with friends, family, or mentors to practice answering questions confidently and concisely.
- **Clarity and Honesty**: Focus on clear, honest answers. Avoid memorizing responses word-for-word; instead, understand the key points you need to convey.

Dress Professionally:

- **Appearance**: Dress appropriately for the interview, as first impressions matter. Business casual or formal attire is typically recommended.

Be Punctual:

- **Timing**: Arrive at the embassy or consulate early to account for security checks and potential delays.
- **Calmness**: Being on time helps you stay calm and composed, reducing last-minute stress.

Stay Calm and Confident:

- **Attitude**: Approach the interview with confidence. Maintain eye contact, speak clearly, and be polite and respectful to the consular officer.
- **Positivity**: Focus on the positive aspects of your application and be ready to address any concerns the officer may have.

Follow Up If Necessary:

- **Post-Interview**: If the consular officer requests additional documentation, provide it promptly. Follow any instructions given to ensure your application is processed smoothly.

By following these tips and thoroughly preparing for your visa interview, you can increase your chances of a successful outcome. Remember, the key is to demonstrate your genuine intent to study, your preparedness for the financial and academic challenges, and your plans for after your studies.

Anecdotes and Expert Insights

Navigating the Visa Maze- Emily's Story

Student Perspective: "When I first decided to study abroad in the UK, I was overwhelmed by the visa application process. I remember spending hours on the internet trying to figure out the requirements for the Tier 4 (General) student visa. There were so many forms to fill out and documents to gather. I had to get a Confirmation of Acceptance for Studies (CAS) from my host university, prove my financial stability, and pay the Immigration Health Surcharge (IHS).

It was daunting, but I made a checklist and tackled each step one by one. Finally, after a few nerve-wracking weeks, I attended my biometric appointment and submitted my application. The day I received my visa was a huge relief and made all the hard work worth it!" – Emily, UK International Student

Expert Insight: The visa application process can indeed be complex but breaking it down into manageable steps can help. Start by thoroughly researching the specific visa requirements for your host country. Create a detailed checklist, including all necessary documents and deadlines. Reach out to your host institution's international office for guidance, as they can provide valuable assistance and ensure you have everything in order. Remember, starting early is key to avoiding last-minute stress.

1.4 Financial Planning

Proper financial planning is essential to ensure you can support yourself during your international experience without unnecessary stress. This involves budgeting for various expenses, exploring potential sources of financial aid, and managing your finances effectively while abroad. A well-thought-out financial plan can make the difference between a smooth, enjoyable experience and one fraught with financial difficulties.

Budgeting for Your International Experience

Creating a detailed budget is the first step in financial planning for your international journey. Understanding the costs involved and planning accordingly will help you manage your finances effectively.

Estimated Costs:

- **Tuition Fees**: Research the tuition fees of your host institution. Some programs may have different fee structures for international students. Additionally, consider any administrative fees or special course fees that may apply.
- **Accommodation**: Consider the cost of living in your host country. Housing options can vary widely, from dormitories and student residences to private apartments and homestays. Do not forget to include utility costs such as electricity, water, and internet.
- **Travel Expenses**: Include the cost of airfare, local transportation, and potential travel within the host country. Consider additional expenses for trips back home if you plan to visit. Also, factor in the cost of travel insurance, which can protect you against cancellations and other unforeseen travel issues.

- **Food and Groceries**: Estimate your monthly food expenses based on local costs and your eating habits. Cooking at home is often cheaper than dining out. Explore local markets and discount stores to stretch your budget further.
- **Health Insurance**: Ensure you have adequate health insurance coverage. Some countries require specific plans, while others may accept international student insurance. Investigate what is covered under your insurance, including dental and vision care, if necessary.
- **Personal Expenses**: Budget for personal items, entertainment, clothing, and any other discretionary spending. Include costs for communication, such as a local SIM card or phone plan. Additionally, consider costs for social activities, cultural events, and excursions that will enhance your experience abroad.

Budgeting Tools:

- **Spreadsheets**: Use spreadsheets to track your income and expenses. This can help you visualize your financial situation and adjust as needed. Create separate categories for different types of expenses to see where your money is going.
- **Budgeting Apps**: Consider using budgeting apps like Mint, YNAB (You Need a Budget), or PocketGuard to manage your finances on the go. These apps can help you track expenses, set savings goals, and receive alerts for overspending. Look for apps that offer currency conversion features if you are dealing with multiple currencies.

Emergency Fund:

- **Purpose**: Set aside an emergency fund to cover unexpected expenses, such as medical emergencies, travel disruptions, or unforeseen costs. This fund can provide a safety net and peace of mind while you are abroad.
- **Amount**: Aim to save at least one to three months' worth of living expenses. Keep this fund in an easily accessible account. Consider opening a savings account specifically for this purpose to avoid dipping into it for non-emergencies.

Sources of Financial Aid

Securing financial aid can significantly ease the burden of expenses during your international program. Explore various options to find the best support available.

Scholarships:

- **Exchange Program Scholarships**: Many exchange programs offer scholarships to support international students. Research and apply for these opportunities early. Keep track of application deadlines and required documents.

- **Government Scholarships**: Check if your home country or host country government offers scholarships for international students. Examples include the Fulbright Program (USA), Erasmus+ (EU), and Chevening Scholarships (UK). These scholarships often have specific eligibility criteria and application processes, so start your research early.
- **Institutional Scholarships**: Many universities provide scholarships for international students. Contact your host institution's financial aid office for information on available grants and scholarships. Look for scholarships specific to your field of study or background.

Financial Aid:

- **Home Institution Aid**: Check if your home institution offers financial aid for studying abroad. This can include grants, loans, or work-study opportunities. Speak with your financial aid office to understand the options and how they can be applied to your international program.
- **Private Grants and Loans**: Research private organizations, foundations, and companies that offer grants and loans to international students. Ensure you understand the terms and conditions before accepting any financial aid. Some organizations might offer specific grants for particular regions or fields of study.

Part-Time Work:

- **Work Regulations**: Explore opportunities for part-time work in your host country. Be sure to check visa regulations and work restrictions for international students. Some countries have strict limitations on the number of hours you can work.
- **On-Campus Jobs**: Many universities offer part-time jobs on campus, such as library assistants, research assistants, or administrative support roles. These jobs often provide flexible hours and are more accommodating to students' schedules.
- **Internships**: Look for paid internships related to your field of study. Internships can provide valuable work experience while helping to cover expenses. Check if your visa allows for internships and if your university has a career services office that can help you find opportunities.

Managing Finances While Abroad

Effective financial management while abroad ensures that you stay within your budget and avoid financial stress.

Bank Accounts:

- **Local Bank Account**: Consider opening a local bank account in your host country for easier access to funds and to avoid international transaction fees. Look for student-friendly accounts with low fees and good online banking options. Some banks may offer special accounts for international students with additional benefits.

- **International Accounts**: If you prefer to keep your home country bank account, ensure it supports international transactions and offers competitive exchange rates. Check for any international transaction fees and consider using a credit card with no foreign transaction fees.

Currency Exchange:

- **Exchange Rates**: Stay informed about exchange rates and the best methods for exchanging currency. Use reputable exchange services to get the best rates. Be aware of the rates offered by airports, which often have less favorable rates.
- **Multi-Currency Accounts**: Some banks offer multi-currency accounts that allow you to hold and manage multiple currencies, which can be beneficial if you travel frequently within the region. These accounts can help you avoid exchange rate fluctuations.

Spending Wisely:

- **Tracking Expenses**: Regularly track your spending to ensure you are staying within your budget. Adjust your spending habits as necessary to avoid overspending. Review your budget monthly to see if any adjustments are needed.
- **Student Discounts**: Take advantage of student discounts on transportation, food, entertainment, and other services. Carry your student ID with you to access these discounts. Many cities have student discount cards that offer significant savings on everyday expenses.
- **Affordable Options**: Look for affordable dining options, such as cooking at home, buying groceries from local markets, and eating at student cafeterias. Explore free or low-cost entertainment options, such as local festivals, student events, and cultural sites. Join social media groups or student networks to find tips on saving money in your host country.

Saving on Travel:

- **Advance Booking**: Book flights and train tickets in advance to secure the best prices. Use fare comparison websites to find deals. Consider budget airlines and off-peak travel times to save money.
- **Public Transportation**: Use public transportation instead of taxis or ride-sharing services. Many cities offer student passes or discounts on public transit. Familiarize yourself with the local transportation system and routes to make the most of it.
- **Travel Insurance**: Purchase travel insurance to cover unexpected travel-related expenses, such as trip cancellations, lost luggage, or medical emergencies. Travel insurance can provide peace of mind and financial protection during your travels.

By carefully planning your finances, securing financial aid, and managing your money effectively while abroad, you can focus on enjoying your international experience without the added stress of financial worries. Remember, financial stability is key to making the most of your time abroad and ensuring a successful and enriching experience. With the right preparation and mindful management, you can create unforgettable memories and achieve your academic and personal goals without financial strain.

Anecdotes and Expert Insights
The Importance of Financial Planning- Luis' Story

Student Perspective: "One of the biggest challenges I faced before my exchange in Canada was financial planning. I underestimated the cost of living in a big city like Toronto. Thankfully, I attended a pre-departure workshop at my home university, where they emphasized creating a detailed budget. I listed all potential expenses, including tuition, rent, food, transportation, and entertainment. I also looked into scholarships and part-time job opportunities. By the time I left, I had a solid financial plan and even set up an emergency fund. This preparation allowed me to enjoy my exchange without constantly worrying about money." – Luis, Canadian International Student

Expert Insight: Thorough financial planning is essential for a successful international experience. Start by creating a detailed budget that includes all potential expenses. Research the cost of living in your host city and factor in tuition, rent, food, transportation, and personal spending. Look into scholarships, grants, and part-time job opportunities to supplement your income. Setting up an emergency fund is also crucial to cover unexpected expenses. Regularly review and adjust your budget to stay on track and ensure financial peace of mind throughout your international program.

Chapter 1 Review

As you complete Chapter 1: Preparing for Your Journey, take a moment to review and reflect on the key points covered. This chapter has provided you with essential information and strategies to effectively plan for your international program. Ensure you have a solid understanding of the following areas before moving on to the next chapter.

Key Points

- **Travel Arrangements**: Importance of booking flights early, using fare comparison tools, and checking for student discounts.

- **Visa and Immigration**: Steps to research, apply for, and secure the appropriate visa for your host country.
- **Financial Planning**: Creating a detailed budget, identifying funding sources, and setting up an emergency fund.
- **Packing**: Tips for packing light, focusing on essentials, and understanding baggage policies.
- **Airport and Customs Procedures**: Navigating check-in, security, customs forms, and inspections smoothly.

Review Questions

1. **Travel Arrangements**:
   - What are the benefits of booking your flight early and using fare comparison websites?
   - How can being flexible with travel dates reduce your flight costs?
2. **Visa and Immigration**:
   - List three key documents required for most student visa applications.
   - Why is it important to start the visa application process early?
3. **Financial Planning**:
   - What are the main components of a comprehensive budget for your international program?
   - Identify two potential sources of financial aid for international students.
4. **Packing**:
   - What is the "pack half" strategy and how can it help with packing for your international journey?
   - Why is it important to understand your airline's baggage policies?
5. **Airport and Customs Procedures**:
   - Describe the 3-1-1 rule for carrying liquids through airport security.
   - What are some common questions you might be asked during a customs inspection?

Invitation to Reflective Exercises

Congratulations on completing Chapter 1! To further solidify your understanding and prepare for your journey, we invite you to explore the companion workbook, "Reflective Exercises: The International Experiences Guide Workbook." This resource provides engaging activities and thought-provoking questions designed to help you internalize the material, apply it to your personal situation, and deepen your learning experience. Dive into the workbook to enhance your preparation and set the stage for a successful and enriching international experience.

{ 2 }

Preparing for Departure

Embarking on an international program is an exhilarating journey that starts long before you step onto the plane. Preparing for departure involves meticulous planning, organization, and a dash of excitement as you ready yourself for new adventures and experiences. This chapter will guide you through the essential steps to ensure you are fully prepared for your journey abroad. From navigating the application process and understanding visa requirements to managing travel arrangements and health considerations, this section provides all the tools you need to embark on your international experience with confidence and ease. As you read through, you will find practical tips, valuable insights, and detailed checklists designed to make your transition as smooth and stress-free as possible. Whether you are a seasoned traveler or venturing out for the first time, this chapter will help you lay a solid foundation for a successful and enriching international experience.

2.1 Travel Arrangements

Planning your travel arrangements is a crucial step in preparing for your international journey. From booking flights to understanding travel logistics, meticulous preparation can make your journey smoother and more enjoyable. Here is how to navigate the complexities of travel planning with confidence and ease.

Booking Flights and Understanding Travel Logistics

Flight Booking

Timing:

Book Early: Securing your flights well in advance can significantly reduce costs and increase your options. Airlines typically release tickets up to a year before departure and booking early often means better deals and more availability.

Fare Comparison: Use fare comparison websites like Skyscanner, Kayak, or Google Flights to explore different options and find the best prices. These tools allow you to compare multiple airlines and routes, ensuring you get the best value for your money. Set up fare alerts to monitor price changes and snag the best deals.

Flexibility:

Flexible Dates: If your schedule allows, being flexible with your travel dates can lead to substantial savings. Midweek flights, especially on Tuesdays and Wednesdays, are often cheaper than weekend flights. Additionally, traveling during off-peak seasons can result in lower airfare and fewer crowds.

Flexible Airports: Consider flying into or out of alternative airports. Sometimes smaller or secondary airports offer lower fares and can be more convenient than major hubs. Check the availability of transport options from these airports to your final destination.

Student Discounts:

Special Rates: Many airlines offer discounted rates for students. Check if they have partnerships with student travel agencies like STA Travel or StudentUniverse, which specialize in providing affordable travel options for students. These agencies can also offer valuable travel advice and support.

Verification: Be prepared to provide proof of your student status, such as a student ID or an enrollment verification letter, to access these discounts. Some airlines may also offer discounts through student organizations or university partnerships.

Direct vs. Connecting Flights:

Direct Flights: While often more expensive, direct flights save time and reduce the hassle of layovers and potential delays. They are a good option if you have a tight schedule or prefer a more straightforward travel experience. Direct flights can also reduce the stress of navigating unfamiliar airports during layovers.

Connecting Flights: These can be significantly cheaper and offer the opportunity to visit another city during your layover. However, they can also extend your travel time and increase the risk of missed connections. When booking connecting flights, ensure you have sufficient layover time to clear customs and security checks, especially if changing airlines or airports.

Baggage Policies:

Review Policies: Each airline has different policies regarding baggage allowances and fees. Ensure you understand these policies to avoid unexpected charges at the airport. Check both the weight and size limits for checked and carry-on luggage.

Weight Limits: Familiarize yourself with the weight and size limits for both checked and carry-on luggage. Overweight or oversized bags can incur hefty fees. Consider using a luggage scale to weigh your bags before heading to the airport.

Luggage

Packing Essentials:

Carry-On: Pack a carry-on with essential items such as important documents (passport, visa, boarding passes), a change of clothes, medications, and personal items like toiletries and electronics. This ensures you have necessities if your checked luggage is delayed or lost.

Important Documents: Keep copies of important documents in both physical and digital formats, stored separately from the originals, for added security. Consider using a secure digital storage service to access your documents anywhere.

Travel Light:

Minimal Packing: Pack only what you need and remember that many items can be purchased in your host country. Traveling light not only makes it easier to move around but also reduces the risk of excess baggage fees. Use packing cubes or compression bags to organize and maximize your luggage space.

Versatile Clothing: Choose clothing that can be mixed and matched. Consider the climate of your destination to avoid overpacking. Pack layers that can be adjusted to different weather conditions.

Luggage Tags:

Clear Labeling: Clearly label all your bags with your contact information, including your name, phone number, and destination address. This helps ensure your luggage can be returned to you if it gets lost.

Distinctive Markings: Add distinctive markings, such as colorful ribbons or stickers, to your luggage to make it easily identifiable on the baggage carousel. This can also deter theft by making your bags more recognizable.

Security:

TSA-Approved Locks: Use TSA-approved locks on your luggage to keep your belongings secure. These locks can be opened by airport security without damaging them.

Valuables: Keep valuable items such as electronics, jewelry, and important documents in your carry-on rather than checked luggage to reduce the risk of loss or theft. Consider investing in anti-theft bags or pouches for added security.

Packing Tips and Essential Items to Bring

Packing for an international program can be both exciting and daunting. Ensuring you have everything you need while avoiding overpacking is key to a smooth transition. Here are comprehensive tips and a checklist of essential items to bring to help you prepare effectively for your journey.

Documentation

Having all necessary documents in order is crucial for a hassle-free experience. Ensure these items are easily accessible yet secure.

- **Passport and Visa**: Your passport should be valid for at least six months beyond your planned stay. Ensure your visa is approved and valid.
- **Acceptance Letter from the Host Institution**: This document is often required at immigration checkpoints and can be useful in other administrative processes.
- **Health Insurance Documents**: Proof of health insurance coverage is essential for accessing medical services in your host country.
- **Emergency Contact Information**: Keep a list of emergency contacts, including family, friends, and local contacts in your host country.
- **Copies of Important Documents**: Make photocopies of your passport, visa, insurance documents, and acceptance letter. Store these copies separately from the originals.
- **Prescriptions with a Doctor's Letter**: If you take prescription medication, bring enough for your entire stay along with a letter from your doctor explaining your medical needs.

Clothing

Packing suitable clothing is essential for comfort and cultural adaptation.

- **Climate-Appropriate Clothing**: Research the climate of your host country and pack accordingly. Layering is useful for varying weather conditions.
- **Versatile Items**: Include clothing that can be mixed and matched to create different outfits, saving space in your luggage.

- **Cultural Norms and Dress Codes**: Respect the cultural norms and dress codes of your host country. This may include more conservative attire or specific clothing for certain settings.
- **Comfortable Shoes**: Pack at least one pair of comfortable walking shoes. You will likely be exploring a lot on foot.

Electronics

Staying connected and equipped for your studies requires the right electronics.

- **Laptop and Charger**: Essential for academic work and staying connected with friends and family.
- **Mobile Phone and Charger**: Ensure your phone is unlocked if you plan to use a local SIM card.
- **Plug Adapters and Voltage Converters**: Electrical outlets and voltage can vary by country. Bring the appropriate adapters and converters for your electronics.
- **Headphones**: Useful for travel, studying, and entertainment.
- **Portable Power Bank**: Handy for keeping your devices charged on the go.

Health and Hygiene

Maintaining your health and hygiene will help you stay comfortable and well.

- **Prescription Medications**: Bring enough for the duration of your stay, as well as a copy of your prescription.
- **Basic First-Aid Kit**: Include band-aids, antiseptic wipes, pain relievers, and any other basic medical supplies.
- **Toiletries**: Pack travel-sized shampoo, conditioner, soap, toothbrush, toothpaste, and other personal care items. These can be replenished locally if needed.
- **Sunscreen and Insect Repellent**: Especially important if you are traveling to a sunny or tropical location.

Personal Items

Bringing a few personal items can make your new place feel more like home and help with any homesickness.

- **Photos or Small Mementos**: Items from home can provide comfort and a sense of familiarity.
- **Small Backpack or Day Bag**: Useful for day trips, classes, and exploring your new city.
- **Reusable Water Bottle**: Stay hydrated and reduce waste by using a reusable water bottle.

Academic Materials

Being prepared academically is just as important as being prepared personally.

- **Notebooks, Pens, and Other Stationery**: Basic supplies for taking notes and completing assignments.
- **Required Textbooks or Course Materials**: Check with your host institution to see if you need to bring any specific books or materials.

Cultural Gifts

Bringing small gifts from your home country can help build connections and show appreciation.

- **Small Gifts or Tokens**: Items like keychains, postcards, or local snacks make great gifts for host families, new friends, or professors.

Final Tips

- **Create a Packing List**: A detailed list can help ensure you do not forget anything important.
- **Check Airline Luggage Policies**: Be aware of weight limits and baggage fees to avoid unexpected charges.
- **Pack Smart**: Use packing cubes or compression bags to maximize space and keep your luggage organized.

By following these packing tips and bringing the essential items listed, you can ensure a smooth and enjoyable start to your international experience. Proper preparation will help you feel confident and ready to embrace all the exciting opportunities ahead.

Travel Logistics

Transportation to the Airport:

Plan Ahead: Decide how you will get to the airport well in advance. Options include public transport, taxis, ride-sharing services, or getting a ride from family or friends. Consider the time of day and traffic conditions when planning your route.

Timing: Aim to arrive at the airport at least three hours before an international flight. This allows ample time for check-in, security screening, and any unforeseen delays. Use online check-in options to save time and choose your preferred seat in advance.

Arrival at Destination:

Research Transportation Options: Familiarize yourself with transportation options from the airport to your accommodation in your host country. Options might include public transportation, airport shuttles, taxis, or ride-sharing services. Research costs, schedules, and routes to choose the most convenient option.

Pre-Book Transport: If possible, pre-book your transportation to avoid the stress of navigating a new city with luggage. Many airports have services that allow you to book shuttles or private cars in advance. Confirm the details and pick-up locations to ensure a smooth arrival.

Local Currency:

Currency Exchange: Consider exchanging a small amount of money into the local currency before you leave, so you have cash on hand for immediate expenses like transportation or food. Exchange rates at airports are often less favorable, so plan accordingly.

ATMs: Research to see if there are ATMs at the airport where you can withdraw local currency upon arrival. Be aware of any international transaction fees your bank may charge. Notify your bank of your travel plans to avoid any issues with accessing your funds.

Accommodation Address:

Know Your Destination: Have the address and contact information of your accommodation readily available. This can be helpful when filling out arrival forms or if you need to ask for directions. Print out a map or save it offline on your smartphone for easy access.

Communication:

SIM Cards and Mobile Plans: Research mobile plans and SIM card options in your host country. Having a local number can make communication easier and more affordable. Some airports offer SIM cards for purchase upon arrival.

Staying Connected: Ensure you have a reliable way to communicate with family and friends back home. Consider using messaging apps like WhatsApp, Viber, or Skype for free or low-cost international calls and texts.

By carefully planning your travel arrangements and understanding the logistics involved, you can ensure a smooth start to your international experience. Proper preparation not only reduces stress but also allows you to focus on the exciting journey ahead. Safe travel!

Anecdotes and Expert Insights
Booking the Perfect Flight- Carlos' Story

Student Perspective: "I thought booking my flight would be the easiest part of my international preparation, but it turned out to be quite a challenge. I was trying to find the best deal and was constantly comparing prices on Skyscanner and Google Flights. I learned that being flexible with my travel dates made a big difference. I ended up booking a midweek flight, which saved me a significant amount of money. Also, I found that student travel agencies like STA Travel offer special rates for students, which was a pleasant surprise. Despite the initial frustration, finding the perfect flight felt like a victory and set a positive tone for my upcoming adventure." – Carlos, Spanish International Student

Expert Insight: Flexibility and research are your best friends when booking flights. Midweek flights are often cheaper than weekend ones, and being open to different departure and return dates can yield substantial savings. Additionally, do not forget to check for student discounts offered by airlines or through student travel agencies like STA Travel and StudentUniverse. Signing up for fare alerts can also help you track price changes and secure the best deals.

Navigating Airports and Customs

Navigating airports and customs can be a daunting part of your journey, especially when traveling internationally. Understanding airport procedures and preparing ahead of time can help you manage this process smoothly and with confidence. Here is a comprehensive guide to ensure your airport experience is as stress-free as possible.

Airport Procedures

Check-In

Arrive Early:

Timing: Arrive at the airport at least three hours before an international flight. This allows ample time for check-in, security screening, and any unexpected delays. Early arrival also gives you time to find your gate, relax before boarding, and handle any last-minute issues calmly.

Benefits: Arriving early reduces stress and gives you a buffer in case of heavy traffic, long lines, or other unforeseen issues. You can use the extra time to grab a snack, read a book, or explore the airport amenities.

Online Check-In:

Convenience: Many airlines offer online check-in starting 24-48 hours before departure. Use this service to save time at the airport and avoid long check-in lines. Online check-in also allows you to confirm flight details and make any last-minute changes if necessary.

Seat Selection: During online check-in, you can often select your seat, which is especially useful if you prefer window or aisle seats or want to ensure you sit with your travel companions. Look for seats with extra legroom if you need more space.

Documentation:

Necessary Documents: Have all necessary documents ready, including your passport, visa, flight itinerary, and any required health certificates or test results. Keep these documents in an easily accessible part of your carry-on bag.

Organization: Use a travel wallet or document organizer to keep everything in one place, ensuring quick access when needed. Make digital copies of important documents and store them securely online or on your phone for backup.

Baggage Drop:

Checked Luggage: If you have checked luggage, drop it off at the airline's designated counter. Make sure your bags are properly tagged with your name, contact information, and destination to prevent loss. Use durable luggage tags that can withstand rough handling.

Weight Check: Ensure your checked bags comply with the airline's weight and size limits to avoid additional fees. Use a luggage scale at home to weigh your bags before leaving for the airport. If necessary, redistribute items between bags to balance the weight.

Security Check

Preparation:

Boarding Pass and ID: Have your boarding pass and identification ready as you approach the security checkpoint. Wear easily removable shoes and avoid excessive jewelry or belts to speed up the screening process. Place all metal items, such as keys and coins, in your carry-on before reaching the checkpoint.

Dress Smart: Consider wearing slip-on shoes and minimal accessories to streamline the security check process. Wear comfortable clothing that is easy to move in, as you might need to walk long distances within the airport.

Liquids and Gels:

3-1-1 Rule: Follow the 3-1-1 rule for liquids and gels: each container must be 3.4 ounces (100 milliliters) or less, all containers must fit in a single quart-sized plastic bag, and each passenger is allowed one bag. This bag should be easily accessible for inspection. Remember to remove this bag from your carry-on during screening.

Exceptions: Be aware of exceptions for medications and infant formula, which may exceed the 3.4-ounce limit but must be declared and inspected separately. Carry a doctor's note for any medical liquids that exceed the limit.

Electronics:

Separate Screening: Remove laptops, tablets, and other large electronics from your carry-on bag and place them in a separate bin for screening. Smaller electronics like smartphones and e-readers can typically stay in your bag. Ensure these devices are charged, as you may be asked to power them on during security checks.

Ease of Access: Pack your electronics in a way that makes them easy to remove and repack quickly. Use padded cases to protect your devices during handling.

Prohibited Items:

Familiarization: Familiarize yourself with the list of prohibited items to ensure you do not carry any restricted items in your carry-on or checked luggage. Common prohibited items include sharp objects, certain liquids, and flammable materials.

Pre-Screening: Double-check your bags at home to remove any items that could cause delays or confiscation at security. Refer to your airline's website for the most updated list of prohibited items.

Boarding

Gate Information:

Check Departure Boards: Regularly check the departure boards for your gate number and any updates to your flight's status. Gates can change, so stay informed and be prepared to move to a different location if necessary. Sign up for airline notifications via text or email for real-time updates.

Announcements: Listen for announcements regarding gate changes or boarding updates, especially if you are in a busy or large airport. Consider downloading the airline's app for instant notifications about your flight.

Boarding Process:

Boarding Groups: Airlines typically board in groups based on seat location or class of service. Listen for your group to be called and have your boarding pass ready. This helps streamline the boarding process and avoid congestion.

Priority Boarding: If you qualify for priority boarding due to frequent flyer status, seat class, or special needs, take advantage of this to get settled in your seat early. Use the extra time to store your carry-on in the overhead bin and organize your personal items.

Final Preparations:

Personal Belongings: Ensure you have all your personal belongings and essential documents before boarding the plane. Double-check that you have your passport, boarding pass, wallet, and any other necessary items.

Comfort Items: Consider having a small bag with comfort items like a neck pillow, headphones, snacks, and a book or tablet for entertainment during the flight. Bring an empty water bottle to fill up after passing through security to stay hydrated during your journey.

By understanding and following these airport procedures, you can navigate the complexities of international travel with greater ease and confidence. Proper preparation and attention to detail will help ensure that your journey begins smoothly, setting a positive tone for your entire international experience. Here are a few additional tips to enhance your airport experience:

Lounge Access: If you have a long layover, consider purchasing a day pass to an airport lounge. Lounges offer comfortable seating, complimentary food and beverages, and a quiet environment to relax or work.

Travel Apps: Use travel apps to track your flight status, find airport maps, and access information about amenities and services at the airport.

Health Precautions: Follow health and safety guidelines, such as wearing a mask and practicing social distancing, to protect yourself and others during your travels.

Tips for Smooth Navigation

Navigating airports can be one of the most stressful parts of your journey, especially when traveling internationally. However, with some preparation and a calm mindset, you can make the process much smoother and even enjoyable. Here are some expert tips to help you navigate airports efficiently and confidently.

Stay Calm

Airports can be overwhelming, particularly if you are in an unfamiliar country where you do not speak the language. However, staying calm is crucial to ensuring a smooth experience.

- **Breathe and Relax**: Take deep breaths and remind yourself that many people are in the same situation. Keeping a clear mind will help you think more clearly and make better decisions.
- **Follow Signs**: Airports are designed to guide you with signs and symbols. Pay close attention to these visual cues—they are often color-coded and universally understood.
- **Ask for Help**: Do not hesitate to approach airport staff for assistance. They are trained to help travelers and can provide directions, answer questions, and help with any issues you may encounter. Remember, they are there to assist you.

Language Barriers

Encountering language barriers can add an extra layer of difficulty to navigating an airport, but with the right tools and strategies, you can overcome this challenge.

- **Translation Apps**: Use translation apps like Google Translate to bridge the communication gap. These apps can translate text, voice, and even images in real-time, making it easier to understand signs and communicate with others.
- **Phrasebook**: Carry a small phrasebook with key phrases related to travel and customs procedures. Simple phrases like "Where is the check-in counter?" or "Can you help me?" can be incredibly useful.
- **Visual Cues**: Pay attention to symbols and pictograms, which are designed to be understood regardless of language. Icons for restrooms, baggage claim, and exits are standardized in many places.

Plan Ahead

Planning ahead is one of the most effective ways to ensure a smooth airport experience. By researching and preparing in advance, you can avoid many common pitfalls.

- **Research Airport Layouts**: Familiarize yourself with the layout of the airports you will be traveling through. Many airports have maps available online or through their mobile apps. Knowing where key areas are located—such as check-in counters, security checkpoints, and gates—can save you time and reduce stress.
- **Understand Procedures**: Each airport may have slightly different procedures for check-in, security, and customs. Research these procedures ahead of time to know what to expect. For example, some airports may have stricter security checks or specific customs regulations.
- **Prepare Documents**: Ensure all your travel documents, such as your passport, boarding pass, visa, and customs forms, are organized and easily accessible. Keeping these documents in a travel wallet can help you quickly present them when needed.

- **Time Management**: Plan to arrive at the airport well in advance of your flight. For international flights, it is generally recommended to arrive at least three hours before departure. This extra time can help accommodate long lines, security checks, and any unexpected delays.
- **Check Flight Status**: Monitor your flight status before and during your trip to stay informed of any changes or delays. Many airlines offer mobile apps that provide real-time updates.

By following these tips for smooth navigation, you can greatly enhance your airport experience. Staying calm, preparing for language barriers, and planning ahead will help you feel more in control and ready to embark on your international experience. Enjoy the journey and embrace the excitement of traveling to a new destination!

Navigating airports and customs does not have to be stressful. With thorough preparation and a positive mindset, you can turn your travel experience into an exciting start to your international adventure.

Anecdotes and Insights

Mastering Airport Navigation- Anna's Story

Student Perspective: "My first international flight to Germany was a whirlwind. The sheer size of the airport and the security procedures were overwhelming. I made sure to arrive three hours early, which gave me plenty of time to navigate through check-in, security, and customs without rushing. I used online check-in the day before to save time and selected my seat. At security, I had all my documents ready and followed the 3-1-1 rule for liquids. My carry-on was packed with essentials, including a change of clothes and important documents. By the time I boarded, I felt prepared and confident, which helped me start my journey on a positive note." – Anna, German International Student

Expert Insight: Navigating airports efficiently can significantly reduce travel stress. Arriving early is crucial for international flights, allowing you ample time to handle check-in, security, and customs. Online check-in and selecting your seat in advance can save time and ensure a smoother experience. Familiarize yourself with security procedures, such as the 3-1-1 rule for liquids, to expedite the process. Pack essential items in your carry-on, including important documents, medications, and a change of clothes, in case of any delays or lost luggage. Being well-prepared will help you feel confident and ready for your adventure.

Customs Procedures

Navigating customs can be one of the more nerve-wracking aspects of international travel, especially for first-time travelers. Understanding what to expect and how to prepare can make the process smooth and stress-free. Here is a detailed guide to help you through customs procedures, ensuring you arrive at your destination ready to start your international experience on the right foot.

Customs Forms

Declaration Form:

Purpose: Most countries require travelers to complete a customs declaration form. This form will ask about items you are bringing into the country, such as food, plants, or large amounts of currency. It helps customs officials identify goods that need to be inspected or taxed.

Honesty: Be honest when filling out the customs declaration form. Failure to declare items can result in fines or confiscation. Even if you are unsure whether an item needs to be declared, it is better to declare it and let the customs officer decide.

How to Fill Out:

Personal Information: Include your name, address, and passport number.

Items to Declare: List any items that need to be declared, such as gifts, food, plants, animal products, or large amounts of money (typically over $10,000 USD or equivalent).

Signature: Sign and date the form to certify that the information provided is true and accurate.

Timing and Convenience:

In-Flight Availability: Many airlines distribute customs declaration forms during the flight. Use this time to fill out the form, so you are ready to proceed upon arrival.

Digital Forms: Some countries offer digital customs declaration forms that can be completed online before your trip. Check if this option is available to save time at the airport.

Prohibited Items

Regulations:

Research: Familiarize yourself with the host country's customs regulations to avoid bringing prohibited or restricted items. Commonly restricted items include certain foods, plants, animals, and large sums of cash. Some countries have strict regulations on products like dairy, meat, fruits, and vegetables to prevent the spread of diseases.

Restricted Items: Items like firearms, drugs, and certain medications may be prohibited or require special permits. Check the specific restrictions of your destination country before packing.

Consequences:

Fines and Legal Action: Understand the consequences of bringing prohibited items, which can range from fines to legal action. In some cases, undeclared items may be confiscated, and you could face prosecution. The severity of the consequences depends on the type of item and the host country's laws.

Special Considerations:

Cultural Artifacts: Be cautious about bringing cultural artifacts or antiques. Some countries have strict laws protecting cultural heritage and may confiscate items that are not properly documented.

Medication: Carry a doctor's note and a copy of your prescription for any medications you need to bring. Some countries have stringent regulations on certain drugs, even those that are commonly prescribed in your home country.

Customs Inspection

Procedure:

Follow Signs: After disembarking, follow signs to the customs area. Present your passport, visa, and completed customs declaration form to the customs officer. Pay attention to announcements and signs that guide you through the process.

Inspection: The customs officer may inspect your luggage to ensure you comply with regulations. Be prepared to open your bags for inspection if asked. Cooperate fully and answer any questions they may have.

Questions:

Prepare Answers: Be prepared to answer questions about your trip, including the purpose of your visit, the duration of your stay, and where you will be staying. Answer clearly and honestly to avoid any misunderstandings. It is helpful to have a copy of your itinerary and accommodation details handy.

Baggage Screening:

Screening Process: Your luggage may be subject to screening or inspection. Cooperate with customs officers and follow their instructions. They may use x-ray machines, sniffer dogs, or manual searches to inspect your belongings.

Tips for Speedy Screening: Pack your carry-on neatly, with liquids and electronics easily accessible. This makes the screening process quicker and more efficient.

Red and Green Channels:

Choose the Right Lane: Some airports have separate lanes for passengers with items to declare (red channel) and those with nothing to declare (green channel). Choose the appropriate lane based on your declaration form. Using the correct lane helps streamline the process and avoid delays.

Post-Customs Procedures

Baggage Claim:

Locating Your Luggage: Follow signs to the baggage claim area. Check the baggage carousel number associated with your flight, which is usually displayed on screens in the baggage claim area. Pay attention to announcements that may indicate changes in the carousel number.

Baggage Tags: Use the tags given at check-in to identify your luggage. Ensure all your bags are collected before leaving the baggage area. Matching your claim tags to the luggage tags helps prevent mix-ups.

Lost Luggage: If your luggage is missing or damaged, report it immediately to the airline's baggage service counter. Provide your baggage claim tags and flight information. The airline will assist you in locating your luggage or compensating you for the loss. Keep a list of the items in your checked baggage to make the claims process smoother.

Currency Exchange:

Airport Exchange Services: If you need local currency, use the currency exchange services available at the airport. Keep in mind that exchange rates at airports might be higher compared to local banks or exchange services. It is often useful to have some local currency on hand for immediate expenses.

ATMs: Consider using ATMs to withdraw local currency, which may offer better exchange rates. Ensure your bank card is compatible and check for international withdrawal fees. Notify your bank of your travel plans to avoid any issues with accessing your funds. Look for ATMs affiliated with your bank to avoid additional fees.

Transportation:

Public Transit: Research the availability of public transportation options such as buses, trains, or metro systems. Many airports have direct connections to public transit, which can be a cost-effective and convenient way to reach your destination.

Taxis and Ridesharing: Official taxi stands and ride-sharing services like Uber or Lyft are usually available at airports. Confirm the fare or estimated cost before starting your journey to avoid any surprises. Some airports have designated pick-up areas for ride-sharing services. It is often safer and more reliable to use official services rather than unlicensed taxis.

Airport Shuttles: Some universities or accommodation providers offer airport shuttle services for new students. Check if this service is available and arrange it in advance if needed. Shuttles can provide hassle-free and direct transfer to your accommodation. Verify the pick-up location and schedule to ensure a smooth transfer.

SIM Cards and Mobile Plans:

Local SIM Cards: Purchasing a local SIM card can help you stay connected and save on roaming charges. Many airports have kiosks where you can buy SIM cards upon arrival. Compare plans to find one that best suits your needs.

International Plans: If you prefer to use your existing mobile plan, check with your provider for international options. Some providers offer plans that include international calling and data at a reasonable cost.

Staying Connected:

Wi-Fi Availability: Most airports offer free Wi-Fi, allowing you to connect with family and friends, update them on your arrival, and access necessary information. Use this opportunity to check maps, confirm transportation details, and communicate with your contacts in the host country.

Communication Apps: Use messaging apps like WhatsApp, Viber, or Skype for free or low-cost international calls and texts. These apps can help you stay in touch without incurring high charges.

Navigating customs and post-customs procedures can seem overwhelming, but with proper preparation and knowledge, you can make the process smooth and efficient. Understanding what to expect and how to prepare will help you handle customs confidently, ensuring a positive start to your international experience. Welcome to your new adventure!

Anecdotes and Expert Insights

Packing Light and Smart- Sofia's Story

Student Perspective: "Packing for a year-long exchange in Japan was a daunting task. I initially wanted to bring everything I thought I might need, but quickly realized that was impractical. I remember my roommate, who had been on an exchange before, gave me the best advice: 'Pack what you think you need, then take out half.' This tip saved me from overpacking. I focused on versatile clothing that could be layered and made sure to pack essential documents and a few personal items to make my new place feel like home. Packing light made my travel day so much easier, and I had no issues with baggage fees or lugging around heavy suitcases." – Sofia, Japanese International Student

Expert Insight: Overpacking is a common mistake for first-time international students. The key is to pack light and focus on essentials. Choose versatile clothing that can be mixed and matched and layered for different weather conditions. Remember, many items can be purchased in your host country, often at a lower cost and more suitable to the local climate and lifestyle. Prioritize important documents, medications, and a few personal items that will help you feel comfortable in your new environment. Using packing cubes or compression bags can help maximize space and keep your luggage organized.

2.2 Health and Safety

Ensuring your health and safety while studying abroad is paramount. Understanding the health insurance requirements and options available to you is a critical step in this process. This section provides detailed insights into securing appropriate health coverage, understanding the types of coverage available, and navigating the specifics of your insurance policy.

Health Insurance Requirements and Options

Insurance Requirements

Host Country Regulations:

Mandatory Coverage: Verify if your host country mandates specific health insurance coverage for international students. Many countries have regulations requiring international students to have health insurance that meets certain criteria. For example, Germany requires students to have health insurance that covers at least €30,000 in medical expenses.

Compliance: Ensure your chosen insurance plan complies with these regulations to avoid any legal issues or enrollment barriers. Contact the embassy or consulate of your host country for detailed information on these requirements.

University Requirements:

Institutional Policies: Check if your host institution has specific insurance requirements. Some universities may mandate that you purchase a student health insurance plan they offer or endorse.

University Health Plans: Evaluate the student health insurance plans offered by your university. These plans are often tailored to meet the needs of international students and ensure compliance with local regulations. They might also provide easier access to on-campus health services.

Types of Coverage

Medical Emergencies:

Hospital Visits: Ensure your insurance covers hospital admissions and treatments. This includes inpatient and outpatient services.

Emergency Room Care: Coverage for emergency room visits is crucial for unexpected illnesses or injuries.

Ambulance Services: Make sure your policy includes emergency transportation services, such as ambulances.

Routine Care:

General Practitioner Visits: Routine check-ups and non-emergency visits to a general practitioner should be covered.

Specialist Consultations: Access to specialists for specific health issues or ongoing care is important. Verify that your insurance plan includes specialist consultations and necessary diagnostic tests.

Mental Health:

Counseling Services: Mental health support is vital, especially when adapting to a new environment. Your insurance should cover counseling and therapy sessions.

Psychiatric Care: Ensure coverage extends to psychiatric consultations and treatments if needed.

Prescription Medications:

Medication Coverage: Your plan should cover prescribed medications, including those needed for ongoing treatments. Check if there are any limits or conditions on this coverage.

Dental and Vision:

Optional Add-ons: Some health insurance plans offer optional coverage for dental and vision care. If not included in your primary plan, consider adding this coverage to manage routine dental check-ups and eye care.

Repatriation:

Medical Evacuation: Coverage for medical evacuation ensures you can be transported back to your home country if you suffer a severe illness or injury.

Repatriation of Remains: In the unlikely event of death, some plans cover the costs associated with repatriating remains to your home country.

Policy Details

Coverage Limits:

Maximum Payouts: Understand the maximum payout amounts for various types of care under your policy. Different services, such as surgeries or hospital stays, may have specific limits.

Annual Limits: Be aware of any annual or lifetime maximums on your policy. These limits could impact your long-term health care costs.

Exclusions:

Non-Covered Services: Familiarize yourself with what is not covered by your insurance, such as pre-existing conditions, elective procedures, or certain high-risk activities like extreme sports.

Policy Specifics: Each policy has unique exclusions, so read the fine print carefully to avoid unexpected expenses.

Claims Process:

Filing Claims: Understand the process for filing a claim, including the necessary documentation and timelines. This often involves submitting medical records, receipts, and sometimes pre-approval forms.

Documentation: Keep copies of all medical records, prescriptions, and receipts. These documents are essential for filing claims and ensuring reimbursement.

Emergency Contact:

Insurance Provider Contact Information: Keep your insurance provider's emergency contact information easily accessible. This includes their phone number, email, and any specific instructions for seeking emergency care.

Travel with Information: Carry a card or document with your insurance details in your wallet or phone for quick access during emergencies.

By thoroughly understanding your health insurance requirements and options, you can ensure that you are well-prepared for any health-related issues that may arise during your international adventure. Adequate coverage not only provides peace of mind but also ensures you receive the necessary care without the burden of unexpected costs. Prioritize your health and safety by making informed decisions about your insurance plan and its coverage.

Vaccinations and Medical Preparations

Ensuring you are medically prepared for your international program is crucial for your health and wellbeing. Vaccinations are an important part of this preparation, protecting you from potential diseases and ensuring you meet the health requirements of your host country. Here is a detailed guide to help you navigate the necessary vaccinations and medical preparations.

Required Vaccinations

Travel Vaccinations:

Research and Verify: Before traveling, check the Centers for Disease Control and Prevention (CDC) and World Health Organization (WHO) websites for the latest recommended and required vaccinations for your host country. These organizations provide comprehensive and up-to-date information tailored to each destination.

Specific Vaccines: Common travel vaccines include:

- **Hepatitis A and B**: These vaccines protect against two types of liver infections caused by the hepatitis A and B viruses, which are more prevalent in certain regions.
- **Typhoid**: Essential if you are traveling to areas where typhoid fever is common, especially in developing countries with limited access to clean water.
- **Yellow Fever**: Required for travel to certain parts of Africa and South America. Some countries may ask for proof of vaccination upon entry.
- **Rabies**: Recommended for travelers who may be exposed to animals in areas where rabies is present.

Booking Appointments: Schedule appointments with a travel health clinic or your healthcare provider well in advance to ensure you receive all necessary vaccinations on time.

COVID-19:

Full Vaccination: Ensure you are fully vaccinated against COVID-19 if it is required by your host country or institution. This often includes the initial vaccination series plus any recommended booster doses.

Proof of Vaccination: Carry proof of vaccination, such as a vaccination card or a digital certificate. Some countries may require this documentation for entry, and it might also be needed for university registration or access to public places.

Health Certificates: In addition to proof of vaccination, some countries might require a negative COVID-19 test result taken within a specified time frame before departure. Stay updated on these requirements as they can change frequently.

Routine Vaccinations

Up-to-Date Immunizations:

Consult Your Healthcare Provider: Schedule a visit with your healthcare provider to review your vaccination history and ensure all routine immunizations are up to date. This is particularly important for vaccines that are given during childhood but may require boosters in adulthood.

Key Vaccines:

- **MMR (Measles, Mumps, Rubella)**: Ensure you have received the full course of MMR vaccines, as outbreaks of these diseases can occur in different parts of the world.
- **Tetanus, Diphtheria, and Pertussis (Tdap)**: Make sure your tetanus and diphtheria vaccinations are current. A booster shot is typically recommended every 10 years.
- **Influenza**: An annual flu shot is advisable, especially if you will be in a region where flu season is prevalent or if you are at higher risk of complications.
- **Polio**: Ensure you are fully vaccinated against polio, particularly if traveling to regions where the disease is still present.

Additional Considerations:

Consultation and Timing: It is best to complete all vaccinations at least 4-6 weeks before your departure to allow your body to build immunity. Some vaccines require multiple doses over a period of time.

Medical Records: Carry a copy of your vaccination records with you. This documentation can be important for medical providers in your host country and may be required by your host institution.

Preparing for Medical Needs

Routine Check-Ups:

General Health Check: Before you leave, have a general health check-up to ensure you are in good health and to discuss any existing medical conditions with your healthcare provider.

Dental Check-Up: Visit your dentist for a routine check-up and any necessary dental work to avoid dealing with dental issues abroad.

Prescriptions and Medications:

Medications: If you take prescription medications, ensure you have enough to last the duration of your stay, along with a doctor's letter explaining your medical needs. Some countries have strict regulations on medication importation.

Over-the-Counter Medications: Consider bringing a supply of over-the-counter medications that you commonly use, such as pain relievers, allergy medication, and stomach remedies. These may not be readily available or might differ in formulation in your host country.

Health Insurance:

Coverage Verification: Confirm that your health insurance covers you while abroad, including emergency care and routine treatments. Understand the procedures for seeking medical care and filing claims.

Emergency Contact Information: Keep the emergency contact information of your health insurance provider readily accessible.

By thoroughly preparing your health and medical needs before departure, you can ensure a safer and more enjoyable international experience. Keeping up with required and routine vaccinations, having a clear understanding of your medical coverage, and being prepared for any health-related issues will provide peace of mind and help you focus on making the most of your time abroad.

2.3 Cultural Preparation

Adapting to a New Cultural Environment

Embarking on an international journey means immersing yourself in a new cultural environment, which can be both exciting and challenging. Successfully adapting to this environment requires a combination of building support networks, understanding cultural differences, and learning the local language. Here's a thorough guide to help you navigate and thrive in your new cultural landscape.

Support Networks

Connecting with Other International Students:

Join Student Groups: Seek out international student groups or associations at your host institution. These groups provide a supportive community where you can share experiences, seek advice, and make friends who understand the unique challenges you face.

- **Example**: Many universities have clubs specifically for international students that host events such as welcome dinners, cultural nights, and sightseeing trips.

Participation in Events: Attend events and activities organized by these groups. They often host social gatherings, cultural outings, and informational sessions that can enhance your understanding of the local culture and provide a sense of belonging.

- **Example**: Participating in a cultural night where students share food, music, and traditions from their home countries can be both educational and a lot of fun.

Local Friends and Mentors:

Making Local Connections: Make an effort to connect with local students and residents. Engaging with locals can offer deeper insights into the culture and help you navigate your new environment more effectively.

- **Example**: Joining study groups or campus organizations where locals are involved can be a great way to make friends.

Mentorship Programs: Many universities offer mentorship programs that pair international students with local mentors. These mentors can provide guidance, share local knowledge, and help you integrate into the community.

- **Example**: A mentor might help you understand local slang, recommend places to visit, or assist with academic challenges.

Support Services:

Utilize Institutional Resources: Take advantage of support services offered by your host institution, such as counseling, academic advising, and cultural integration programs. These services are designed to help international students adjust to their new surroundings and succeed academically and socially.

- **Example**: Attending a workshop on cultural adjustment can provide strategies for coping with culture shock and making the most of your experience.

Health and Wellness Services: Do not hesitate to use health and wellness services if you feel overwhelmed or need someone to talk to. Mental health support is crucial during significant transitions.

- **Example**: Many universities offer free or low-cost counseling services for students.

Understanding Cultural Differences and Norms

Research:

Cultural Norms:

Local Customs: Learn about the cultural norms, values, and social behaviors of your host country. This includes understanding local customs related to greetings, dining etiquette, gift-giving, and personal space. For example, in Japan, bowing is a common greeting, while in many European countries, a kiss on the cheek may be customary.

- **Example**: Research how different cultures handle punctuality. In some places, being on time is critical, while in others, a more relaxed approach is taken.

Daily Life: Understanding these customs can help you navigate social interactions smoothly and avoid unintentional faux pas.

Social Etiquette:

Appropriate Topics: Study common social etiquettes, such as appropriate topics for conversation, gestures to avoid, and behavior in public places. In some cultures, discussing politics or religion might be considered taboo, while in others, such discussions are normal.

- **Example**: In some cultures, it is considered rude to talk loudly in public places or to make direct eye contact with strangers.

Behavior: Being aware of these norms will help you engage in conversations respectfully and appropriately.

Work and Study Habits:

Academic Culture: Understand the work and study habits in your host country, including attitudes towards punctuality, deadlines, and collaboration. For instance, some cultures place a high value on punctuality and expect you to be on time for classes and meetings.

- **Example**: In some countries, students are expected to participate actively in class discussions, while in others, a more passive approach is the norm.

Group Work: Knowing these habits can help you adapt to the academic expectations and perform better in your studies.

Cultural Sensitivity:

Open-Mindedness:

Curiosity: Approach new experiences with curiosity and an open mind. Be respectful of different perspectives and practices, even if they differ significantly from your own. This openness will enrich your experience and help you build meaningful relationships.

- **Example**: Trying new foods or participating in local festivals can provide deeper cultural insights.

Observation:

Learning by Watching: Observe how locals interact and behave in various situations. This can provide valuable insights into acceptable social conduct and help you adapt more easily. Pay attention to body language, tone of voice, and other non-verbal cues.

- **Example**: Notice how people queue in lines, handle public transportation, or behave in social gatherings.

Avoid Assumptions:

Avoiding Stereotypes: Avoid making assumptions based on stereotypes or your own cultural background. Each individual and situation can be unique. Approach each interaction with an open mind and a willingness to learn.

- **Example**: Rather than assuming everyone in a country acts a certain way, get to know individuals and their personal experiences.

Anecdotes and Insights

Embracing Cultural Differences in Brazil- Aisha's Story

Student Perspective: Aisha, a sociology student from the UK, was excited about her international program in São Paulo, Brazil. She had always been fascinated by Brazilian culture and was eager to immerse herself in it. However, adapting to the local customs and social norms was more challenging than she expected.

"In Brazil, people are very warm and expressive. They greet each other with hugs and kisses, which is very different from the UK. At first, I found it uncomfortable and a bit intrusive. But over time, I started to understand and appreciate this aspect of Brazilian culture. It is all about showing affection and building close relationships. Embracing this difference helped me connect with people on a deeper level."

Expert Insight: Aisha's experience highlights the importance of cultural sensitivity and open-mindedness. Adapting to different social norms and communication styles is crucial for successful cultural integration. Observing and respecting local customs can help you build stronger connections and enhance your overall experience.

Actionable Tip: Take the time to learn about the cultural norms and social etiquette of your host country. Observe how locals interact and try to mimic their behaviors respectfully. If you are unsure about a particular custom, do not hesitate to ask for guidance from local friends or mentors. Being open and adaptable will enrich your experience and help you build meaningful relationships.

Learning the Local Language or Basic Phrases

Language Basics:

Key Phrases:

Essential Vocabulary: Learn essential phrases such as greetings, polite expressions, and basic questions. This includes phrases like "hello," "thank you," "please," "excuse me," and "how much does this cost?" These basics will help you navigate daily interactions more smoothly.

- **Example**: Knowing how to ask for directions or order food in the local language can be very helpful.

Practical Usage: Use these phrases frequently to build confidence and improve your pronunciation.

Pronunciation:

Correct Pronunciation: Practice correct pronunciation to improve communication and avoid misunderstandings. Use language learning apps or listen to native speakers to hear accurate pronunciation. Recording yourself and comparing it to native speakers can also be helpful.

- **Example**: Pronouncing names correctly shows respect and effort in learning the language.

Language Resources:

Apps and Online Courses:

Digital Tools: Use language learning apps like Duolingo, Babbel, or Rosetta Stone to build vocabulary and grammar skills. These apps make learning engaging and accessible anywhere.

- **Example**: Duolingo offers gamified lessons that make learning fun and interactive.

Structured Learning: Online courses from platforms like Coursera or edX can provide more structured language learning experiences, often with the opportunity to earn certificates.

Language Guides:

Reference Materials: Carry a pocket dictionary or phrasebook for quick reference. Apps like Google Translate can also be useful for on-the-go translations, especially for more complex phrases or unexpected situations.

- **Example**: A phrasebook can be invaluable when you do not have internet access to use translation apps.

Language Classes:

Formal Education: Consider enrolling in a language course offered by your host institution or a local language school. These classes can provide formal instruction and opportunities for practice with other learners.

- **Example**: Many universities offer beginner language courses tailored for international students.

Practice:

Conversational Practice:

Speaking with Locals: Practice speaking with native speakers or language exchange partners. Engaging in conversation is one of the best ways to improve your language skills.

- **Example**: Participating in language exchange programs or conversation clubs can provide a supportive environment for practice.

Social Settings: Join language clubs or meet-up groups to practice in a social setting. These environments provide a relaxed atmosphere where you can practice without fear of making mistakes.

- **Example**: Many cities have "language cafes" where people meet to practice languages in an informal setting.

By building strong support networks, understanding cultural differences, and learning the local language, you can effectively adapt to your new cultural environment. These steps will help you feel more comfortable and integrated, enhancing your overall international experience. Embrace the journey with an open mind and a willingness to learn, and you will gain invaluable insights and skills that will stay with you long after your international program ends.

Adapting to a New Cultural Environment

Open-Mindedness

Embrace Differences:

Cultural Immersion:

Active Engagement: Actively engage with the local culture by participating in various cultural activities. Attend local festivals, join traditional celebrations, and visit cultural landmarks. These experiences will give you a deeper understanding of your host country's heritage and customs.

- **Example**: In India, participating in Holi, the festival of colors, can provide a vibrant and immersive cultural experience that highlights the significance of the celebration.

Trying Local Cuisine: Food is a significant part of any culture. Be adventurous with your palate and try local dishes. This not only helps you appreciate the local cuisine but also opens doors to conversations and connections with locals.

- **Example**: In Thailand, tasting street food like Pad Thai or Mango Sticky Rice at local markets can enhance your cultural experience and provide a taste of everyday life.

Acceptance:

Understanding Differences: Accept that cultural differences are natural and that embracing them will enrich your experience. Instead of comparing everything to your home country, appreciate the uniqueness of your host culture. Each culture has its own values and traditions that contribute to its identity.

- **Example**: Embracing the siesta culture in Spain can help you understand the local rhythm of life and the value placed on rest and family time.

Non-Judgmental Approach:

Avoid Quick Judgments: Refrain from making quick judgments about cultural practices that may seem strange or unfamiliar. Instead, approach these practices with curiosity and a desire to understand the underlying reasons.

- **Example**: In Japan, the practice of removing shoes before entering a home or certain public buildings is rooted in the value placed on cleanliness and respect for shared spaces.

Adaptability:

Flexible Attitude:

Behavioral Adjustments: Be willing to adapt your behavior and expectations to fit the local norms. This might involve adjusting your daily routines, communication style, or social behaviors to align with those of your host country.

- **Example**: In many Middle Eastern countries, it is customary to greet with a handshake and sometimes a kiss on the cheek. Adjusting to these norms shows respect and willingness to integrate.

Resilience:

Positive Outlook: Understand that adapting to a new culture can be challenging and that setbacks are a normal part of the process. Developing resilience involves maintaining a positive outlook and being patient with yourself as you navigate cultural adjustments.

- **Example**: If you accidentally offend someone by not following a local custom, use it as a learning experience and seek to understand how to avoid similar situations in the future.

Cultural Activities

Participation:

Local Events:

Engagement: Attend local festivals, fairs, and cultural events to immerse yourself in the culture and meet new people. These events are a fun and engaging way to learn about traditions and customs.

- **Example**: Participating in Oktoberfest in Germany offers a unique opportunity to experience local traditions, music, and cuisine.

Cultural Organizations:

Involvement: Join cultural clubs or organizations at your host institution. These groups often organize activities, excursions, and social events that can help you integrate and learn more about the local culture.

- **Example**: Joining a university's international student association can provide access to trips, social events, and cultural workshops.

Local Etiquette:

Greetings and Introductions:

Appropriate Greetings: Learn the appropriate ways to greet people and introduce yourself. This may vary significantly from your home country and can include different forms of address, handshakes, bows, or other gestures.

- **Example**: In Thailand, a respectful wai (a slight bow with palms pressed together) is the traditional way to greet someone.

Dining Etiquette:

Table Manners: Familiarize yourself with local dining customs, including table manners, tipping practices, and typical mealtimes. Understanding these norms can help you navigate social situations and avoid misunderstandings.

- **Example**: In France, it is customary to keep your hands (but not elbows) on the table during a meal, and tipping is often included in the bill.

Behavioral Norms:

Observational Learning: Observe and adopt local behaviors, such as how to queue, the appropriate volume for speaking in public, and gestures to avoid. Respecting these norms shows your willingness to integrate and adapt.

- **Example**: In Japan, it is important to queue patiently and quietly when waiting for public transportation, reflecting the local value of orderliness and respect for others.

Support Networks

Connecting with Other International Students:

International Student Associations:

Join Associations: Join international student associations or groups at your host institution. These organizations provide a community of peers who share similar experiences and challenges.

- **Example**: Being part of an international student group can offer support through shared experiences and collective activities.

Peer Support Groups:

Engage in Peer Support: Join peer support groups organized by your host institution or local community organizations. These groups often provide a platform for international students to share experiences, offer advice, and support each other through common challenges.

- **Example**: Participating in regular meetups can create a sense of belonging and provide practical tips for navigating daily life.

Online Communities:

Utilize Online Platforms: Participate in online forums and social media groups dedicated to international students. These platforms can be valuable resources for finding information, asking questions, and connecting with others in similar situations.

- **Example**: Joining Facebook groups or Reddit communities focused on international students can offer quick access to advice and peer support.

Local Friends and Mentors:

Cultural Ambassadors:

Seek Ambassadors: Look for programs where local students act as cultural ambassadors or buddies for international students. These ambassadors can help you understand local customs, introduce you to new friends, and assist with everyday challenges.

- **Example**: A cultural buddy might help you navigate the city, explain cultural nuances, or invite you to local events.

Community Engagement:

Get Involved: Engage in community activities, such as volunteering or joining local clubs and organizations. This can help you build relationships with locals and gain a deeper understanding of the host culture.

- **Example**: Volunteering at a local charity or participating in community clean-up events can provide meaningful interactions and insights into local life.

Support Services:

Health Services:

Access Health Services: Utilize health services provided by your host institution for physical and mental health support. Knowing where to go for medical assistance is crucial in case of illness or emergency.

- **Example**: Familiarize yourself with the location of the nearest campus health center and the procedures for accessing care.

Student Affairs Office:

Seek Assistance: Contact the student affairs office for assistance with housing, academic issues, and personal concerns. They can provide resources and support tailored to international students.

- **Example**: The student affairs office can help resolve housing issues, offer academic advising, or provide information on campus resources.

Emergency Contacts:

Keep Emergency Information: Keep a list of important emergency contacts, including local emergency numbers, your country's embassy or consulate, and contacts at your host institution.

- **Example**: Having a readily accessible list of emergency contacts can be a lifesaver in critical situations.

By embracing open-mindedness, actively participating in cultural activities, and building robust support networks, you can effectively adapt to your new cultural environment. These strategies will help you feel more integrated and enhance your overall international experience. Approach your journey with curiosity, flexibility, and resilience, and you will gain invaluable insights and skills that will stay with you long after your international journey ends.

Anecdotes and Insights

Building a Support Network in Germany- Liam's Story

Student Perspective: Liam, an engineering student from Canada, embarked on an international program in Berlin. He was eager to explore the rich history and vibrant culture of Germany. However, he soon found himself struggling to connect with others.

"Germany was everything I had imagined, but I felt lonely. Making friends was harder than I thought, especially because I did not speak German fluently. I attended my classes and explored the city, but I missed having a social circle. It was not until I joined a local soccer club that things started to change. Playing soccer with locals broke the ice and helped me form meaningful connections. I also started attending international student meetups, which made a big difference."

Expert Insight: Liam's proactive approach to joining local activities is a powerful strategy for building a support network. Engaging in social activities that align with your interests can help break down barriers and create a sense of belonging. Sports, clubs, and student organizations provide excellent opportunities for meeting new people and forming friendships.

Actionable Tip: Identify activities or groups that interest you and get involved early in your stay. Whether it is sports, arts, or academic societies, these platforms offer great opportunities to meet like-minded individuals. Do not hesitate to attend social events organized by your university or local community centers. Building a support network is crucial for emotional well-being and cultural adaptation.

Coping with Culture Shock

Adapting to a new cultural environment can be both exhilarating and challenging. Culture shock is a common experience for international students, encompassing a range of emotional and psychological responses to living in a new country. Understanding the stages of culture shock and developing effective coping strategies can help you navigate this transition smoothly and enrich your overall experience.

Understanding Culture Shock

Adjustment Phase:

Initial Excitement: The journey often begins with a honeymoon phase where everything new feels exciting and intriguing. You might be eager to explore your surroundings and embrace new experiences.
Example: On arriving in Paris, you might be thrilled by the sight of iconic landmarks, the sound of the French language, and the aroma of fresh pastries from local bakeries.

Emerging Challenges: As the novelty wears off, you may start encountering challenges such as language barriers, unfamiliar social norms, and homesickness. This is a natural part of the adjustment phase.
Example: Navigating complex public transportation systems or understanding local bureaucratic procedures can feel daunting at first.

Developing Routines: Gradually, you will start developing routines and finding comfort in daily activities. Establishing a sense of normalcy helps in adapting to the new environment.
Example: Regular visits to a favorite café, morning jogs in the park, or weekly markets for fresh produce can become comforting routines.

Acceptance Phase:

Cultural Adaptation: Over time, you begin to understand and appreciate the deeper aspects of the culture. You become more adept at navigating social situations and develop a more nuanced understanding of local customs.

Example: You might start understanding the subtleties of local humor, participating in traditional festivals, or adopting local dining habits.

Integration: In the acceptance phase, you feel integrated into the community. You maintain your own cultural identity while comfortably engaging with the new culture.

Example: Balancing your traditional celebrations with local holidays or blending cuisines from both cultures in your meals signifies this integration.

Anecdotes and Insights

Coping with Homesickness in South Africa- Sara's Story

Student Perspective: Sara, a medical student from France, was excited about her international program in Cape Town, South Africa. However, as time passed, she began to feel the weight of homesickness.

"I missed my family and friends a lot, especially during special occasions. The time difference made it hard to keep in touch regularly. I felt isolated and longed for the comfort of home. To cope, I started joining local volunteer groups and got involved in community projects. Helping others and staying busy helped me feel more connected and less lonely."

Expert Insight: Homesickness is a common challenge for many international students. Staying connected with family and friends back home is important but immersing yourself in the local community can also provide a sense of belonging and purpose. Volunteering and participating in community activities can help mitigate feelings of isolation.

Actionable Tip: Establish a routine for staying in touch with loved ones through regular video calls, social media, or messaging apps. Additionally, find local volunteer opportunities or community projects to get involved in. Engaging in meaningful activities can provide a sense of purpose and help you build new connections in your host country.

Coping Strategies

Stay Positive:

Focus on Positives: Concentrate on the positive aspects of your experience and the reasons you chose to study abroad. Keeping a positive outlook can help you overcome challenges and appreciate the unique opportunities available to you.

- **Example**: When feeling homesick, remind yourself of the unique experiences, such as learning a new language or making friends from around the world, that would not be possible without this journey.

Keep a Journal: Document your journey and reflect on your growth. Writing about your experiences can help you process your emotions and track your progress.

- **Example**: Journaling about a successful interaction in the local language or a new friendship can boost your confidence and reinforce positive experiences.

Celebrate Small Wins: Acknowledge and celebrate small victories, like successfully navigating a cultural nuance or making a new friend.

- **Example**: Successfully ordering a meal in the local language without help can be a confidence booster and a reminder of your progress.

Stay Connected:

Regular Communication: Maintain regular communication with family and friends back home through calls, video chats, or social media. Staying connected can provide emotional support and help reduce feelings of isolation.

- **Example**: Schedule weekly video calls with your family to share your experiences and stay updated on their lives.

Share Your Journey: Sharing your experiences with loved ones can help you feel supported and less isolated.

- **Example**: Posting photos and updates on social media can keep your friends and family engaged in your journey and provide a sense of connection.

Virtual Support Networks: Engage in online communities for international students. These platforms can be valuable for sharing experiences, advice, and support.

- **Example**: Joining a Facebook group for international students in your city can provide tips, event notifications, and peer support.

Build a Routine:

Daily Stability: Establish a daily routine to create a sense of normalcy and stability. Include activities that you enjoy and help you relax, such as exercise, hobbies, or socializing with friends.

- **Example**: Joining a local gym or a sports club can provide regular physical activity and social interaction.

Balanced Schedule: Balance your academic responsibilities with leisure activities to maintain overall well-being.

- **Example**: Dedicate specific times to study, but also ensure you have time for exploring the city, relaxing, and pursuing hobbies.

Personalized Routine: Customize your routine to include elements from both your home and host cultures.

- **Example**: Incorporate traditional meals from your home country into your weekly menu while also exploring local cuisine.

Seek Support:

Reach Out for Help: Do not hesitate to seek support from friends, mentors, or counseling services if you feel overwhelmed. Sharing your experiences can provide comfort and advice.

Example: Many universities offer counseling services specifically for international students, providing a safe space to discuss your feelings and challenges.

Well-being Activities: Engage in activities that promote well-being, such as mindfulness, meditation, or yoga.

Example: Practicing mindfulness or meditation can help you stay grounded and manage stress more effectively.

Support Services: Utilize the support services offered by your host institution, including health services, academic advising, and cultural integration programs.

Example: Attending workshops on cultural adjustment or stress management can provide practical tools and support.

Learn and Reflect:

Continuous Learning: Take time to learn from each experience, reflect on what you have learned, and appreciate the growth you are undergoing. This reflective practice can help you adapt more quickly and fully to your new environment.

- **Example**: After an interaction that felt challenging, reflect on what went well and what you could do differently next time.

Appreciate Growth: Recognize and celebrate your achievements and progress, no matter how small they might seem.

- **Example**: Acknowledge your courage in navigating a new city, mastering basic phrases in a new language, or making new friends.

Personal Development: Use your experiences to build resilience, adaptability, and a deeper understanding of yourself and the world.

- **Example**: Reflect on how overcoming cultural challenges has strengthened your problem-solving skills and cultural empathy.

Engage with the Local Community:

Volunteer: Volunteering in your host community can provide a sense of purpose and connection.

- **Example**: Volunteering at local shelters, schools, or environmental initiatives can help you make a positive impact and meet new people.

Cultural Exchange: Participate in cultural exchange programs or activities that allow you to share your culture with others.

- **Example**: Hosting a cultural night where you cook traditional dishes from your home country can foster mutual understanding and appreciation.

Practice Self-Care:

Healthy Lifestyle: Maintain a healthy lifestyle through regular exercise, balanced nutrition, and adequate rest.

- **Example**: Join a local yoga class or jogging group to stay active and meet new people.

Mental Health: Prioritize your mental health by practicing stress-relief techniques and seeking professional help if needed.

- **Example**: Engaging in hobbies that you enjoy, such as reading, painting, or hiking, can provide a much-needed mental break.

By understanding and navigating the phases of culture shock and employing these comprehensive coping strategies, you can enhance your adaptation process and enrich your overall experience. Embrace the journey with an open mind, seek support when needed, and continuously reflect on your growth. These practices will help you thrive in your new cultural environment and make the most of your international experience.

Anecdotes and Insights

Overcoming Culture Shock in Japan- Maria's Story

Student Perspective: Maria, an art student from Spain, had always dreamed of experiencing life in Japan. She was thrilled when she received an acceptance letter from a prestigious university in Tokyo. However, upon arrival, Maria quickly realized that the reality of living in Japan was different from her expectations.

"Initially, everything was so exciting—the food, the people, the sights. But after the first few weeks, the excitement faded, and I started to feel overwhelmed. The language barrier was much more challenging than I had anticipated. Simple tasks like grocery shopping or asking for directions became daunting. I felt isolated and frustrated because I couldn't communicate effectively."

Expert Insight: Maria's experience is a common one among international students. The initial "honeymoon" phase of excitement can quickly give way to the "frustration" phase of culture shock. This phase is characterized by feelings of isolation, frustration, and homesickness. The key to managing this transition is preparation and proactive engagement with the new culture.

Actionable Tip: To manage culture shock, it is essential to take small steps towards integration. Start by learning basic phrases in the local language, and do not be afraid to use them. Engage in daily activities that involve interaction with locals, such as shopping at local markets or joining community events. Additionally, seek out support groups for international students where you can share experiences and coping strategies.

Chapter 2 Conclusion

As you prepare to embark on your international journey, Chapter 2 has equipped you with essential strategies and insights to navigate the early stages of your international experience with confidence and ease. Adapting to a new cultural environment involves understanding and overcoming culture shock, building supportive networks, and embracing cultural differences with an open mind.

Embracing Cultural Immersion

Engaging deeply with the local culture is the cornerstone of a transformative international experience. By participating in local events, trying new cuisines, and visiting cultural landmarks, you will not only learn about your host country but also develop a profound appreciation for its unique traditions and customs. Embracing these experiences with curiosity and enthusiasm will enrich your journey and help you form lasting memories.

Developing an Open-Minded Attitude

A successful cultural adaptation hinges on your willingness to embrace differences and remain open-minded. Recognize that cultural norms and behaviors may differ significantly from what you are accustomed to. Approach these differences with curiosity rather than judgment. This mindset will not only facilitate smoother interactions but also foster deeper connections with locals and fellow international students.

Building Resilience Through Coping Strategies

Navigating culture shock is an inevitable part of the international process. By understanding the stages of culture shock—honeymoon, frustration, adjustment, and acceptance—you can better manage your emotions and expectations. Employ coping strategies such as maintaining a positive outlook, building a routine, and seeking support from friends, mentors, or counseling services. These strategies will help you stay resilient and focused on the positive aspects of your experience.

Cultivating Support Networks

Establishing strong support networks is crucial for a successful and enjoyable international experience. Connect with other international students through associations and peer support groups. These communities offer a shared understanding of the challenges you face and provide valuable advice and camaraderie. Additionally, building relationships with local friends and mentors can offer insights into the culture and provide a support system that extends beyond the academic environment.

Continuous Learning and Reflection

Adapting to a new culture is an ongoing process that requires continuous learning and reflection. Take the time to reflect on your experiences, appreciate your growth, and celebrate your achievements, no matter how small. This reflective practice not only enhances your cultural adaptation but also contributes to your personal development and global awareness.

Final Thoughts

Your journey as an international student is a unique opportunity to expand your horizons, develop intercultural competencies, and grow both personally and academically. By embracing cultural differences, building supportive networks, and employing effective coping strategies, you will navigate the challenges of cultural adaptation with resilience and grace. Remember, every experience, whether positive or challenging, is a valuable part of your journey that contributes to your growth and understanding.

As you move forward, keep an open mind, stay curious, and continue to seek new experiences. The skills and insights you gain during your international program will stay with you long after you return home, enriching your perspective and shaping your future endeavors. Welcome this adventure with enthusiasm and confidence, knowing that you are well-prepared to make the most of your international experience.

Thank you for engaging deeply with the content of Chapter 2. Your proactive approach to cultural preparation sets a strong foundation for the exciting journey ahead. Continue to build on these insights as you explore the diverse and vibrant world around you. Safe travels and enriching experiences await!

Chapter 2 Review

As you complete Chapter 2: Navigating and Adapting to a New Cultural Environment, take a moment to review and reflect on the key points covered. This chapter has provided you with essential strategies to adapt successfully and make the most of your international experience. The insights gained here will help you build resilience, foster connections, and fully embrace the cultural richness of your host country. Ensure you have a solid understanding of the following areas before moving on to the next chapter.

Key Points

Understanding Culture Shock:

Stages of Culture Shock: Recognize the phases of culture shock—honeymoon, frustration, adjustment, and acceptance—and understand the emotional and psychological responses associated with each stage.

Adjustment and Acceptance: Learn how to navigate the adjustment phase by developing routines and finding comfort in daily activities. Understand that acceptance is about finding a balance between your own cultural identity and the new culture.

Coping Strategies:

Staying Positive: Focus on the positive aspects of your experience, keep a journal to document your journey, and celebrate small wins.

Maintaining Connections: Regular communication with family and friends back home, as well as engaging in virtual support networks, can provide emotional support and reduce feelings of isolation.

Building Routines: Establishing a daily routine creates a sense of normalcy and stability. Balance academic responsibilities with leisure activities to maintain overall well-being.

Seeking Support: Do not hesitate to reach out to friends, mentors, or counseling services if you feel overwhelmed. Engage in activities that promote well-being, such as mindfulness, meditation, or yoga.

Continuous Learning and Reflection: Reflect on your experiences, appreciate your growth, and use your experiences to build resilience and adaptability.

Open-Mindedness:

Embracing Cultural Differences: Understand that cultural differences are natural and embracing them will enrich your experience. Avoid making quick judgments and approach new experiences with curiosity.

Developing an Open-Minded Attitude: Recognize and appreciate the unique values and traditions of your host culture. Engage with locals and seek to understand the reasons behind cultural practices.

Cultural Activities:

Participation in Local Events: Attend local festivals, fairs, and cultural events to immerse yourself in the culture and meet new people.

Joining Cultural Organizations: Engage with cultural clubs or organizations at your host institution to learn more about the local culture and build connections.

Understanding Local Etiquette: Learn the appropriate ways to greet people, introduce yourself, and navigate dining customs and behavioral norms.

Support Networks:

Connecting with International Students: Join international student associations or peer support groups to share experiences and find camaraderie.

Building Relationships with Locals: Establish connections with local friends and mentors who can provide insights into the culture and support you through everyday challenges.

Utilizing Support Services: Make use of the support services provided by your host institution, including health services, academic advising, and cultural integration programs.

Review Questions

Understanding Culture Shock:

- What are the stages of culture shock, and how can recognizing these stages help you navigate your adjustment to a new culture?
- How does the adjustment phase differ from the acceptance phase, and why is it important to understand both?

Coping Strategies:

- Describe two coping strategies that can help you manage feelings of homesickness or cultural frustration. How can these strategies be applied in your daily life?
- Why is maintaining a positive outlook important during your cultural adaptation, and how can keeping a journal assist in this process?

Open-Mindedness:

- Why is it important to approach cultural differences with curiosity rather than judgment? Provide an example of how this mindset can enhance your experience.
- How can developing an open-minded attitude help you build deeper connections with locals?

Cultural Activities:

- What are some benefits of participating in local events and cultural organizations during your international program? How can these activities help you integrate into the community?
- Describe the importance of understanding local etiquette and provide an example of a cultural practice you might need to adapt to.

Support Networks:

- How can building a support network with other international students and local mentors enhance your international experience? Provide specific benefits of these relationships.
- What types of support services should you seek out at your host institution, and how can they assist you in your adaptation process?

Invitation to Reflective Exercises

Congratulations on completing Chapter 2! To further solidify your understanding and prepare for your journey, we invite you to explore the companion workbook, "Reflective Exercises: The International Experiences Guide Workbook." This resource provides engaging activities and thought-provoking questions designed to help you internalize the material, apply it to your personal situation, and deepen your learning experience.

Reflective Exercises Highlights:

- **Personal Reflections**: Engage in exercises that prompt you to reflect on your experiences with culture shock and adaptation.
- **Practical Applications**: Develop action plans for building routines, seeking support, and participating in cultural activities.
- **Continuous Learning**: Use the workbook to track your progress, set goals, and celebrate your achievements.

Dive into the workbook to enhance your preparation and set the stage for a successful and enriching international experience. Embrace the adventure with confidence, knowing you are equipped with the knowledge and strategies to navigate and thrive in your new cultural environment. Safe travels and enriching experiences await!

{ 3 }

Settling In

Introduction

Welcome to Chapter 3 of "International Experiences: A Comprehensive Guide." This chapter is dedicated to helping you settle into your new environment smoothly and confidently. Settling in effectively is crucial for your overall well-being and success during your time abroad. It sets the foundation for your academic, social, and personal life in a new country, allowing you to make the most of this transformative experience.

Moving to a new country can be both exciting and daunting. You have navigated the initial stages of preparation, tackled the challenges of travel, and now you are here, ready to embark on your journey as an international student. This chapter will guide you through the essential aspects of settling in, ensuring that you feel at home in your new surroundings.

Overview of the Importance of Settling in Effectively

Settling in effectively involves more than just unpacking your bags and attending your first class. It is about creating a sense of belonging and stability in your new environment. This process is fundamental to your emotional and psychological well-being, as it helps reduce feelings of homesickness, anxiety, and isolation. When you feel settled, you are more likely to engage fully in your academic and social activities, making your international experience richer and more fulfilling.

Key Areas to Focus on for a Smooth Transition

To ensure a smooth transition, there are several key areas to focus on:

Finding and Setting Up Your Accommodation:

- Securing a comfortable and convenient place to live is the first step to feeling at home.
- Personalizing your space can create a sense of familiarity and comfort.

Navigating Local Transportation:

- Understanding the local public transportation system will make it easier to get around and explore your new city.
- Familiarizing yourself with routes, schedules, and transportation apps can save time and reduce stress.

Understanding Local Culture and Social Norms:

- Immersing yourself in the local culture helps you adapt more quickly and build meaningful connections.
- Learning about social norms, etiquette, and common practices will enhance your interactions with locals.

Building a Support Network:

- Establishing a network of friends, mentors, and support services is essential for your emotional and social well-being.
- Participating in social activities and joining student organizations can help you make new friends and feel connected.

Managing Finances and Administrative Tasks:

- Understanding local banking, budgeting, and administrative requirements ensures you stay organized and financially stable.
- Keeping track of important documents and deadlines is crucial for avoiding unnecessary stress.

Encouragement and Reassurance

Embarking on an international journey is a significant step that requires courage, adaptability, and resilience. It is natural to feel a mix of excitement and apprehension as you navigate this new chapter in your life. Remember, you are not alone—many students have walked this path before you and have successfully settled into their new environments.

Take it one step at a time, and do not hesitate to seek support when needed. Use the resources available to you, be open to new experiences, and give yourself grace as you adjust. The challenges you face will be opportunities for growth, and each small victory will build your confidence.

Settling in is a process that takes time, but with patience and perseverance, you will find your rhythm and create a fulfilling life abroad. Embrace the journey, and let each experience enrich your understanding of the world and yourself. Welcome to your new home away from home—exciting adventures and opportunities await you!Top of Form

3.1 Finding Accommodation

Settling into your new home is one of the most important steps in your journey as an international student. Finding the right accommodation can significantly impact your overall experience, from your daily comfort to your ability to study and relax. This section will guide you through the various types of accommodation available, how to secure a place to live, and tips for setting up your new home efficiently.

Types of Accommodation

University Dormitories:

Benefits and Drawbacks:

- *Benefits*: University dormitories offer convenience and a built-in community. They are usually located on or near campus, making it easy to attend classes and participate in university activities. Dorms often provide furnished rooms and include utilities in the rent, reducing the hassle of setting up services. Additionally, living in a dorm can help you quickly form friendships with other students who are in the same situation as you.
- *Drawbacks*: However, dormitory living can come with downsides such as less privacy, stricter rules, and potential noise from other students. Shared facilities like bathrooms and kitchens might not meet everyone's comfort levels. Also, space can be limited, which means you will need to be strategic about what to bring and how to organize your belongings.

How to Apply and Secure a Spot:

- *Application Process*: Begin the application process as early as possible. University housing departments often have specific deadlines and limited availability. Ensure you complete all necessary forms and provide any required documentation.
- *Requirements*: Prepare necessary documentation, which may include proof of enrollment, identification, and sometimes a deposit. Some universities may also require a personal statement or interview as part of the application process.
- *Selection*: Housing is often allocated on a first-come, first-served basis or through a lottery system, so timely application is crucial. Keep track of deadlines and respond promptly to any communication from the housing office.

Private Rentals:

Searching for Apartments or Houses:

- *Resources*: Utilize online platforms like Zillow, Craigslist, or local real estate websites. University housing offices may also have listings or partnerships with local landlords. Additionally, social media groups and forums for international students can be valuable resources for finding rental properties.
- *Viewing*: Schedule viewings, either in person or virtually, to assess the condition and suitability of the accommodation. Take note of important factors such as safety, proximity to campus, and local amenities like grocery stores and public transportation.

Understanding Rental Agreements and Leases:

- *Lease Terms*: Carefully read the lease agreement, paying attention to the duration, rent amount, payment schedule, and termination clauses. Understand your responsibilities for maintenance, repairs, and any penalties for breaking the lease early.
- *Deposits and Fees*: Understand the requirements for security deposits and any additional fees. Ensure you know the conditions for getting your deposit back at the end of the lease. Ask about policies for wear and tear versus damages to avoid misunderstandings later.

Homestays:

Benefits of Living with a Local Family:

- *Cultural Immersion*: Homestays offer a unique opportunity to immerse yourself in the local culture, practice the language, and gain insights into daily life. This can enhance your understanding and appreciation of the host country's traditions and customs.
- *Support*: Living with a host family can provide a supportive environment, especially helpful for those adjusting to a new country. Hosts can offer guidance, support, and a sense of security.

How to Find and Arrange Homestays:

- *Programs*: Look for homestay programs affiliated with your university or reputable organizations like Homestay.com. These programs typically vet families and ensure they provide a safe and welcoming environment.
- *Screening*: Ensure the program conducts thorough background checks and matches you with a compatible family. Consider having an introductory meeting or conversation with the host family to establish expectations and build rapport before moving in.

Shared Housing:

Living with Roommates or Other Students:

Cost-Effective: Sharing a house or apartment can be more affordable than living alone. It also offers a chance to make friends and share responsibilities. This arrangement can foster a sense of community and support.

Social Aspect: Shared housing can be a great way to build a social network quickly. Living with others can help ease the transition to a new environment and provide companionship.

Tips for Finding and Maintaining a Good Roommate Relationship:

Compatibility: Choose roommates who have similar lifestyles and habits. Clear communication about expectations from the start can prevent conflicts. Discuss topics such as cleanliness, noise levels, guests, and shared expenses.

Agreements: Draft a roommate agreement outlining responsibilities for cleaning, paying bills, and other shared duties. This agreement can serve as a reference point in case of disagreements and help ensure everyone is on the same page.

Anecdotes and Insights

Finding the Perfect Accommodation -Emma's Story

Student Perspective: "When I first arrived in London, finding a place to live was daunting. I opted for a private rental because I wanted a bit more independence than university dorms could offer. The process involved a lot of research, but I found a cozy flat in a student-friendly neighborhood. My tip? Start your search early and use trusted websites to avoid scams. Also, visiting potential places in person helped me feel more confident in my choice." — Emma, International Student from Australia

Expert Insight: Emma's experience underscores the importance of thorough research and early planning. Utilize reputable rental websites and, if possible, visit properties in person or arrange virtual tours. Make sure you understand the lease terms and check reviews of landlords or property managers. Having a clear understanding of your housing contract can prevent future issues and ensure a comfortable living situation.

Securing Accommodation

Application Processes for Different Types of Housing:

University Dormitories: Follow the university's specific application process, which typically involves submitting an online form and required documents. Be sure to check if there are any additional steps, such as interviews or placement tests.

Private Rentals: Contact landlords or property managers to apply. This usually involves a background check and proof of income or financial support. Prepare references from previous landlords if available.

Homestays: Apply through a homestay program, which may include interviews or questionnaires to ensure a good match. Be prepared to provide personal information and preferences to help find a compatible host family.

Shared Housing: Use platforms like SpareRoom or Roomster to find roommates. Meet potential roommates and visit the property before making a decision. Consider using social media groups or university bulletin boards to find housing opportunities.

Necessary Documentation and Deposits:

Documentation: Commonly required documents include identification (passport, visa), proof of enrollment, financial statements, and references. Some landlords may also request a credit check or proof of employment.

Deposits: Be prepared to pay a security deposit, which is typically one to two months' rent. Understand the terms for the return of your deposit, including any conditions related to the state of the property at the end of the lease.

Tips for Avoiding Scams and Ensuring Safety:

- **Verification**: Always verify the legitimacy of the listing and the landlord. Use trusted platforms and avoid properties that seem too good to be true. If possible, visit the property in person or request a virtual tour.
- **Contracts**: Never sign a lease or send money without a signed contract. Ensure all agreements are in writing and read the terms carefully. Seek clarification on any points that are unclear.
- **Visits**: If possible, visit the property in person. If not, request a virtual tour and check reviews from previous tenants. Look for red flags such as unusually low prices or requests for payment before viewing the property.

Initial Setup

Moving In and Setting Up Your Living Space:

Inspection: Upon moving in, inspect the property for any damage and report it immediately to avoid being held responsible later. Take photos or videos as evidence.

Organization: Arrange your living space to make it feel like home. This might include bringing personal items like photos, decorations, and favorite books. Consider creating zones for studying, relaxing, and sleeping to maximize comfort and productivity.

Purchasing Essential Items:

Essentials: Depending on your accommodation, you may need to purchase furniture, kitchenware, bedding, and cleaning supplies. Make a list of essential items and prioritize purchases based on your budget.

Where to Shop: Look for affordable options at stores like IKEA, Walmart, or local second-hand shops. Online marketplaces like Amazon or eBay can also be useful. Consider joining local buy/sell/trade groups on social media for deals on gently used items.

Understanding Utilities and Services:

Utilities: Understand how to set up and pay for utilities like electricity, water, and internet. Some rentals include these in the rent, while others require you to arrange them separately. Contact utility providers in advance to set up accounts and schedule installation if needed.

Contacts: Keep a list of important contacts such as your landlord, utility providers, and emergency services. Familiarize yourself with the procedures for reporting issues or emergencies.

By understanding your options and following these steps, you can secure the right accommodation and set up your living space efficiently. This will help you create a comfortable, safe, and welcoming home away from home, allowing you to focus on your studies and enjoy your international experience to the fullest.

3.2 Navigating Your New Environment

Settling into your new environment involves more than just finding a place to live; it is about familiarizing yourself with your surroundings and feeling confident in navigating your daily life. This section will guide you through the essentials of getting oriented on campus, understanding local transportation, and exploring your city's layout. By the end, you will feel more connected and capable of moving around your new home with ease.

Campus Orientation

Attending Orientation Sessions:

Importance of Orientation: Think of orientation as your crash course in university life. These sessions are designed to help you acclimate quickly by providing vital information about academic expectations, campus resources, and social opportunities. It is your chance to get a head start.

Making Connections: Orientation is also a golden opportunity to meet other new students. Everyone is in the same boat, eager to make friends and share tips. Building a network early can offer emotional support and practical advice throughout your journey.

Getting Informed: Pay close attention during these sessions. They typically cover crucial topics such as course registration, academic advising, student organizations, and campus policies. Do not hesitate to ask questions and take plenty of notes—you will thank yourself later.

Campus Tours and Resources:

Guided Tours: Take advantage of any guided tours offered during orientation. These tours are a great way to get acquainted with the campus layout and key facilities without feeling overwhelmed.

Self-Guided Exploration: If guided tours are not available or you prefer exploring on your own, carve out some time to wander around the campus. Use campus maps or mobile apps to help you locate important buildings and services.

Resources: Make a list of key resources such as academic support centers, IT services, and student services. Knowing where to find help can save you a lot of time and stress down the road.

Key Locations:

Libraries: Libraries are more than just places to study; they are treasure troves of resources. Find out where the main library and any specialized libraries are located. Familiarize yourself with their hours, borrowing policies, and available study spaces.

Student Centers: Student centers are the heartbeat of campus life. They often house essential services such as career counseling, international student offices, and social spaces. Check out bulletin boards and information desks for events and opportunities.

Health Services: Locate the campus health center and understand what services are offered. Knowing where to go for medical care or counseling is crucial for maintaining your well-being. It is better to know before you need it!

Local Transportation

Public Transit Options:

Buses, Trains, Subways: Most cities offer a variety of public transit options. Learn the routes, schedules, and costs of buses, trains, and subways. Download transit apps to get real-time updates and plan your trips. Take a few practice runs to familiarize yourself with the system.

Navigating Transit: Practice using the transit system by taking short trips. This will build your confidence and help you understand the layout of the city. Do not be afraid to ask locals or fellow students for advice—they are usually happy to help.

Understanding Transportation Passes and Student Discounts:

Passes and Cards: Many cities offer transportation passes that can be more cost-effective than single tickets. Look into options such as monthly or semester passes. Some passes may even offer unlimited travel within a certain period.

Student Discounts: Check if there are student discounts available for public transportation. Often, universities partner with transit authorities to provide discounted passes for students. Make sure to carry your student ID for verification.

Purchasing Passes: Find out where and how to purchase these passes. Some universities sell them directly to students, while others can be bought at transit stations or online. Look for any early bird specials or seasonal discounts.

Biking and Walking as Alternatives:

Cycling: Many cities are bike-friendly with dedicated bike lanes and bike-sharing programs. Consider cycling as an eco-friendly and healthy way to get around. Invest in a good lock, safety gear, and learn local biking rules and safety practices.

Walking: Walking is a great way to explore your new environment and stay active. Use pedestrian maps to discover walking routes and nearby amenities. It is also a wonderful way to stumble upon hidden gems and local favorites.

Anecdotes and Insights
Navigating Your New Environment -Lucas's Story

Student Perspective: "Getting around Munich was initially overwhelming, but the orientation sessions at my university were incredibly helpful. I also downloaded a local transit app which made public transportation much easier to navigate. I made it a point to explore a bit every weekend, which helped me get to know the city better. One of my favorite finds was a hidden park that became my go-to study spot." — Lucas, International Student from Brazil

Expert Insight: Lucas's proactive approach to exploring his new environment is exemplary. Attending orientation sessions and using local transit apps are excellent ways to familiarize yourself with your new surroundings. Regularly exploring your city, whether it is through weekend adventures or daily walks, helps you become more comfortable and integrated into your new home. These explorations can lead to delightful discoveries and a stronger sense of belonging.

City Layout and Key Areas

Exploring the City Layout:

City Map: Get a map of the city to familiarize yourself with its layout. Identify major streets, neighborhoods, and landmarks. Apps like Google Maps can be incredibly helpful for navigation and discovering points of interest.

Neighborhood Exploration: Spend time exploring different neighborhoods. Each area may have its own unique character and amenities. Take note of areas you enjoy and frequent spots that cater to your needs, like grocery stores and coffee shops.

Identifying Important Areas:

Shopping Districts: Locate major shopping areas where you can buy essentials, groceries, and personal items. This might include supermarkets, malls, and local markets. Knowing where to shop can make your daily life much more convenient.

Cultural Sites: Explore cultural sites such as museums, theaters, historical landmarks, and art galleries. These can enrich your experience and understanding of the local culture. Plus, they are great spots to take visiting friends and family.

Recreational Areas: Find parks, sports facilities, and recreational areas where you can relax, exercise, and socialize. Being aware of these spaces can improve your quality of life and provide outlets for stress relief.

Safety Tips for Navigating the City:

- **Personal Safety**: Stay aware of your surroundings, especially at night. Stick to well-lit and populated areas. Avoid using headphones or being distracted by your phone while walking. Trust your instincts and do not take unnecessary risks.
- **Emergency Contacts**: Keep a list of emergency contacts, including local emergency services and your university's emergency number. Program these into your phone for quick access. It is also a good idea to know the location of the nearest hospital or clinic.

- **Local Customs**: Be aware of local customs and laws to ensure you do not inadvertently offend or get into trouble. This might include jaywalking rules, tipping practices, or public behavior norms. Respecting these customs will help you integrate more smoothly.
- **Transportation Safety**: When using public transportation, keep your belongings secure and be aware of your surroundings. Avoid traveling alone late at night if possible, and always be cautious in crowded areas to prevent theft.

By familiarizing yourself with these aspects of your new environment, you will gain the confidence and knowledge needed to navigate your new home successfully. This preparation will help you feel more settled and allow you to focus on enjoying your international experience to the fullest. Embrace the journey, stay curious, and make the most of every opportunity to explore and learn.

3.3 Managing Daily Life

Adjusting to daily life in a new country involves mastering a variety of practical tasks that can significantly impact your comfort and success. This section will provide you with essential information and tips on grocery shopping, health and wellness, banking and finances, and communication. By understanding how to manage these aspects of daily life, you will be better equipped to thrive in your new environment.

Grocery Shopping

Local Supermarkets and Markets:

Supermarkets: Familiarize yourself with the major supermarket chains in your area. Whether it is Tesco in the UK, Carrefour in France, or Walmart in the USA, these stores often have everything you need under one roof, including international sections. It is like a one-stop-shop for all your grocery needs.

Markets: Do not overlook local markets. They can be treasure troves of fresh produce, meats, and unique local goods. Plus, they often offer more affordable prices and a more authentic shopping experience. Take a stroll through the market and soak in the vibrant atmosphere—it is a great way to feel more connected to your new community.

Tips for Finding International Foods or Specialty Items:

- **Specialty Stores**: If you are craving a taste of home, look for specialty stores or international supermarkets that cater to specific cuisines. These stores often carry a range of imported goods that can make you feel more at home. Imagine finding that favorite spice blend or snack you thought you would have to live without!
- **Online Shopping**: Many specialty items can be found online. Websites like Amazon or local equivalents might offer the international foods and specialty items you are looking for. It is convenient and often provides a broader selection than physical stores.
- **Ask Locals**: Do not hesitate to ask fellow international students or locals where they find certain foods or products. They can often provide insider tips on the best places to shop. Building this network can lead to discovering hidden gems in your new city.

Budgeting for Groceries:

Plan Ahead: Create a weekly meal plan to avoid impulse buys and ensure you purchase only what you need. This can also help you balance your diet and enjoy a variety of foods. Plus, it makes grocery shopping quicker and less stressful.

Compare Prices: Compare prices between different supermarkets and markets to find the best deals. Many cities have price comparison apps that can help you save money. It is like having a personal assistant for your grocery shopping!

Bulk Buying: Buying in bulk can save money in the long run, especially for non-perishable items. Look for stores that offer bulk purchasing options. Just make sure you have enough storage space to keep everything.

Anecdotes and Insights
Managing Daily Life -Akira's Story

Student Perspective: "In Tokyo, managing daily life was a mix of excitement and confusion. Grocery shopping was particularly challenging at first because I could not read the labels. I joined a local cooking class which not only helped me understand the ingredients better but also introduced me to new friends. For banking, I found it essential to open a local bank account to avoid international fees. The bank staff were very helpful and walked me through the process." — Akira, International Student from the USA

Expert Insight: Akira's experience highlights the value of immersing yourself in local activities, such as cooking classes, to better manage daily tasks and build connections. Opening a local bank account can simplify financial transactions and save on fees. When grocery shopping in a foreign language, apps that translate labels or even learning a few key phrases can be incredibly helpful. Engaging with local services and asking for assistance when needed can make daily life much smoother.

Health and Wellness

Registering with Local Health Services:

University Health Services: Many universities offer health services for students. Register as soon as possible to take advantage of these resources. It is a convenient way to access medical care without having to navigate the local health system on your own.

Local Health Clinics: Find out where the nearest health clinics and hospitals are located. Register with a local GP (General Practitioner) if required by your host country's health system. Knowing where to go before you need care can save valuable time in an emergency.

Finding Doctors, Dentists, and Mental Health Resources:

Doctors and Dentists: Use university recommendations or online directories to find local doctors and dentists. Check if they accept your health insurance. It is always good to have a trusted professional lined up for routine care and any unexpected issues.

Mental Health Resources: Mental health is just as important as physical health. Universities often provide counseling services, but there are also many local resources available. Do not hesitate to seek help if you need it—adjusting to a new environment can be stressful, and there is no shame in reaching out for support.

Staying Active (Gyms, Sports Clubs, Outdoor Activities):

Gyms: Find a gym that suits your needs and budget. Many offer student discounts or trial memberships. Regular exercise can boost your mood and help you stay healthy.

Sports Clubs: Joining a sports club is a great way to stay active and meet new people. Universities often have a variety of clubs to choose from, ranging from soccer to yoga. It is a fun way to integrate into the community and make friends.

Outdoor Activities: Explore local parks, hiking trails, and other outdoor spaces. Regular physical activity is crucial for maintaining your health and well-being. Plus, spending time in nature can be incredibly refreshing and rejuvenating.

Banking and Finances

Opening a Local Bank Account:

Choosing a Bank: Research local banks and their offerings for international students. Look for accounts with low fees and convenient online banking options. A local account can simplify your financial transactions and save on foreign transaction fees.

Documentation: Prepare the necessary documents, which typically include your passport, visa, proof of address, and proof of enrollment. Having these ready can expedite the process and help you get your account set up smoothly.

Benefits: A local bank account can help you avoid foreign transaction fees and make managing your finances easier. It is also useful for receiving payments if you take on part-time work or internships.

Understanding Local Currency and Exchange Rates:

Currency Familiarization: Get to know the local currency and common denominations. Practice calculating exchange rates so you are comfortable with the value of money. This knowledge can help you budget more effectively and avoid overspending.

Exchange Services: Use reputable exchange services for converting money. Avoid high-fee services often found at airports and tourist areas. Look for banks or exchange offices with competitive rates and transparent fee structures.

Managing Expenses and Budgeting:

Track Your Spending: Use budgeting apps to keep track of your expenses and ensure you are staying within your budget. Apps like Mint, YNAB (You Need A Budget), or local equivalents can be very helpful. They can provide insights into your spending habits and help you make adjustments as needed.

Set a Budget: Establish a monthly budget for essentials like rent, groceries, and transportation, as well as discretionary spending for entertainment and travel. Setting financial goals can keep you focused and help you avoid unnecessary debt.

Emergency Fund: Maintain an emergency fund to cover unexpected expenses. This provides a financial safety net and peace of mind. Even a small cushion can make a big difference in a pinch.

Communication

Setting Up a Local Mobile Phone Plan:

Plan Options: Research mobile phone plans and providers to find the best option for your needs. Look for plans that offer good data allowances and coverage. Prepaid plans can be a flexible option if you are unsure of your usage patterns.

Student Discounts: Many providers offer student discounts, so be sure to ask. Prepaid plans can be a flexible option if you are unsure of your usage patterns. It is worth comparing a few different options to find the best deal.

International Calls: If you need to make international calls frequently, consider plans that offer discounted rates or use apps that provide low-cost calling options. Apps like Skype, WhatsApp, and Zoom can also be great for staying in touch with family and friends back home.

Using Communication Apps for Staying in Touch:

Popular Apps: Apps like WhatsApp, Skype, and Zoom are widely used for staying in touch with family and friends back home. These apps are often free and easy to use. They can also be used for group chats, video calls, and sharing photos and videos.

Social media: Social media platforms can also be a great way to keep connected with loved ones and share your experiences. Just be mindful of time zones and data usage. It is easy to feel connected to home while building your new life abroad.

Accessing Reliable Internet:

Home Internet: If your accommodation does not include internet, research local providers to set up a home connection. Look for plans that offer good speeds and reliable service. Having a stable internet connection is essential for studying, staying in touch, and enjoying your favorite online activities.

Public Wi-Fi: Many cafes, libraries, and public spaces offer free Wi-Fi. Use these to stay connected when you are out and about. Just be cautious with your personal information when using public networks.

University Resources: Take advantage of the university's internet resources, including on-campus Wi-Fi and computer labs. These resources can be incredibly helpful for completing assignments and staying connected.

By mastering these daily life essentials, you will create a stable and comfortable foundation for your stay abroad. Embrace the opportunity to learn, adapt, and remember that these skills will serve you well throughout your international experience and beyond. With careful planning and a proactive approach, managing your daily life in a new country can be both rewarding and empowering. Enjoy every moment of this journey—it is a unique and enriching chapter of your life!

3.4 Social Integration

Social integration is a crucial part of your experience as an international student. Building friendships, adjusting to a new culture, and improving language skills will help you feel more connected and confident in your new environment. This section provides valuable insights and tips on making friends, cultural adjustment, and enhancing your language skills.

Making Friends

Joining Clubs and Student Organizations:

Campus Clubs: Universities are bustling with clubs and organizations tailored to various interests—academic, cultural, sports, and hobbies. Joining these clubs is like opening the door to a new world of friendships. Whether you are into chess, debate, hiking, or cooking, there is likely a club that fits your interests. Plus, participating in club activities can help you form lasting friendships with people who share your passions.

Special Interest Groups: Look for groups that match your passions. If photography is your thing, find a photography club. If you love volunteering, join a community service organization. These groups provide a sense of belonging and a ready-made community where you can share and grow your interests.

International Student Associations: Many universities have associations specifically for international students. These associations often organize social events, trips, and cultural exchanges, making it easier to connect with fellow international students. It is a fantastic way to share experiences and support each other.

Participating in Social Events and Activities:

University Events: Do not miss out on university-sponsored events like orientation programs, cultural festivals, sports events, and workshops. These events are designed to help students socialize and integrate into campus life. They are fun, informative, and perfect for making new friends.

Local Festivals and Events: Dive into local culture by participating in festivals, fairs, and community events. These activities not only offer fun experiences but also provide insights into local traditions. Imagine the stories you will have to share!

Social media and Apps: Use social media platforms and event apps to stay in the loop about upcoming events and activities in your area. Websites like Meetup can help you find gatherings and groups that match your interests. It is like having a social calendar in your pocket.

Building a Social Network:

Networking: Networking is not just for professional settings; it is also crucial for building a social circle. Attend networking events, seminars, and informal gatherings where you can meet people and expand your connections. You never know who you might meet!

Social media: Use social media platforms to stay connected with new friends and keep up with social activities. Join university and community groups on Facebook, Instagram, or LinkedIn. It is a great way to keep track of events and stay engaged.

Roommates and Neighbors: Do not overlook the people living around you. Building a good relationship with your roommates or neighbors can lead to close friendships and a support network. Plus, they can be great sources of local tips and advice.

Anecdotes and Insights

Social Integration – Sofia's Story

Student Perspective: "Making friends in a new country seemed daunting at first but joining the international student association at my university in Paris made all the difference. We organized regular meetups and cultural exchange events which were fantastic icebreakers. I also made an effort to join local clubs, like a hiking group, which helped me meet people outside the university." — Sofia, International Student from Italy

Expert Insight: Sofia's strategy of joining both international and local groups is a great way to build a diverse social network. Engaging in university clubs and local community groups can provide support and enrich your social life. Regular meetups and participating in activities you enjoy will help you form meaningful connections and integrate more smoothly into your new environment. Being proactive in social settings and open to new friendships can significantly enhance your international experience.

Cultural Adjustment

Understanding and Adapting to Cultural Differences:

Cultural Research: Spend some time researching the cultural norms and values of your host country. Understanding these can help you navigate social interactions more smoothly and avoid misunderstandings. It is like having a cultural cheat sheet.

Observing and Learning: Pay attention to how locals behave in different situations—how they greet each other, what gestures they use, and their dining etiquette. Mimicking these behaviors can help you fit in better. Think of it as a fun cultural experiment.

Asking Questions: Do not be afraid to ask questions about cultural practices that are unfamiliar to you. Most people appreciate the effort you are making to understand and will be happy to explain. It is a great conversation starter, too!

Overcoming Culture Shock:

Acknowledge Your Feelings: Culture shock is a common experience. Acknowledge your feelings and understand that it is okay to feel overwhelmed or homesick. Everyone goes through it—you are not alone.

Stay Connected: Keep in touch with family and friends back home. Regular communication can provide emotional support and help ease feelings of isolation. Thanks to technology, home is just a call away.

Seek Support: Utilize support services offered by your university, such as counseling and international student offices. Sharing your experiences with other international students can also provide comfort and practical advice. There's strength in numbers!

Respecting Local Customs and Traditions:

Being Respectful: Show respect for local customs and traditions, even if they differ significantly from what you are used to. This includes dress codes, religious practices, and public behaviors. Respect earns respect.

Participating in Traditions: Whenever possible, participate in local customs and traditions. This not only shows respect but also provides a deeper understanding and appreciation of the culture. Plus, it can be a lot of fun!

Open-Mindedness: Approach cultural differences with an open mind. Embrace the opportunity to learn and grow from these new experiences. Remember, every cultural quirk is a chance to broaden your horizons.

Language Skills

Improving Language Proficiency:

Regular Practice: Make a habit of practicing the local language daily. This can include speaking with locals, watching local TV shows or movies, and reading newspapers or books. Think of it as immersing yourself in a linguistic adventure.

Language Apps: Use language learning apps like Duolingo, Babbel, or Rosetta Stone to enhance your proficiency. These apps offer structured lessons and practice exercises that can be very effective. It is like having a personal language tutor in your pocket.

Study Groups: Form or join study groups with other students who are also learning the language. Group study sessions can provide mutual support and motivation. Plus, they are a great way to make new friends.

Language Exchange Programs and Classes:

Language Exchange: Participate in language exchange programs where you can practice the local language with native speakers who want to learn your language. This mutual learning setup is beneficial and often leads to friendships. It is a win-win!

Language Classes: Enroll in language classes offered by your university or local language schools. These classes provide structured learning and can significantly boost your language skills. Plus, they often come with the added bonus of meeting other language learners.

Conversation Partners: Find a conversation partner through university programs or local organizations. Regular practice with a native speaker can improve your fluency and confidence. It is like having a local guide and a language coach rolled into one.

Practicing with Locals and Other Students:

Everyday Conversations: Take every opportunity to practice the language in everyday situations—ordering food, asking for directions, or chatting with classmates. These interactions can help you become more comfortable and fluent. Practice makes perfect!

Cultural Immersion: Immerse yourself in the local culture by attending events, participating in activities, and spending time with locals. Immersion is one of the most effective ways to improve language skills. Plus, it is a great way to experience the local way of life.

Volunteer Work: Consider volunteering in the community. This not only helps you practice the language but also provides meaningful interactions and a sense of contribution. It is a wonderful way to give back while learning.

By actively engaging in these aspects of social integration, you will build a robust support network, adapt smoothly to cultural differences, and enhance your language skills. These efforts will enrich your international experience, making it more enjoyable and fulfilling. Embrace the journey with curiosity and openness, and you will find that integrating into your new environment can be one of the most rewarding parts of your time abroad.

3.5 Academic Success

Academic success is a cornerstone of your journey as an international student. Adapting to a new education system, developing effective study habits, and engaging with professors and peers are crucial for achieving your academic goals. This section provides valuable insights and practical tips to help you navigate these aspects and thrive in your studies.

Understanding the Education System

Differences in Academic Culture and Expectations:

Cultural Nuances: Every education system has its unique culture and set of expectations. In some countries, education might be more lecture-based with a focus on exams, while in others, there might be a greater emphasis on participation and continuous assessment. Understanding these differences can help you adapt more quickly. Think of it as learning the rules of a new game.

Self-Directed Learning: Many Western education systems place a significant emphasis on self-directed learning. This means you will need to take the initiative to study independently, complete assignments on time, and seek help when needed. It is an excellent opportunity to develop your critical thinking and problem-solving skills. Embrace the freedom to manage your own learning!

Academic Integrity: Academic integrity is taken very seriously. Plagiarism and cheating are strictly prohibited and can have severe consequences. Make sure you understand what constitutes academic dishonesty in your host country and always strive to produce original work. It is all about maintaining your reputation and credibility.

Course Structure and Grading System:

Course Format: Courses might be structured differently than what you are used to. Some may have a mix of lectures, seminars, labs, and tutorials. Each component serves a specific purpose, so attend all sessions to get the most out of your education. Think of each type of session as a piece of the puzzle.

Grading System: Grading systems can vary significantly. Familiarize yourself with the local grading scale and what each grade represents. This will help you set realistic academic goals and understand where you stand. Knowing how you are being evaluated can reduce anxiety and help you focus on what matters most.

Assessment Methods: Assessments can include exams, essays, projects, and presentations. Each method tests different skills, so be prepared to adapt your study strategies accordingly. Embrace the variety—it keeps things interesting!

Key Academic Resources (Libraries, Study Groups, Tutoring Services):

Libraries: Libraries are invaluable resources. They offer access to textbooks, academic journals, and study spaces. Take advantage of library orientations to learn how to navigate and utilize these resources effectively. The library is your academic treasure trove.

Study Groups: Joining or forming study groups can enhance your learning experience. Discussing material with peers can deepen your understanding and provide different perspectives. Plus, it is a great way to make friends!

Tutoring Services: Many universities offer tutoring services for various subjects. Do not hesitate to seek help if you are struggling with a particular topic. Tutors can provide personalized assistance and help you improve your academic performance. It is like having a personal coach.

Effective Study Habits

Time Management and Organization:

Creating a Schedule: Develop a study schedule that balances class time, study sessions, and personal activities. Use tools like planners, calendars, or time management apps to keep track of deadlines and commitments. A well-planned schedule can be your best friend.

Prioritizing Tasks: Learn to prioritize your tasks based on urgency and importance. Break down larger projects into manageable chunks and set deadlines for each part. This will help you stay on top of your workload and reduce stress. Remember, the key is to work smarter, not harder.

Avoiding Procrastination: Procrastination can be a major barrier to academic success. Identify what triggers your procrastination and develop strategies to overcome it. Setting specific goals and rewarding yourself for meeting them can be motivating. It is all about finding what works for you.

Study Techniques and Tools:

Active Learning: Engage actively with the material by summarizing information in your own words, creating mind maps, or teaching concepts to a friend. Active learning techniques can improve retention and understanding. Make studying an interactive experience.

Effective Notetaking: Develop a note-taking system that works for you. Whether it is the Cornell method, mind mapping, or bullet points, good notes are essential for effective study sessions. Clear, organized notes can be a game-changer.

Utilizing Technology: Take advantage of technology to enhance your study habits. Apps like Anki for flashcards, Evernote for organization, and Quizlet for practice tests can be incredibly helpful. Your smartphone can be a powerful study tool.

Balancing Academics with Social Life:

Setting Boundaries: While it is important to enjoy your social life, setting boundaries can help you maintain a healthy balance. Allocate specific times for studying and socializing to ensure neither aspect is neglected. It is all about finding the right balance.

Stress Management: Engaging in social activities can be a great way to relieve stress. Make time for hobbies, exercise, and relaxation to keep your mind and body healthy. Remember, a happy student is a productive student.

Support Systems: Build a support system of friends, family, and mentors who understand your academic goals and can offer encouragement and advice when needed. Having a strong support network can make a world of difference.

Engaging with Professors and Peers

Building Relationships with Professors:

Office Hours: Take advantage of professors' office hours to ask questions, seek clarification on topics, and discuss your progress. Building a rapport with your professors can provide valuable insights and guidance. They are there to help you succeed.

Email Etiquette: When communicating with professors via email, be respectful and concise. Use proper salutations and clearly state your questions or concerns. Professional communication reflects well on you and fosters a positive relationship. It is all about making a good impression.

Class Participation: Actively participating in class shows your interest and engagement. Do not be afraid to ask questions or contribute to discussions. Professors appreciate students who are actively involved in their learning. Your voice matters!

Participating in Class and Group Discussions:

Preparation: Come to class prepared by completing readings and assignments beforehand. This allows you to contribute meaningfully to discussions and enhances your understanding of the material. Preparation is key.

Active Listening: Practice active listening during lectures and discussions. Take notes and ask follow-up questions to deepen your understanding. Engaging fully in class can make learning more effective and enjoyable.

Respecting Diverse Opinions: Be open to different perspectives and respectful of diverse opinions during group discussions. Engaging with a variety of viewpoints can enrich your learning experience and foster a collaborative environment. Diversity is a strength.

Networking with Peers for Academic Support:

Study Groups: Form study groups with classmates to review material, prepare for exams, and work on projects. Collaborative learning can provide different perspectives and enhance your understanding. It is also a great way to build friendships.

Peer Mentoring: Seek out peer mentoring programs where more experienced students offer guidance and support. Mentors can share valuable tips and strategies for academic success. It is like having a trusted guide.

Academic Events: Attend academic events such as seminars, workshops, and guest lectures. These events provide opportunities to network with peers and professors and stay informed about developments in your field of study. Knowledge is power.

Anecdotes and Insights
Academic Success -Priya's Story

Student Perspective: "Studying in a different academic system in Toronto was challenging, but I found attending all the orientation sessions and using campus resources really helped. I regularly visited the library and joined study groups, which improved my understanding of the coursework. Engaging with professors during office hours was also beneficial—they were very approachable and provided valuable insights." — Priya, International Student from India

Expert Insight: Priya's proactive approach to academic success is commendable. Making the most of campus resources like libraries, study groups, and professor office hours can greatly enhance your understanding and performance. Understanding the local education system and developing effective study habits are crucial. Do not hesitate to ask for help and seek academic support services if needed. Building good relationships with professors and peers can provide a strong academic support network.

By understanding the education system, developing effective study habits, and engaging actively with professors and peers, you will be well-equipped to achieve academic success. Embrace these strategies to make the most of your educational experience and remember that perseverance and a positive attitude are key components of success. Enjoy the journey of learning and growing in your new academic environment!

3.6 Staying Safe and Legal

As an international student, ensuring your safety and understanding legal requirements are paramount. This section will guide you through essential personal safety tips, emergency procedures, and legal obligations to help you navigate your new environment confidently and responsibly.

Personal Safety

General Safety Tips for Living in a New City:

Stay Aware of Your Surroundings: Always keep an eye on what is happening around you, especially in unfamiliar areas. Avoid getting too engrossed in your phone while walking and be cautious in crowded places to prevent pickpocketing. It is all about staying alert and aware.

Know the Safe Routes: Familiarize yourself with the safest routes to your accommodation, campus, and other frequently visited places. Stick to well-lit, populated areas, especially at night. A little planning goes a long way in keeping you safe.

Blend In: Try not to draw unnecessary attention to yourself. Avoid flashing expensive items like jewelry or gadgets in public. Blending in with the locals can help you feel more at ease and reduce the likelihood of becoming a target.

Trust Your Instincts: If something feels off, trust your gut. It is better to be safe and take precautions than to ignore potential dangers. Your intuition is a powerful tool—use it!

Emergency Apps: Download local safety apps that provide real-time updates on safe routes, emergency contacts, and alerts. These tools can be incredibly useful in unfamiliar surroundings. Think of them as your digital safety net.

Emergency Contacts and Procedures:

Emergency Numbers: Memorize the local emergency numbers for police, fire, and medical services. These numbers can vary by country, so ensure you know the correct ones for your location. It is one of those things you hope you never need, but it is crucial to know.

University Contacts: Keep the contact details of your university's emergency services, international student office, and student support services handy. They can offer assistance in various situations. Having these numbers saved in your phone can be a lifesaver.

Emergency Plan: Develop a personal emergency plan. Know the location of the nearest hospital, police station, and embassy or consulate. Share your plan with friends or roommates so they are aware of your emergency contacts. Preparation is key to staying calm in a crisis.

Safety Drills: Participate in any safety drills conducted by your university. These drills prepare you for different emergency scenarios, ensuring you know what to do and where to go. It is always better to be over-prepared than underprepared.

Staying Informed About Local News and Alerts:

Local News Sources: Regularly check local news websites, newspapers, or radio stations to stay updated on current events, weather forecasts, and safety alerts. Staying informed helps you make better decisions.

Social media: Follow official local authorities and your university on social media for real-time updates and important announcements. It is a quick and easy way to stay in the loop.

Alert Systems: Sign up for local emergency alert systems if available. These systems provide notifications about natural disasters, safety threats, and other emergencies directly to your phone. It is like having a personal alert system in your pocket.

Legal Requirements

Registering with Local Authorities if Required:

Local Registration: Some countries require international students to register with local authorities upon arrival. This process can involve registering your residence, getting a local ID, or informing the local immigration office of your presence. It is usually a straightforward process, but essential for staying compliant.

Timelines and Documents: Be aware of the timelines and documents required for registration. Commonly needed documents include your passport, visa, proof of address, and university enrollment certificate. Having everything ready in advance can make the process smoother.

Procedure: Follow the registration procedure carefully to avoid legal issues. Your university's international office can usually provide guidance on this process. Do not hesitate to ask for help if you are unsure about any steps.

Understanding Visa Regulations and Maintaining Legal Status:

Visa Conditions: Familiarize yourself with the conditions of your student visa. This includes the duration of your stay, work restrictions, and any mandatory reporting requirements. Keeping track of these details ensures you stay on the right side of the law.

Renewals and Extensions: Keep track of your visa expiration date and start the renewal or extension process well in advance. Delays can lead to complications and affect your legal status. It is all about staying ahead of the game.

Legal Work: If you plan to work while studying, understand the work restrictions and ensure any employment complies with your visa conditions. Unauthorized work can jeopardize your visa status. It is not worth the risk—stick to the rules.

Knowing Your Rights and Responsibilities as an International Student:

Student Rights: Understand your rights as an international student. This includes the right to fair treatment, access to educational resources, and protection under local laws. Knowing your rights can help you advocate for yourself if needed.

University Policies: Familiarize yourself with your university's policies regarding academic integrity, campus conduct, and dispute resolution. Adhering to these policies helps maintain a positive academic record. It is all part of being a responsible student.

Legal Aid: Know where to seek legal aid if needed. Some universities offer legal advice services to students, or you may find local legal aid organizations that can assist you. Having access to legal support can provide peace of mind.

Anecdotes and Insights
Staying Safe and Legal – Carlos's Story
Student Perspective: "In Berlin, I quickly learned the importance of staying informed about local safety guidelines. I registered with the local authorities as soon as I arrived and downloaded a few safety apps that provided real-time updates on any incidents. It was also helpful to keep

emergency contact numbers handy. Knowing I had a plan in place made me feel much more secure." — Carlos, International Student from Mexico

Expert Insight: Carlos's emphasis on staying informed and prepared is essential for safety. Registering with local authorities and using safety apps are excellent practices. Always keep a list of emergency contacts and familiarize yourself with local emergency procedures. Being aware of your surroundings and staying informed through local news sources can enhance your personal safety. Proactively managing your legal and safety responsibilities ensures a worry-free stay.

By prioritizing personal safety, staying informed, and adhering to legal requirements, you can ensure a secure and compliant stay in your host country. Embrace these practices to navigate your new environment confidently, focusing on your studies and enriching your international experience. Remember, being proactive and prepared can make all the difference in staying safe and legal while studying abroad. Stay vigilant, stay informed, and most importantly, enjoy your time as an international student!

3.7 Exploring and Enjoying Your New Home

As an international student, you have a unique opportunity to explore and immerse yourself in a new culture. Balancing your academic responsibilities with leisure activities can enrich your experience and help you make the most of your time abroad. This section will provide valuable insights and tips on travel and exploration, cultural experiences, and leisure activities to help you enjoy your new home to the fullest.

Travel and Exploration

Local Attractions and Must-See Places:

Research and Recommendations: Start by doing a little homework on your new city's top attractions. Guidebooks, travel websites, and local tourism offices are great resources. Do not forget to ask locals and fellow students for their favorite spots—they often know the hidden gems that are not in the guidebooks.

Historical and Cultural Sites: Make it a point to visit historical landmarks, monuments, and cultural sites. These places offer a deeper understanding of the local history and heritage. Create a list of must-see spots and plan your visits. You might discover a newfound love for history or art!

Parks and Nature Reserves: Do not overlook local parks, gardens, and nature reserves. These are perfect places to relax, enjoy nature, and get some fresh air. A stroll through a beautiful park can be just the break you need from studying.

Weekend Trips and Travel Tips:

Short Getaways: Plan weekend trips to nearby towns or cities. These short trips can provide a refreshing change of scenery and an opportunity to explore different regions. Look for affordable accommodation options like hostels or budget hotels. Sometimes, a quick escape is all you need to recharge.

Travel Deals: Keep an eye out for travel deals and discounts. Many travel websites and apps offer special rates for students. Booking in advance can also save you money. It is always exciting to find a great deal on a trip!

Packing Light: Pack light for weekend trips to make travel easier. Bring essentials like a change of clothes, toiletries, and any necessary travel documents. A small backpack or carry-on is usually sufficient. You will be surprised how liberating it can be to travel light.

Balancing Exploration with Academics: While it is exciting to travel and explore, remember to balance these activities with your academic responsibilities. Plan your trips around your study schedule and avoid traveling during critical exam periods or project deadlines. The goal is to enjoy yourself without compromising your studies.

Cultural Experiences

Engaging in Local Festivals and Events:

Community Festivals: Participate in local festivals and community events. These gatherings are a fantastic way to experience the culture, meet new people, and have fun. Check local event calendars and join in the celebrations. Imagine the stories you will have to tell!

University Events: Many universities organize cultural events, international fairs, and themed weeks. Get involved in these activities to connect with other students and learn about different cultures. It is like traveling the world without leaving campus.

Visiting Museums, Galleries, and Cultural Sites:

Museums and Galleries: Spend time visiting museums and art galleries. These venues often showcase the local history, art, and culture. Many offer student discounts or free entry on certain days. It is a great way to spend a rainy afternoon.

Historical Sites: Explore historical sites and landmarks. These places provide insights into the country's past and its cultural evolution. Guided tours can offer additional information and enrich your visit. You will feel like you have stepped back in time.

Cultural Performances: Attend cultural performances such as theater plays, dance shows, and music concerts. These events offer a glimpse into the local artistic scene and are often highly enjoyable. It is a wonderful way to experience the creative heartbeat of your new home.

Trying Local Cuisine and Learning About Food Culture:

Local Restaurants: Try out local restaurants and eateries. Sampling traditional dishes is a delightful way to experience the culture. Do not be afraid to try new foods—you might discover some new favorites! Eating out is also a great way to socialize.

Street Food: Explore the street food scene. Many cities have vibrant street food markets offering delicious and affordable meals. Street food can provide an authentic taste of local cuisine. It is often some of the best food you will find.

Cooking Classes: Consider taking a cooking class to learn how to prepare local dishes. It is a fun activity and a great skill to bring back home. Plus, you will get to enjoy a delicious meal at the end. Cooking classes are also a fantastic way to meet new people.

Leisure Activities

Finding Hobbies and Interests:

Hobby Groups: Join hobby groups or clubs that match your interests. Whether it is painting, knitting, photography, or gardening, there are usually groups or classes available. These activities are great for relaxation and meeting like-minded people. Pursuing your hobbies abroad can make you feel more at home.

University Clubs: Participate in university clubs and societies. They often offer a range of activities, from debate clubs to dance classes. Getting involved can help you build a sense of community on campus. It is a chance to explore new interests and talents.

Participating in Sports and Recreational Activities:

Sports Teams: Join a sports team or club. Playing sports is an excellent way to stay active, relieve stress, and make new friends. Whether you are into soccer, basketball, or tennis, there is likely a team or group you can join. It is also a great way to stay fit.

Outdoor Activities: Take advantage of outdoor recreational activities like hiking, cycling, or kayaking. These activities can be both exhilarating and refreshing. Many universities organize outdoor trips and activities for students. It is a wonderful way to see the natural beauty of your new home.

Fitness Classes: Enroll in fitness classes such as yoga, Pilates, or dance. These classes are not only good for your physical health but also a great way to unwind and meet new people. Staying active is crucial for your well-being, especially when balancing academics and exploration.

Enjoying Local Entertainment Options (Theaters, Concerts, Cinemas):

Theater and Cinema: Check out local theaters and cinemas. Watching a play or a movie can be a relaxing way to spend an evening. Many theaters offer student discounts or special rates for certain performances. It is a great way to enjoy local culture and unwind.

Live Music and Concerts: Attend live music events and concerts. Local music venues often host a variety of performances, from classical concerts to rock bands. It is a fantastic way to experience the local music scene and discover new artists.

Cultural Centers: Visit cultural centers that host a range of events, including workshops, exhibitions, and performances. These centers can be hubs of cultural activity and a great place to learn and have fun. They often offer unique insights into the local culture and traditions.

By exploring and enjoying your new home, you will enrich your international experience and create lasting memories. Embrace every opportunity to learn, discover, and immerse yourself in the local culture. Balancing academics with exploration and leisure activities will help you make the most of your time abroad. So, get out there, explore, and enjoy all that your new home has to offer!

Chapter 3 Conclusion

Key Points for Settling in Effectively

As you embark on this exciting journey, settling into your new environment effectively is crucial. Remember, it is all about finding the right balance between academic responsibilities and enjoying your new surroundings. Here is a quick recap of the key points covered in this chapter:

Finding Accommodation: Whether you choose university dormitories, private rentals, home-stays, or shared housing, it is important to understand the pros and cons of each option. Make sure you know how to apply, what documents you will need, and how to avoid common pitfalls like scams. It is all about finding a place where you feel comfortable and safe.

Navigating Your New Environment: Get to know your campus and city. Attend orientation sessions, take campus tours, and use local transit apps to familiarize yourself with transportation options. Knowing where the libraries, health services, and student centers can make a big difference in your daily life. The more you explore, the more at home you will feel.

Managing Daily Life: From grocery shopping and health services to banking and communication, mastering these daily tasks will help you settle in smoothly. Learn where to find local supermarkets, how to access healthcare, open a bank account, and set up a mobile phone plan. These practical skills are essential for your independence and peace of mind.

Social Integration: Join clubs, participate in social events, and engage in cultural activities. Building a strong social network and adapting to cultural differences are essential for a fulfilling experience. Making friends and understanding the local culture will enrich your stay and help you feel more connected.

Academic Success: Understand the education system, develop effective study habits, and engage actively with professors and peers. Balancing academics with social life and utilizing available resources will help you thrive. Remember, your studies are the main reason you are here, so make sure you stay on top of them.

Staying Safe and Legal: Prioritize your personal safety, stay informed about local news, and adhere to legal requirements. Register with local authorities, if necessary, maintain your visa status, and know your rights as an international student. Staying safe and compliant will ensure a trouble-free experience.

Exploring and Enjoying Your New Home: Embrace the opportunity to travel, explore local attractions, and immerse yourself in cultural experiences. Engage in leisure activities, try local cuisine, and enjoy the local entertainment options. Balance is key—make sure to enjoy yourself while keeping up with your studies.

Encouragement to Embrace New Experiences and Challenges

Your time as an international student is a unique opportunity filled with new experiences and challenges. Embrace every moment with an open mind and a positive attitude. Each experience, whether exciting or challenging, is a chance to learn and grow. Do not be afraid to step out of your comfort zone and try new things. Whether it is participating in a local festival, joining a new club, or simply navigating daily life in a new city, these experiences will enrich your life and broaden your perspective.

Remember, it is okay to feel overwhelmed at times. Adjusting to a new environment takes time, and it is normal to face ups and downs. Lean on your support network—friends, family, and university resources are there to help you. Stay connected with loved ones back home while building new relationships in your host country. Every challenge you overcome will make you more resilient and adaptable.

Final Tips for a Successful and Enjoyable International Experience

- **Stay Organized**: Keeping track of your academic and personal responsibilities with a planner or digital tools can make life much easier. Stay on top of deadlines, appointments, and social events. Organization reduces stress and helps you manage your time effectively.
- **Be Proactive**: Do not wait for opportunities to come to you. Seek them out, whether it is academic help, social activities, or exploring new places. Taking initiative can open doors and create memorable experiences.
- **Maintain Balance**: Balance is key. Make sure to prioritize your studies, but also take time to relax and enjoy your new surroundings. Find a rhythm that works for you and stick to it. A healthy balance between work and play will enhance your overall experience.
- **Stay Curious**: Cultivate a sense of curiosity. Learn about the local culture, try new foods, and engage in conversations with locals. This curiosity will lead to a richer and more

fulfilling experience. Every new thing you try is a step towards understanding your new home better.

- **Take Care of Yourself**: Your physical and mental health are crucial for a successful international experience. Eat well, exercise regularly, and seek support if you are feeling stressed or overwhelmed. Self-care is not a luxury; it is a necessity.
- **Reflect on Your Journey**: Take time to reflect on your experiences and what you have learned. Keeping a journal can be a great way to document your journey and track your personal growth. Reflecting helps you appreciate how far you have come and the challenges you have overcome.

Your journey as an international student is a remarkable adventure. Embrace the opportunities, overcome the challenges, and make the most of every moment. This experience will not only enhance your academic and professional prospects but also shape you into a more adaptable, open-minded, and resilient individual. Enjoy your time abroad and remember that every step you take is a valuable part of your international adventure!

Chapter 3 Review

As you navigate your new environment as an international student, it is important to reflect on the key points we have covered in this chapter. Settling in effectively involves finding suitable accommodation, understanding your new environment, managing daily life, integrating socially, achieving academic success, staying safe and legal, and exploring and enjoying your new home.

Short Answer Questions

1. **Accommodation Options**:
   - What are the benefits and drawbacks of living in university dormitories versus private rentals?
   - Describe two key factors you should consider when choosing accommodation.
2. **Navigating Your Environment**:
   - What are two strategies for mastering the local public transportation system?
   - Why is it important to familiarize yourself with key locations on and around your campus?
3. **Managing Daily Life**:
   - List three essential daily tasks you need to manage and describe how you can efficiently handle each one in your new environment.
   - What are the benefits of setting up a local bank account?

4. **Social Integration**:
   ◦ How can joining student clubs and organizations help with social integration?
   ◦ Name two cultural activities you are interested in participating in and explain why.

5. **Academic Success**:
   ◦ What are the benefits of attending professor office hours?
   ◦ Describe one effective study habit that can help you balance academic and social life.

6. **Staying Safe and Legal**:
   ◦ Why is it important to register with local authorities and keep emergency contacts handy?
   ◦ List two ways to stay informed about local safety guidelines and legal requirements.

7. **Exploring and Enjoying Your New Home**:
   ◦ What are the advantages of planning weekend trips and participating in local cultural experiences?
   ◦ Describe one local dish you have tried or would like to try and its cultural significance.

Reflective Questions

1. What has been your biggest challenge in settling into your new environment, and how did you overcome it?
2. How has participating in local cultural activities enriched your experience as an international student?
3. Reflect on a recent interaction with a local student or resident. What did you learn from this interaction?

By engaging with these questions, you can solidify your understanding of the chapter's key points and reflect on your personal experiences. Remember, your journey as an international student is unique and full of opportunities for growth and discovery. For more in-depth exercises and reflections, refer to the companion " Reflective Exercises: The International Experiences Guide Workbook." This workbook is designed to help you further internalize the concepts discussed in this chapter and apply them to your personal situation, enhancing your overall learning experience. Enjoy your adventure and make the most of every moment!

{ 4 }

Academic and Social Integration

Introduction

As an international student, one of the key challenges you will face is balancing academic responsibilities with social activities. Both aspects are crucial for a fulfilling and successful international experience. In this chapter, we will explore the importance of finding this balance, provide an overview of effective strategies for successful integration, and encourage you to make the most of your time abroad.

Importance of Balancing Academic and Social Life

Balancing academic and social life is essential for several reasons. Academically, maintaining good grades and understanding your coursework is vital for your success and future opportunities. Socially, engaging with peers and participating in local activities can enrich your experience, help you build a support network, and enhance your cultural understanding.

Academic Success: Your primary goal as a student is to excel academically. Attending classes, completing assignments on time, and preparing for exams are fundamental. However, overloading yourself with academic work without taking breaks can lead to burnout.

Social Well-being: Engaging in social activities helps you build friendships, reduce stress, and create lasting memories. It is a chance to experience the culture of your host country firsthand and integrate more fully into the community.

Holistic Development: A balanced approach fosters holistic development. While academic achievements are crucial, soft skills such as communication, teamwork, and adaptability are equally important and often developed through social interactions.

Overview of Strategies for Successful Integration

Navigating a new academic environment while building a social life requires strategic planning and effort. Here are some strategies to help you integrate successfully:

Time Management: Create a schedule that allocates time for both study and social activities. Prioritize tasks and set realistic goals to ensure you are productive without feeling overwhelmed.

Engage in Campus Life: Join clubs, societies, and student organizations that interest you. This not only helps you meet new people but also allows you to pursue hobbies and interests.

Active Participation in Class: Engage actively in your classes by participating in discussions, group work, and projects. Building a rapport with your professors and classmates can enhance your academic experience.

Cultural Adaptation: Learn about the local culture and social norms. Respecting and understanding these can make your interactions smoother and more meaningful.

Seek Support: Utilize university resources such as counseling services, academic advisors, and peer support groups. Do not hesitate to ask for help if you are struggling with any aspect of your integration.

Encouragement to Make the Most of the International Experience

Your time as an international student is a unique opportunity to grow both personally and academically. Here are some final words of encouragement to help you make the most of your international experience:

Embrace Opportunities: Take advantage of every opportunity that comes your way, whether it is an academic project, a social event, or a cultural experience. Each opportunity is a chance to learn and grow.

Stay Open-Minded: Keep an open mind and be willing to step out of your comfort zone. You may face challenges, but each one is a learning experience that will make you stronger and more adaptable.

Reflect and Adapt: Regularly reflect on your experiences and adapt your strategies as needed. What worked for you in the past may need adjustment as you continue to integrate into your new environment.

Build Lasting Connections: The friendships and connections you make during your international program can last a lifetime. Invest time and effort in building these relationships.

Enjoy the Journey: Finally, enjoy the journey. Studying abroad is a once-in-a-lifetime experience filled with adventures, challenges, and unforgettable moments. Make the most of it and create memories that you will cherish forever.

Balancing academic and social life may seem challenging, but with the right approach and mindset, you can achieve a fulfilling and successful international experience. Embrace the journey, make the most of the opportunities, and enjoy every moment of this incredible adventure.

4.1 Understanding the Academic System

Educational Structure

Differences Between Home and Host Country Education Systems:

When you step into a new academic environment, one of the first things you will notice is how different the education system might be from what you are used to. This can be both exciting and challenging. Here is what to keep an eye on:

Teaching Methods: In some countries, education is more lecture-based, where professors do most of the talking, while in others, there is a strong emphasis on interactive or group-based learning. Understanding this difference can help you adjust your study habits and make the most of your classes.

Classroom Dynamics: Participation levels and the role of students in the classroom can vary widely. For example, in some places, students are expected to actively engage in debates and discussions, while in others, the norm might be more about listening and taking detailed notes.

Support Systems: The level of support and resources available to students can differ significantly. Some institutions offer extensive tutoring services and academic support centers, while others expect students to be more independent. Knowing what is available can help you seek the support you need.

Types of Degrees and Courses Offered:

Understanding the different types of degrees and courses available at your host institution will help you navigate your academic journey more effectively.

Undergraduate vs. Graduate Programs: Get to know the distinctions between undergraduate (bachelor's degrees) and graduate programs (master's and doctoral degrees). Each has its own set of requirements, duration, and expected outcomes.

Course Varieties: Courses can range from foundational (introductory) to specialized (advanced) topics. Be aware of the progression and prerequisites for each course. This will help you plan your academic path strategically.

Academic Calendar and Key Dates:

Knowing the academic calendar is crucial for planning your studies and balancing your personal life.

Semesters and Terms: Find out how the academic year is structured. Many universities operate on a semester system (fall and spring), while others might have trimesters or quarters. Each structure has its own rhythm, so getting familiar with it early on will help you manage your time better.

Important Dates: Mark down key dates such as the start and end of terms, exam periods, and holidays. This helps you manage your time effectively and ensures you do not miss critical deadlines. It is also helpful to note any registration deadlines for courses and other important events.

Course Registration

How to Register for Courses:

The course registration process can vary, but here are some general steps to guide you:

Online Systems: Most universities use online platforms for course registration. Take some time to familiarize yourself with the platform and important deadlines well in advance. Missing a deadline can be a hassle, so it is best to be prepared.

Advisor Meetings: Schedule meetings with your academic advisor to discuss your course selections. They can help ensure that your choices align with your academic goals and degree requirements, and they might offer insights into courses that suit your interests and strengths.

Choosing the Right Courses for Your Program and Interests:

Selecting the right courses is a crucial part of your academic success.

Core vs. Elective Courses: Understand the difference between core (required) courses and electives (optional). Core courses are essential for your degree, while electives allow you to explore other areas of interest. Balancing both can keep your studies engaging.

Balance and Load: Choose a mix of courses that balance your workload and keep you engaged. Avoid overloading yourself in one term to prevent burnout. Remember, it is about quality learning, not just quantity.

Understanding Prerequisites and Course Loads:

Each course might have prerequisites that you need to complete beforehand.

Prerequisites: Check the requirements for each course and ensure you have completed any necessary prerequisites. This ensures you are adequately prepared for the coursework and can keep up with the class.

Course Load: Be realistic about how many courses you can handle. A typical full-time load might be around four to five courses per term, but this can vary. Listen to your body and mind—do not push yourself too hard.

Grading and Assessment

Grading Scales and What They Mean:

Grading systems can differ significantly from one country to another.

Letter Grades vs. Percentages: Some systems use letter grades (A, B, C), while others use percentages or a combination. Understand what each grade represents and what is considered a passing grade. This will help you set realistic goals and track your progress.

GPA Calculation: If your host institution uses a GPA system, learn how it is calculated and what it means for your academic standing. Understanding this can help you gauge your performance and set targets.

Types of Assessments (Exams, Essays, Presentations):

Your performance will be evaluated through various forms of assessment.

Exams: Exams can be written, oral, or practical. Understanding the format and expectations for each type of exam is crucial. Make sure you know what materials and knowledge are being tested.

Essays: Essays often require a deep understanding of the subject and strong writing skills. Pay attention to the structure, argumentation, and referencing style required. Developing good writing habits early on can save you time and stress.

Presentations: Presentations assess your ability to communicate ideas clearly and confidently. Practice and preparation are key to delivering effective presentations. Engaging with your audience and using visual aids can enhance your delivery.

Academic Integrity and Avoiding Plagiarism:

Maintaining academic integrity is essential in all your academic work.

Understanding Plagiarism: Plagiarism is using someone else's work without proper attribution. This can be intentional or unintentional, so it is important to understand what constitutes plagiarism and how to avoid it. Familiarize yourself with the rules and always give credit where it is due.

Citation and Referencing: Learn the required citation style (e.g., APA, MLA, Chicago) and use it consistently. Proper referencing shows respect for the original authors and helps you avoid plagiarism. Using citation tools can simplify this process.

University Policies: Familiarize yourself with your university's policies on academic integrity. Penalties for violations can be severe, so it is crucial to adhere to these guidelines. If in doubt, always ask your professors for clarification.

By understanding the academic system at your host institution, you can navigate your studies more effectively and make the most of your educational experience. Balancing your course load, engaging actively in your classes, and maintaining academic integrity will set you up for success in your international academic journey. Embrace the learning process, seek help when needed, and enjoy the unique educational experiences that come with studying abroad.

Anecdotes and Insights

Navigating Academic Expectations- Ana's Story

Student Perspective: "When I first started my exchange program in Germany, I was overwhelmed by the different academic expectations. In my home country, the education system focused more on continuous assessment through assignments and projects. However, in Germany, the emphasis was on final exams and independent study. This shift required me to adapt my study habits significantly." – Ana, International Student in Germany

Expert Insight: Understanding and adapting to different academic systems is crucial for success. In countries like Germany, where final exams play a significant role, it is important to develop effective study strategies and manage your time efficiently. Seek advice from local students or academic advisors to understand what is expected. Using resources like libraries and study groups can also help you adjust to the new academic environment.

4.2 Engaging with Professors and Academic Staff

Building Relationships

Importance of Connecting with Professors:

Building strong relationships with your professors and academic staff can significantly enhance your academic experience. Professors are not just there to teach; they can also provide guidance, support, and valuable insights into your field of study.

Academic Success: Professors can help clarify complex topics, guide your research, and provide insights that go beyond the textbook. A good relationship with your professors can lead to better understanding and improved grades.

Career Opportunities: Professors often have extensive networks and can offer advice on career paths, internships, and job opportunities. They can also write strong letters of recommendation if they know you well.

Personal Growth: Interacting with professors can help you develop critical thinking skills, gain different perspectives, and build confidence in your academic abilities.

How to Approach and Communicate with Academic Staff:

Approaching and communicating with professors can be daunting, but it is a crucial skill to develop.

Be Respectful and Professional: Always address your professors formally unless they specify otherwise. Use titles such as "Professor" or "Dr." and be polite in your communications.

Be Prepared: Before approaching a professor, make sure you have a clear idea of what you want to discuss. Whether it is a question about the lecture, a request for feedback, or a discussion about your research, being prepared shows that you respect their time.

Use Email Etiquette: When emailing professors, keep your messages clear and concise. Start with a formal greeting, state your purpose, and end with a polite closing. For example:

Dear Professor [Last Name],

I hope this email finds you well. I am writing to seek clarification on [specific topic] discussed in your recent lecture. I have reviewed my notes and the reading materials but would appreciate your further explanation.

Thank you for your time and assistance.

Best regards,

[Your Name]

Office Hours and Seeking Help:

Office hours are a valuable resource and knowing how to utilize them effectively can make a big difference in your academic journey.

Take Advantage of Office Hours: Professors set aside office hours specifically to help students. Use this time to ask questions, seek clarification, and discuss any challenges you are facing in the course.

Be Specific: When you visit during office hours, be specific about what you need help with. This allows the professor to provide targeted assistance.

Follow-Up: If your professor gives you advice or resources, follow up to show that you have taken their suggestions seriously. This can further strengthen your relationship with them.

Academic Mentorship

Finding a Mentor or Advisor:

Having a mentor or academic advisor can provide you with personalized guidance and support throughout your studies.

Identify Potential Mentors: Look for professors whose research interests align with yours or who you feel comfortable with. Attend their lectures, engage in their discussions, and express your interest in their work.

Make the Ask: Do not hesitate to ask a professor to be your mentor. A simple and respectful request can go a long way. You might say something like, "I'm really interested in your research on [topic]. Would you be willing to mentor me as I explore this field further?"

Benefits of Academic Mentorship:

An academic mentor can offer numerous benefits beyond just academic guidance.

Personalized Guidance: Mentors can provide tailored advice based on their knowledge of your strengths, weaknesses, and interests.

Professional Development: They can offer insights into career paths, help you build your professional network, and provide recommendations for internships and job opportunities.

Emotional Support: A mentor can be a source of encouragement and support, helping you navigate the challenges of academic life.

How to Make the Most of Mentorship Opportunities:

Once you have a mentor, it is important to make the most of this relationship.

Be Proactive: Take the initiative to schedule regular meetings and come prepared with questions or topics for discussion.

Set Goals: Work with your mentor to set short-term and long-term goals. This provides a clear direction and purpose for your meetings.

Be Open to Feedback: Mentors are there to help you grow, so be open to their feedback and willing to make changes based on their suggestions.

Anecdotes and Insights

Building Relationships with Professors- Tom's Story

Student Perspective: "In Japan, I initially found it challenging to build relationships with my professors because of the cultural differences. However, I learned that attending office hours and showing genuine interest in their research helped me connect with them. This not only improved my understanding of the coursework but also opened up opportunities for research projects." – Tom, International Student in Japan

Expert Insight: Building relationships with professors can enhance your academic experience and open doors to new opportunities. In cultures where respect and hierarchy are emphasized, such as in Japan, showing interest and attending office hours can demonstrate your dedication and respect. Do not be afraid to ask questions and seek feedback—professors appreciate engaged and motivated students.

Feedback and Improvement

Receiving and Responding to Feedback:

Feedback from professors is a critical part of the learning process.

Listen Carefully: When receiving feedback, listen carefully and take notes. Avoid getting defensive and try to understand the constructive points being made.

Ask for Clarification: If something is not clear, do not hesitate to ask for further explanation. Understanding the feedback fully is crucial for improvement.

Thank Your Professors: Always thank your professors for their feedback. It shows appreciation for their time and effort.

Using Feedback to Improve Your Academic Performance:

Feedback is only valuable if you use it to improve.

Reflect on the Feedback: Take time to reflect on the feedback and identify specific areas for improvement.

Create an Action Plan: Develop a plan to address the areas of improvement. This could involve revising your study methods, seeking additional resources, or practicing certain skills.

Monitor Your Progress: Keep track of your progress and continue to seek feedback. This on-going process will help you continuously improve.

Seeking Additional Support When Needed:

Do not be afraid to seek additional help if you are struggling.

Tutoring Services: Many universities offer tutoring services for free or at a reduced cost. Take advantage of these resources if you need extra help.

Study Groups: Joining a study group can provide additional support and make learning more interactive.

Counseling Services: If academic stress is impacting your mental health, do not hesitate to seek support from your university's counseling services.

By actively engaging with your professors and academic staff, seeking mentorship, and using feedback constructively, you can significantly enhance your academic experience. These relationships and strategies will not only help you succeed academically but also support your overall personal and professional development. Remember, your professors and academic staff are there to help you, so make the most of these valuable resources.

4.3 Effective Study Habits and Time Management

Study Techniques

Active Learning Methods:

Active learning is all about engaging deeply with the material, and it can make a huge difference in how well you retain information.

Summarization: After reading a chapter or attending a lecture, take a few minutes to summarize the key points in your own words. This helps reinforce what you have learned and identify any gaps in your understanding.

Questioning: Challenge yourself by asking questions about the material. Try to answer them without looking at your notes. This method can deepen your comprehension and improve recall.

Teaching Others: Try explaining the material to a friend or classmate. Teaching forces you to organize your thoughts and clarify concepts, which can enhance your understanding.

Practice Problems: If you are studying subjects like math or science, practice problems are your best friends. They help reinforce concepts and improve your problem-solving skills.

Note-Taking Strategies:

Good notetaking can transform your study sessions from stressful to seamless.

Cornell Method: This technique involves dividing your paper into three sections: a narrow-left column for keywords or questions, a larger right column for detailed notes, and a summary section at the bottom. It encourages active engagement and makes reviewing easier.

Mind Mapping: Create visual diagrams that connect different concepts. This method is especially useful for visual learners and for subjects that involve complex relationships.

Outlining: Use an outline format with headings and subheadings to organize your notes. This structure helps in logically organizing the material and makes reviewing more efficient.

Digital Tools: Consider using apps like Evernote, OneNote, or Notion to take and organize your notes. These tools offer features like search functions, tags, and multimedia integration, making your notes more versatile and accessible.

Preparing for Exams and Assessments:

Preparation is key to conquering exams and assessments with confidence.

Start Early: Begin reviewing material well before the exam date. This reduces stress and gives you plenty of time to thoroughly understand the content.

Practice Tests: Take practice tests under exam conditions to get used to the format and timing. This can help reduce anxiety and improve your performance.

Review Sessions: Join or organize review sessions with classmates. Discussing the material with others can provide new insights and reinforce your understanding.

Healthy Habits: Don't forget to take care of your body and mind. Ensure you get enough sleep, eat well, and exercise regularly. A healthy body supports a healthy mind, which is crucial during exam periods.

Time Management

Creating a Study Schedule:

A well-planned study schedule can help you manage your time effectively and ensure you cover all your material.

Set Priorities: Identify the most important tasks and tackle them first. Use a planner or digital calendar to organize your time. Prioritizing tasks helps you focus on what is essential and reduces the risk of falling behind.

Break it Down: Divide your study sessions into manageable chunks. For example, study for 25 minutes and then take a 5-minute break (the Pomodoro Technique). This approach helps maintain focus and prevents burnout.

Be Realistic: Set achievable goals for each study session. Overloading yourself can lead to burnout and decreased productivity. It is better to study consistently and steadily rather than cramming all at once.

Regular Reviews: Periodically review and adjust your schedule to ensure it remains effective and realistic. Flexibility is key to managing unforeseen changes and staying on track.

Balancing Study Time with Social and Personal Activities:

Maintaining a balance between your academic responsibilities and personal life is crucial for overall well-being.

Set Boundaries: Allocate specific times for studying and for social or personal activities. This helps ensure you do not neglect either area. Balance is key to avoiding burnout and keeping your life well-rounded.

Stay Flexible: Be prepared to adjust your schedule if unexpected events arise. Flexibility can help you maintain balance and reduce stress. Life happens and being adaptable is an essential skill.

Prioritize Self-Care: Make time for activities that relax and rejuvenate you, such as exercise, hobbies, and spending time with friends. Self-care is not a luxury but a necessity for sustained academic and personal success.

Avoiding Procrastination and Staying Motivated:

Procrastination can derail your study plans and lead to unnecessary stress.

Understand Your Triggers: Identify what causes you to procrastinate and develop strategies to counteract these triggers. This might involve creating a more conducive study environment or setting specific, short-term goals.

Use Positive Reinforcement: Reward yourself for completing tasks. This can be something small like a treat or a break to do something you enjoy. Positive reinforcement can help build good study habits.

Stay Connected: Surround yourself with motivated peers who can encourage and support you. Study groups can provide accountability and reduce the temptation to procrastinate.

Anecdotes and Insights

Effective Time Management- Luis' Story

Student Perspective: "Balancing my studies and social life was a challenge during my exchange in Canada. I realized early on that I needed to improve my time management skills. Using a planner and setting realistic goals each week helped me stay on top of my academic responsibilities while still enjoying my time with friends." – Luis, International Student in Canada

Expert Insight: Effective time management is key to balancing academic and social life. Use tools like planners, digital calendars, and to-do lists to organize your tasks and commitments. Set achievable goals and prioritize your workload to avoid last-minute stress. Remember to allocate time for relaxation and social activities to maintain a healthy balance.

Study Resources

Utilizing Libraries and Online Databases:

Libraries and online databases are treasure troves of information that can support your studies.

Library Resources: Take advantage of the books, journals, and study spaces available at your university library. Librarians can also assist with finding resources and conducting research.

Online Databases: Use academic databases like JSTOR, PubMed, and Google Scholar to access scholarly articles and papers. These resources are invaluable for research projects and assignments.

Digital Tools: Many libraries offer digital tools and resources such as e-books, online journals, and research databases. Familiarize yourself with these tools to enhance your research capabilities.

Joining Study Groups and Academic Clubs:

Collaborative learning can be highly effective and enjoyable.

Study Groups: Join or form study groups with classmates. Discussing material with peers can provide new perspectives and aid understanding.

Academic Clubs: Participate in academic clubs or societies related to your field of study. These clubs often organize events, guest lectures, and study sessions that can enrich your learning experience.

Accessing Tutoring and Academic Support Services:

Do not hesitate to seek additional help if you need it.

Tutoring Services: Many universities offer free or low-cost tutoring services. Tutors can provide personalized assistance and help clarify difficult concepts.

Academic Support Centers: Utilize academic support centers for help with writing, math, and other subjects. These centers often offer workshops and one-on-one consultations.

Online Resources: There are numerous online resources available, including instructional videos, practice exercises, and forums where you can ask questions and get help from other students and educators.

By developing effective study habits and time management skills, you can enhance your academic performance and reduce stress. Balancing your studies with social and personal activities, using a variety of study techniques, and accessing available resources will support your success as an international student. Embrace these strategies to make the most of your academic journey and enjoy a well-rounded, enriching experience.

4.4 Navigating Campus Life

Campus Facilities

Important Locations on Campus:

Knowing your way around campus is key to a smooth and enjoyable university experience. Here are some spots you will want to familiarize yourself with:

Libraries: Think of the library as your academic hub. It is not just a place to borrow books; it is also a great spot for studying, accessing academic journals, and using computers. Many libraries offer quiet study areas, group study rooms, and even cafes. Get to know the library's layout and resources early on—it can be your best friend during exam season. Make a habit of checking out the library's events and workshops; they often host sessions on research skills, citation styles, and more.

Study Areas: Besides the library, look out for dedicated study areas around campus. These can include lounges, common rooms, and specific buildings designed for quiet study. Knowing where these are can help you find the perfect spot for different types of study sessions. Some students prefer a bustling café for a bit of background noise, while others need complete silence—find what works best for you.

Cafeterias and Dining Halls: Eating well is crucial for maintaining your energy and focus. Explore the dining options on campus, from cafeterias to food courts. Check out what meal plans are available and see if there are spots that cater to specific dietary needs. Dining halls can also be great places to meet people and catch up with friends between classes. Do not forget to check if your campus has food trucks or farmers' markets for some fresh and exciting meal options.

Recreational Facilities and Gyms:

Staying active is essential for your overall well-being, and most campuses offer excellent recreational facilities.

Gyms: Campus gyms usually provide a range of equipment and classes, from cardio machines to weightlifting, yoga, and Pilates. Memberships are often included in your student fees or offered at a reduced rate. Make it a habit to visit regularly; it is a great way to relieve stress. Many gyms also offer free fitness assessments or personal training sessions to help you create a workout plan that fits your goals.

Sports Facilities: Whether you are into basketball, tennis, swimming, or track and field, check out what sports facilities your campus has to offer. Joining intramural sports teams can be a fun way to stay fit and make friends. Even if you are not a serious athlete, casual games can be a great way to unwind and meet new people.

Recreational Programs: Many universities offer recreational programs and clubs, such as hiking, dance, or martial arts. Participating in these can provide a nice break from academic pressures and help you maintain a balanced lifestyle. Look out for weekend trips or adventure outings organized by the recreation department—they can be a fantastic way to explore the area around your university.

Health and Wellness Centers:

Taking care of your physical and mental health is vital during your time at university.

Health Centers: Most campuses have health centers that provide medical services, including general practice, vaccinations, and sexual health services. Knowing where the health center is and what services it offers can save you time and stress if you fall ill. Many health centers also provide wellness check-ups, which can help you stay on top of your health.

Counseling Services: Mental health is just as important as physical health. Campus counseling services offer support for stress, anxiety, depression, and other mental health issues. Do not hesitate to make an appointment if you need someone to talk to. Often, these services are included in your student fees, so take advantage of them without worrying about extra costs.

Wellness Programs: Look for wellness programs that promote healthy living, such as stress management workshops, mindfulness meditation sessions, and nutrition advice. Participating in these can help you stay healthy and balanced. Keep an eye out for events like wellness fairs, yoga sessions on the quad, or cooking classes focused on healthy eating.

Student Services

Academic Advising and Career Counseling:

These services can be instrumental in helping you navigate your academic journey and prepare for your future career.

Academic Advising: Academic advisors can help you choose courses, understand degree requirements, and plan your academic path. They can also provide support if you are facing academic challenges. Regularly check in with your advisor to stay on track with your goals. Do not wait until you are in trouble—proactively seeking advice can help you avoid issues before they arise.

Career Counseling: Career counselors offer guidance on resume writing, job search strategies, and interview preparation. They can also connect you with internship opportunities and career fairs. Start engaging with career services early to make the most of these resources. They often offer workshops on topics like networking skills, job search strategies, and how to leverage LinkedIn effectively.

Mental Health Resources:

Your mental health is a priority, and universities provide various resources to support you.

Counseling Services: As mentioned earlier, counseling services are available for a wide range of mental health issues. These services are usually confidential and provided by trained professionals. If you are feeling overwhelmed, reaching out can make a big difference.

Peer Support Programs: Some universities offer peer support programs where you can talk to fellow students who are trained to provide support. This can be a more informal and relatable way to get help. Sometimes, just knowing that others have been through similar experiences can be incredibly reassuring.

Workshops and Seminars: Look out for workshops and seminars on topics like stress management, mindfulness, and building resilience. These can provide valuable tools for maintaining your mental health. Universities often bring in guest speakers or mental health experts for these events, offering you access to top-notch advice and strategies.

Accessibility Services for Students with Disabilities:

If you have a disability, your university will have resources to ensure you can fully participate in campus life.

Disability Services Office: Contact the disability services office to learn about the accommodations and support available to you. This can include things like note-taking assistance, extended time on exams, and accessible housing.

Technology and Tools: There are many assistive technologies available to support students with disabilities. The disability services office can help you access these resources.

Advocacy and Support: Do not hesitate to advocate for yourself and seek support. Universities are committed to creating inclusive environments and will work with you to meet your needs. Many campuses also have student groups or organizations dedicated to supporting students with disabilities, providing both resources and a sense of community.

Campus Involvement

Joining Student Organizations and Clubs:

Getting involved in student organizations and clubs is a great way to meet new people, pursue your interests, and develop new skills.

Finding Clubs: Most universities have a wide range of clubs and organizations, from academic and professional societies to hobby groups, cultural associations, and sports teams. Attend club fairs and check out online directories to find groups that interest you. Do not be afraid to try something new. College is the perfect time to explore different interests.

Benefits of Joining: Joining a club can help you make friends, build your resume, and find a sense of community. It is also an opportunity to develop leadership skills and take on responsibilities in a low-pressure environment. Plus, being active in clubs can provide a much-needed break from academic pressures.

Participating in Campus Events and Activities:

Campus events and activities provide opportunities for fun, relaxation, and learning outside the classroom.

Social Events: Look out for social events like parties, movie nights, and cultural festivals. These are great ways to unwind and meet people from different backgrounds. Universities often host themed events, cultural nights, and festivals that showcase the diversity of the student body.

Academic Events: Attend lectures, seminars, and workshops hosted by your university. These events can deepen your understanding of your field and introduce you to new ideas. Guest lectures by industry professionals or prominent academics can offer valuable insights and networking opportunities.

Volunteer Opportunities: Volunteering is a fantastic way to give back to the community, gain experience, and meet new people. Look for volunteer opportunities both on and off-campus. Engaging in community service can also provide a sense of fulfillment and purpose, and it looks great on your resume.

Leadership Opportunities and Student Government:

If you are interested in developing your leadership skills, consider getting involved in student government or other leadership roles.

Student Government: Joining student government allows you to represent your peers, influence university policies, and organize events. It is a great way to make a tangible impact on campus life. You will gain experience in leadership, teamwork, and public speaking, all of which are valuable skills for your future career.

Leadership Roles in Clubs: Many student organizations offer leadership positions, such as president, treasurer, or event coordinator. Taking on a leadership role can be a rewarding experience that enhances your resume and personal growth. It also provides an excellent opportunity to develop organizational and management skills.

Leadership Development Programs: Some universities offer programs specifically designed to develop leadership skills. These can include workshops, retreats, and mentorship opportunities. These programs often involve training sessions on topics like conflict resolution, project management, and effective communication.

Navigating campus life is about making the most of the resources and opportunities available to you. By familiarizing yourself with campus facilities, utilizing student services, and getting involved in campus activities, you can create a fulfilling and well-rounded university experience. Embrace every opportunity to learn, grow, and enjoy your time as a student. Remember, your university experience is what you make of it—get involved, stay curious, and make the most of this exciting time!

4.5 Social Integration and Building Relationships

Making Friends

Strategies for Meeting New People:

Meeting new people can be both exciting and a bit nerve-wracking, but it is a crucial part of your social integration. Here are some friendly strategies to help you get started:

Join Clubs and Organizations: This is one of the easiest and most fun ways to meet people with similar interests. Whether it is an academic club, a sports team, or a hobby group, getting involved can help you connect with others who share your passions. Clubs often host regular events, meetings, and social gatherings, giving you plenty of chances to mingle.

Attend Campus Events: Universities host a variety of events, from cultural festivals to career fairs. These are great opportunities to meet new people in a relaxed setting. Do not worry about going alone—chances are, many others are there to meet new friends too.

Use social media and Apps: Many campuses have social media groups or apps designed to connect students. Platforms like Facebook, Instagram, or campus-specific apps can help you stay informed about upcoming events and find study buddies or social groups. Join these groups to stay in the loop and find people with similar interests.

Social Events and Activities:

Engaging in social events and activities is a fun and effective way to build friendships. Here are some ideas to get you started:

Orientation Week: Take full advantage of orientation week. This period is specifically designed to help new students get to know each other. Attend as many events as you can to meet a wide variety of people. From icebreaker games to campus tours, these activities are perfect for making new friends.

Cultural Nights and Festivals: Participating in cultural nights or international festivals can expose you to new traditions and help you meet students from different backgrounds. These events often include food, music, and dance, creating a lively atmosphere for socializing.

Volunteer Work: Volunteering is a fantastic way to meet like-minded individuals while contributing to the community. Many universities have volunteer programs or partnerships with local organizations where you can get involved. Plus, volunteering can give you a great sense of accomplishment and purpose.

Building a Diverse Network of Friends:

Having a diverse group of friends can enrich your experience and broaden your perspectives. Here is how to build and nurture such a network:

Be Open-Minded: Approach new friendships with an open mind. Embrace differences and be willing to learn from others. Diverse friendships can offer unique insights and help you grow as a person. Celebrate the diversity around you by trying new foods, learning about different cultures, and sharing your own experiences.

Participate in Study Groups: Study groups are not only great for academic support but also for social interaction. They provide a structured environment to get to know your classmates better. Discussing coursework together can lead to deeper conversations and friendships.

Network Beyond Your Comfort Zone: Make an effort to step out of your comfort zone and interact with people from different cultures and backgrounds. This can lead to meaningful and lasting friendships. Attend events or join clubs that you would not normally consider expanding your horizons.

Anecdotes and Insights
Social Integration and Cultural Adjustment- Emily's Story

Student Perspective: "During my exchange in Spain, integrating socially was initially tough due to the language barrier. I joined a language exchange program where I taught English and learned Spanish from local students. This not only improved my language skills but also helped me make friends and understand the local culture better." – Emily, International Student in Spain

Expert Insight: Language exchange programs are excellent for improving language skills and integrating socially. Participating in these programs allows you to practice the local language in a real-world context and build meaningful relationships. Additionally, engaging in cultural activities and showing interest in local traditions can enhance your cultural understanding and help you feel more at home.

Cultural Adjustment

Understanding Cultural Norms and Values:

Understanding and respecting the cultural norms and values of your host country is essential for smooth social integration. Here is how to navigate this aspect:

Research: Before you arrive, do some research on the cultural norms and values of your host country. This can help you avoid misunderstandings and show respect for local customs. Websites, travel guides, and even YouTube videos can be valuable resources.

Observe and Ask: Pay attention to how locals behave in different situations and do not hesitate to ask questions if you are unsure about something. Most people will appreciate your interest in their culture and be happy to help. Observing daily interactions, like how people greet each other or how they behave in public spaces, can provide useful clues.

Participate in Cultural Activities: Engage in cultural activities, such as festivals, traditional ceremonies, and local events. This will give you a deeper understanding of the culture and help you connect with locals. Trying local cuisine, learning traditional dances, or attending local sports events can be both fun and educational.

Navigating Cultural Differences in Social Settings:

Cultural differences can sometimes lead to misunderstandings but navigating them effectively can enrich your social interactions. Here are some tips on how to handle this gracefully:

Be Patient and Tolerant: Understand that cultural differences are natural and be patient when you encounter them. Tolerance and openness are key to building positive relationships. If you find certain customs puzzling, approach them with curiosity rather than judgment.

Adapt Your Communication Style: Different cultures have different communication styles. Some may be more direct, while others are more indirect. Observing and adapting to these styles can help you communicate more effectively. For instance, in some cultures, maintaining eye contact is crucial, while in others, it might be seen as confrontational.

Avoid Assumptions: Avoid making assumptions based on stereotypes or your own cultural background. Each individual is unique, and it is important to treat everyone with respect and understanding. When in doubt, ask for clarification rather than jumping to conclusions.

Overcoming Culture Shock and Homesickness:

It is normal to experience culture shock and homesickness, but there are ways to manage these feelings effectively:

Stay Connected to Home: Regularly communicate with family and friends back home through calls, video chats, or social media. This can provide comfort and reduce feelings of isolation. Sharing your experiences with loved ones can also help them understand what you are going through.

Create a Routine: Establishing a daily routine can create a sense of normalcy and stability. Include activities that you enjoy and that help you relax. Whether it is a morning jog, a weekly movie night, or a study schedule, routines can provide structure.

Seek Support: Do not hesitate to seek support if you are struggling with culture shock or homesickness. Many universities offer counseling services and connecting with other international students can also provide mutual support. Joining support groups or talking to a mentor can make a big difference.

Communication Skills

Improving Interpersonal Communication:

Good communication skills are essential for building strong relationships. Here are some tips to enhance your interpersonal communication:

Be Clear and Concise: When communicating, try to be as clear and concise as possible. Avoid using slang or idiomatic expressions that might be confusing to non-native speakers. Clear communication reduces the chances of misunderstandings and ensures that your message is understood.

Ask Questions: Show interest in others by asking questions about their experiences, opinions, and backgrounds. This not only helps you get to know them better but also shows that you value their perspective. Asking open-ended questions can lead to more meaningful conversations.

Share About Yourself: Do not be afraid to share your own experiences and thoughts. This can help others understand you better and create a more balanced experience. Sharing your own cultural practices, traditions, and stories can make interactions more engaging.

Active Listening and Empathy: Active listening and empathy are crucial for effective communication. Here is how you can practice these skills:

Listen More Than You Speak: Make an effort to listen more than you speak. This shows that you value the other person's input and are genuinely interested in what they have to say. Nodding, maintaining eye contact, and giving verbal affirmations can show that you are engaged.

Use Non-Verbal Cues: Non-verbal communication, such as nodding, maintaining eye contact, and using appropriate facial expressions, can enhance your interactions and show that you are engaged. These cues can help convey understanding and empathy.

Be Empathetic: Try to understand things from the other person's perspective. Empathy can help you build deeper connections and navigate social interactions more smoothly. If someone is sharing a problem or concern, acknowledge their feelings and offer support.

Navigating Language Barriers:

Language barriers can be challenging, but they can also be an opportunity to learn and grow. Here is how to handle them:

Use Simple Language: When communicating with non-native speakers, use simple language and avoid jargon. This makes it easier for others to understand you. Speaking slowly and clearly can also help.

Be Patient: Patience is key when dealing with language barriers. Give the other person time to express themselves and do not rush them. Encourage them and make them feel comfortable.

Learn the Local Language: Making an effort to learn the local language can go a long way. Even if you are not fluent, knowing some basic phrases can help you connect with others and show that you respect their culture. Phrases like "hello," "thank you," and "excuse me" can make a big difference.

Use Technology: Do not hesitate to use translation apps and tools to aid communication. They can be very helpful in bridging language gaps and ensuring that your messages are understood correctly. Apps like Google Translate can be lifesavers in tricky situations.

By focusing on making friends, understanding cultural norms, and honing your communication skills, you can build meaningful relationships and integrate smoothly into your new environment. Embrace the opportunity to learn from others, share your experiences, and grow both personally and academically. Social integration is a journey, and each interaction is a step towards a richer and more fulfilling university experience. Enjoy every moment and take full advantage of the vibrant, diverse community around you!

4.6 Extracurricular Activities and Hobbies

Exploring Interests

Finding Clubs and Organizations that Match Your Interests:

University life offers a plethora of clubs and organizations tailored to a wide array of interests. Here is how to find the perfect fit:

Club Fairs and Open Houses: At the beginning of the semester, universities often host club fairs or open houses where you can meet members of different clubs and learn about their activities. These events are great for exploring what is available and signing up for what interests you. Do not be shy—approach the tables, ask questions, and grab some flyers.

Campus Websites and social media: Most universities have websites or social media pages dedicated to student organizations. These resources can provide a comprehensive list of clubs, their meeting times, and contact information. Take some time to browse these resources and make a list of clubs that catch your eye.

Ask Around: Do not hesitate to ask classmates, roommates, or academic advisors about clubs they recommend. Personal recommendations can lead you to hidden gems you might not find on your own. Sometimes the best clubs are the ones you hear about through word of mouth.

Trying New Activities and Stepping Out of Your Comfort Zone:

University is a time for exploration and growth, so why not try something new?

Be Open-Minded: Do not limit yourself to activities you are already familiar with. Trying new things can lead to unexpected interests and talents. Attend a meeting or a trial class of something completely new—whether it is salsa dancing, debate club, or a coding workshop. You might discover a new passion.

Attend Workshops and Events: Universities often host workshops, guest lectures, and events that can introduce you to new hobbies and activities. These are low-commitment ways to explore new interests. Check your campus events calendar regularly.

Challenge Yourself: Stepping out of your comfort zone can be intimidating, but it is also rewarding. Pushing your boundaries can help you develop new skills, meet new people, and grow as a person. Remember, the best experiences often come from trying something outside your usual routine.

Anecdotes and Insights

Exploring Extracurricular Activities- Raj's Story

Student Perspective: "I joined the university's photography club during my international program in Australia. It was a fantastic way to explore the country and meet people with similar interests. Through club outings and events, I developed my photography skills and built a strong network of friends." – Raj, International Student in Australia

Expert Insight: Joining clubs and extracurricular activities can significantly enhance your international experience. These activities provide opportunities to pursue your interests, develop new skills, and meet like-minded individuals. Look for clubs and organizations that align with your passions and be proactive in participating in events and activities.

Balancing Extracurriculars with Academic Responsibilities:

Balancing your academic responsibilities with extracurricular activities is crucial for a fulfilling university experience.

Time Management: Create a schedule that allows you to manage your time effectively. Use planners or digital calendars to keep track of your commitments and deadlines. Prioritize your tasks and set aside specific times for studying and extracurricular activities. Find a system that works for you and stick to it.

Set Realistic Goals: While it is great to be involved, it is important not to overcommit. Set realistic goals for both your academics and extracurriculars to avoid burnout. Know your limits and learn to say no when necessary. It is better to do a few things well than to stretch yourself too thin.

Combine Interests: Look for ways to combine your academic interests with extracurricular activities. For example, if you are studying environmental science, joining an eco-club, or participating in sustainability projects can enrich both your academic and extracurricular life. This can make your extracurricular activities more meaningful and relevant.

Sports and Fitness

Joining Intramural and Varsity Sports Teams:

Engaging in sports can be a fantastic way to stay active, make friends, and relieve stress.

Intramural Sports: Intramural sports are organized within the university and are usually more relaxed and recreational. They offer a great way to stay active and socialize without the intense commitment of varsity sports. Whether it is soccer, basketball, or ultimate frisbee, there is likely an intramural team for you. Plus, the friendly competition can be a lot of fun.

Varsity Sports: If you are more serious about athletics, consider trying out for a varsity team. Varsity sports require a higher level of commitment and skill but offer the chance to compete at a higher level and represent your university. The camaraderie and team spirit can be incredibly rewarding.

Recreational Leagues: Many universities also have recreational leagues that are open to all skill levels. These leagues are a great way to stay active and have fun without the pressure of competitive sports. It is also a wonderful way to meet people who share your interest in sports.

Accessing Gym Facilities and Fitness Classes:

Most universities offer excellent gym facilities and a variety of fitness classes to keep you in shape.

Gym Membership: Check if your student fees include a gym membership. Campus gyms typically offer a range of equipment, from cardio machines to weights, and may also include swimming pools, basketball courts, and other facilities. Make it a habit to visit regularly; it is a great way to relieve stress and stay fit.

Fitness Classes: Many gyms offer group fitness classes like yoga, Pilates, spin, and Zumba. These classes are a fun way to stay fit and meet new people. Look out for classes that fit your schedule and interests. Trying different classes can keep your workout routine exciting and diverse.

Personal Training: If you prefer more personalized guidance, many gyms offer personal training services. Trainers can help you set fitness goals, create workout plans, and stay motivated. It can be a worthwhile investment in your health and well-being.

Outdoor Activities and Recreational Sports:

If you prefer being outdoors, there are plenty of recreational activities to enjoy.

Hiking and Biking: Many campuses are located near parks or nature reserves that offer great trails for hiking and biking. Joining a hiking or biking club can provide a structured way to explore the outdoors and stay active. It is also a great way to discover beautiful spots around your campus.

Water Sports: If your university is near a body of water, investigate opportunities for kayaking, canoeing, or sailing. These activities can be both relaxing and exhilarating. Many universities have clubs or rental facilities that make it easy to get involved.

Recreational Sports: Beyond traditional team sports, many universities offer recreational activities like rock climbing, disc golf, and even martial arts. These can be great ways to try something new and enjoy the outdoors. Check out your campus recreation center for more information.

Creative Pursuits

Participating in Arts and Cultural Clubs:

Engaging in creative activities can provide a wonderful outlet for expression and relaxation.

Arts Clubs: Many universities have clubs dedicated to various forms of art, including painting, sculpture, and photography. These clubs often provide supplies and space for you to work on your projects and may host exhibitions to showcase members' work. It is a fantastic way to meet other creative minds and share your passion.

Cultural Clubs: Joining cultural clubs can give you a deeper appreciation for different traditions and customs. These clubs often host events such as cultural nights, dance performances, and food festivals. Participating in these events can broaden your horizons and provide a sense of community.

Opportunities for Music, Theater, and Dance:

If you have a passion for the performing arts, university is a great place to nurture that interest.

Music Groups: Whether you play an instrument, sing, or enjoy composing, there are usually numerous musical groups to join. From orchestras and bands to choirs and a cappella groups, you will find plenty of opportunities to perform. Do not miss out on the chance to showcase your musical talents and collaborate with others.

Theater: Drama clubs and theater groups are fantastic for those interested in acting, directing, or stagecraft. Many universities put on several productions a year, giving you the chance to audition for roles or get involved behind the scenes. The experience of working on a production can be incredibly rewarding and memorable.

Dance: Dance clubs and teams often cater to various styles, from ballet and jazz to hip-hop and salsa. These groups typically offer regular classes and opportunities to perform at campus events. Dancing is not only a great workout but also a wonderful way to express yourself.

Showcasing Your Talents in Student Exhibitions and Performances:

Showcasing your talents can be a rewarding experience and a great confidence booster.

Art Exhibitions: Many universities have galleries or spaces where students can display their artwork. Participating in exhibitions allows you to share your creations with a wider audience and receive feedback. It is a fantastic way to gain recognition for your work and connect with other artists.

Concerts and Recitals: Music departments and clubs often organize concerts and recitals where you can perform solo or as part of an ensemble. These events provide a platform to showcase your skills and hard work. Performing in front of an audience can be exhilarating and fulfilling.

Theater Productions: Being part of a theater production, whether onstage or behind the scenes, is an exhilarating experience. The process of rehearsing and performing can create strong bonds with your fellow cast and crew members. The excitement of opening night and the applause from the audience are moments to cherish.

Dance Performances: Dance showcases and competitions offer a stage for you to express yourself and demonstrate your talent. Whether it is a formal recital or an informal jam session, performing can be incredibly fulfilling. It is also a wonderful way to celebrate your hard work and dedication.

Engaging in extracurricular activities and hobbies is a vital part of the university experience. It not only enriches your life but also helps you develop new skills, make lasting friendships, and create a balanced lifestyle. By exploring your interests, staying active, and pursuing creative endeavors, you will enhance your university journey and make the most of this exciting time. Remember, university is a unique opportunity to discover new passions and grow as an individual, so dive in and enjoy every moment!

4.7 Networking and Professional Development

Career Services

Utilizing Career Counseling and Job Placement Services:

Career services can be an invaluable resource as you navigate your professional journey during and after university. Here is how to make the most of them:

Career Counseling: Think of career counselors as your personal guides to the professional world. Schedule appointments to discuss your career goals, explore different career paths, and get personalized advice. They can help you identify your strengths, interests, and values, which is crucial for making informed career choices. Do not wait until you are about to graduate—start early to get the most out of these services.

Job Placement Services: Take full advantage of job placement services offered by your university. These services often include job boards, resume reviews, mock interviews, and job search strategies. The staff can also connect you with potential employers and help you navigate the job application process. Regularly check the job boards and attend any workshops or seminars they offer.

Workshops and Events: Career services frequently host workshops and events on topics like resume writing, interview skills, and job search strategies. Attending these can provide you with valuable insights and practical skills to boost your employability. Keep an eye on your university's event calendar and make it a habit to attend these sessions.

Attending Career Fairs and Networking Events:

Career fairs and networking events are excellent opportunities to connect with potential employers and expand your professional network.

Prepare in Advance: Before attending a career fair, do some homework. Research the companies that will be present and identify the ones you are interested in. Prepare your resume, practice your elevator pitch, and come up with questions to ask the recruiters. Being well-prepared can make you stand out.

Dress Professionally: First impressions matter, so dress in professional attire that reflects your seriousness about finding a job or internship. A neat, polished appearance can make a lasting impression. Remember, it is always better to be slightly overdressed than underdressed.

Follow Up: After meeting with recruiters, follow up with a thank-you email to express your appreciation and reiterate your interest. This can help keep you on their radar and demonstrate your professionalism. Mention something specific from your conversation to make your email more personal.

Building a Professional Resume and LinkedIn Profile:

A strong resume and LinkedIn profile are essential tools in your job search arsenal.

Resume Writing: Your resume should be clear, concise, and tailored to the job you are applying for. Highlight your relevant skills, experiences, and accomplishments. Use action verbs and quantify your achievements when possible. Keep it to one page if you are an undergraduate with limited work experience. Do not forget to proofread!

LinkedIn Profile: Your LinkedIn profile should complement your resume and provide a more comprehensive view of your professional background. Include a professional photo, a compelling summary, and detailed descriptions of your experiences and skills. Do not forget to ask for

recommendations from professors, supervisors, or colleagues. Engage with content and join groups related to your field to increase your visibility.

Consistency: Ensure that the information on your resume and LinkedIn profile is consistent. Any discrepancies can raise red flags with potential employers. Double-check dates, job titles, and descriptions to make sure everything matches up.

Internships and Work Experience

Finding and Applying for Internships:

Internships are a great way to gain practical experience, develop new skills, and enhance your resume.

Start Early: Begin your internship search well in advance. Many companies have early application deadlines and starting early gives you a better chance of securing a position. Use your university's career services, job boards, and personal network to find opportunities.

Use Multiple Resources: Utilize various resources to find internships, including university job boards, company websites, and professional associations. Networking can also be a powerful tool —let your professors, career counselors, and peers know you are looking for an internship. Do not be afraid to reach out to alumni or professionals in your field for advice or opportunities.

Tailor Your Applications: Customize your resume and cover letter for each internship you apply for. Highlight the skills and experiences that are most relevant to the position and show your enthusiasm for the role. Use specific examples to demonstrate your qualifications and achievements.

Balancing Work and Academic Commitments:

Balancing work and academics can be challenging, but it is essential for maintaining your well-being and achieving success in both areas.

Time Management: Create a schedule that includes dedicated time for work, study, and relaxation. Use tools like planners, calendars, and apps to keep track of your commitments and deadlines. Prioritize your tasks and set aside specific times for studying and extracurricular activities. Find a system that works for you and stick to it.

Set Realistic Goals: While it is great to be involved, it is important not to overcommit. Set realistic goals for both your academics and extracurriculars to avoid burnout. Know your limits and learn to say no when necessary. It is better to do a few things well than to stretch yourself too thin.

Communicate: If you are struggling to balance work and academics, communicate with your supervisors and professors. They may be able to offer flexibility or support to help you manage your workload. Do not wait until you are overwhelmed—reach out for help early.

Gaining Valuable Skills and Experience:

Internships and part-time jobs can provide valuable skills and experiences that will benefit you in your future career.

Take Initiative: Show your enthusiasm and dedication by taking on additional responsibilities and seeking out new challenges. This can help you develop new skills and demonstrate your value to your employer. Look for ways to contribute beyond your job description.

Reflect on Your Experience: Regularly reflect on what you are learning and how it applies to your career goals. Keep a journal or portfolio of your achievements and skills to track your progress and accomplishments. This can also be helpful when updating your resume or preparing for interviews.

Seek Feedback: Do not be afraid to ask for feedback from your supervisors and colleagues. Constructive criticism can help you improve and grow in your role. Use feedback to identify areas for improvement and set goals for your professional development.

Building Professional Relationships

Networking with Professors, Alumni, and Industry Professionals: Building a strong professional network can open doors to new opportunities and provide valuable support and guidance.

Engage with Professors: Take the time to build relationships with your professors. Attend their office hours, ask questions, and show interest in their research. They can provide valuable advice, references, and connections in your field. Remember, professors can be mentors and advocates for your career.

Connect with Alumni: Many universities have alumni networks that you can tap into. Attend alumni events, join alumni groups on LinkedIn, and reach out to alumni working in your desired industry. They can offer insights, advice, and potential job leads. Do not be shy about reaching out—alumni are often eager to help current students.

Industry Events: Attend industry events, such as conferences, seminars, and workshops. These events are excellent opportunities to meet professionals in your field, learn about industry trends, and expand your network. Bring business cards and be prepared to follow up with new contacts.

Joining Professional Associations and Student Chapters:

Being part of professional associations can enhance your knowledge, skills, and network.

Professional Associations: Join professional associations related to your field of study. These organizations often offer student memberships at reduced rates and provide access to resources, events, and networking opportunities. Membership can also look impressive on your resume.

Student Chapters: Many professional associations have student chapters on university campuses. Joining a student chapter can help you build connections with peers and professionals, gain leadership experience, and stay informed about industry developments. Get involved in chapter activities and take on leadership roles if possible.

Certifications and Training: Take advantage of any certifications, training programs, or workshops offered by professional associations. These can enhance your skills and make you more attractive to potential employers. Continuous learning is key to staying competitive in your field.

Attending Seminars, Workshops, and Conferences:

Participating in seminars, workshops, and conferences can be incredibly beneficial for your professional development.

Seminars and Workshops: These events often focus on specific topics or skills and provide in-depth learning opportunities. Look for seminars and workshops that align with your career interests and goals. They can provide practical knowledge and hands-on experience.

Conferences: Conferences bring together professionals from various fields to share knowledge, discuss trends, and network. Attending conferences can help you stay current with industry developments, learn from experts, and expand your professional network. Consider presenting your research or volunteering to increase your visibility.

Presenting and Volunteering: Consider presenting your research or volunteering at conferences. This can increase your visibility, demonstrate your expertise, and create networking opportunities. Volunteering can also give you behind-the-scenes access and help you build relationships with organizers and speakers.

Networking and professional development are crucial components of your university experience. By utilizing career services, seeking internships, and building professional relationships, you can enhance your skills, gain valuable experience, and create a strong foundation for your future career. Remember, the connections you make and the experiences you gain during your university years can have a lasting impact on your professional journey. So, take advantage of every opportunity, stay proactive, and enjoy the process of building your career!

4.8 Maintaining Health and Wellbeing

Physical Health

Importance of Regular Exercise and Healthy Eating:

Taking care of your physical health is essential to performing well academically and enjoying your university experience to the fullest.

Regular Exercise: Think of exercise as your daily energy boost. It does not have to be intense; even a 30-minute walk can make a big difference. Explore campus facilities like gyms, swimming pools, and sports courts. Join fitness classes such as yoga, Pilates, or spin to make exercise fun and social. If you are not into traditional workouts, consider activities like dancing, hiking, or biking. You will feel more energetic, less stressed, and ready to tackle your studies.

Healthy Eating: Your diet plays a huge role in how you feel and function. Focus on a balanced diet that includes a variety of fruits, vegetables, lean proteins, and whole grains. Avoid relying too heavily on fast food or instant meals, as they can be high in unhealthy fats, sugars, and sodium. Learn some basic cooking skills to prepare your own meals. Many universities offer nutrition workshops or cooking classes—take advantage of these resources to learn how to make healthy and delicious meals on a budget. Cooking for yourself can be fun and rewarding, plus it is often healthier and cheaper than eating out all the time.

Accessing Medical Services and Health Insurance:

Being aware of the medical services available on campus and understanding your health insurance are key components of staying healthy.

Campus Health Services: Familiarize yourself with the medical services offered by your university's health center. These typically include general health check-ups, vaccinations, sexual health services, and emergency care. Keep the contact information for the health center handy in case you need it. Knowing where to go and what is available can save you a lot of stress if you ever need medical help.

Health Insurance: Ensure you have health insurance coverage that meets your needs. Many universities offer student health plans, which can be an affordable option. If you have coverage through a parent or guardian, check that it extends to your location and covers necessary services. Understand what your insurance covers and how to use it, including the process for filing claims and accessing emergency services. Do not wait until you are sick to figure this out—being prepared can make a big difference.

Preventative Health Measures: Regular check-ups and preventive care can help catch potential health issues early. Stay up to date with vaccinations, get regular dental check-ups, and attend annual physical exams. Practice good hygiene, such as regular handwashing, to prevent the spread of illness. Prevention is often easier and cheaper than treatment, so take care of your health proactively.

Mental Health

Recognizing Signs of Stress and Mental Health Issues:

Mental health is just as important as physical health, and university life can sometimes be stressful. Here is how to recognize and address potential issues.

Signs of Stress: Stress can manifest in various ways, including irritability, difficulty concentrating, changes in sleep patterns, and physical symptoms like headaches or stomachaches. Pay attention to these signs and take them seriously. Everyone experiences stress differently, so learn to recognize your own warning signs.

Mental Health Issues: More severe mental health issues might include persistent feelings of sadness or hopelessness, withdrawal from social activities, changes in appetite, and thoughts of self-harm. If you or someone you know is experiencing these symptoms, it is important to seek help. Mental health issues are common and treatable, so do not hesitate to reach out.

Self-Assessment: Regularly check in with yourself about how you are feeling. Journaling can be a useful tool for tracking your mood and identifying stressors. Do not ignore persistent or severe symptoms—early intervention can make a big difference. Talking about your feelings, even just to yourself in a journal, can help clarify what is going on and what you need.

Accessing Counseling and Mental Health Support:

Universities offer a range of mental health resources to support students.

Counseling Services: Most universities have counseling centers that offer free or low-cost services to students. These might include individual counseling, group therapy, and workshops on topics like stress management and resilience. Do not hesitate to make an appointment if you need someone to talk to. Counselors are trained to help you navigate challenges and develop coping strategies.

Mental Health Hotlines: Keep a list of mental health hotlines and emergency contacts. Many universities have 24/7 hotlines for immediate support. National and local mental health organizations also offer helplines and chat services. These resources are there for you—do not be afraid to use them if you need immediate help.

Peer Support: Sometimes, talking to a peer who understands your experience can be very helpful. Look for peer counseling programs or support groups on campus. These can provide a more informal, relatable form of support. Sharing your experiences with someone who has been through similar things can be incredibly validating and comforting.

Practicing Mindfulness and Stress Management Techniques:

Incorporating mindfulness and stress management techniques into your routine can help maintain mental well-being.

Mindfulness Practices: Mindfulness involves focusing on the present moment without judgment. Practices like meditation, deep breathing exercises, and yoga can help reduce stress and improve mental clarity. Apps like Headspace and Calm offer guided meditations and mindfulness exercises that are easy to incorporate into your day. Even a few minutes of mindfulness practice each day can make a big difference in how you feel.

Stress Management Techniques: Find what works best for you to manage stress. This might include physical activity, creative hobbies, spending time in nature, or talking to friends. Make sure to take regular breaks and engage in activities that you enjoy. Balancing work with fun and relaxation is key to maintaining mental health.

Healthy Habits: Maintaining a regular sleep schedule, eating well, and staying hydrated are foundational to managing stress. Avoid excessive caffeine and alcohol, which can exacerbate stress and anxiety. Create a relaxing bedtime routine to ensure you get quality sleep. Good physical health supports good mental health, so take care of your body to take care of your mind.

Anecdotes and Insights
Maintaining Health and Wellbeing- Maria's Story

Student Perspective: "During my exchange in the UK, I struggled with the gloomy weather and homesickness. I found that maintaining a regular exercise routine and exploring the beautiful parks helped lift my spirits. Additionally, attending counseling sessions at the university's health center provided valuable support during tough times." – Maria, International Student in the UK

Expert Insight: Maintaining your health and wellbeing is essential for a positive international experience. Regular exercise, healthy eating, and mental health support can help you cope with stress and homesickness. Utilize campus health services and seek counseling if needed. Exploring your surroundings and staying active can also boost your mood and overall well-being.

Work-Life Balance

Finding a Balance Between Academics, Work, and Social Life:

Balancing academics, work, and social life is essential for overall well-being and success.

Prioritize and Plan: Use planners or digital calendars to manage your time effectively. Prioritize tasks based on deadlines and importance and break larger projects into manageable steps. Schedule time for classes, study sessions, work, and social activities, ensuring you do not overcommit. A well-balanced schedule helps you stay on top of your responsibilities without feeling overwhelmed.

Quality Over Quantity: Focus on the quality of your study and work time rather than the quantity. Efficient study techniques and focused work sessions can help you get more done in less time, leaving you with more free time. It is not about how long you study but how effectively you use that time.

Social Connections: Make time for socializing and building relationships. Maintaining strong social connections is crucial for mental health and can provide a support system during stressful times. Balance group activities with solo relaxation time to recharge. Being around friends and loved ones can help you unwind and feel supported.

Setting Boundaries and Managing Time Effectively:

Setting boundaries and managing your time effectively can help prevent burnout and maintain a healthy balance.

Learn to Say No: It is important to recognize your limits and not take on more than you can handle. Politely declining extra commitments when your schedule is full can help you avoid unnecessary stress. It is okay to say no to protect your well-being.

Designate Study and Relaxation Times: Create a clear distinction between study time and relaxation time. This can help you stay focused and productive during study sessions and fully unwind during breaks. Use techniques like the Pomodoro Technique to break study time into focused intervals with short breaks in between. Having set times for work and relaxation can help you be more productive and less stressed.

Communicate Boundaries: Let friends, family, and colleagues know your availability and limits. Clear communication can help manage expectations and prevent misunderstandings. For example, let your roommates know your study schedule to minimize interruptions. Being upfront about your needs helps others respect your time and space.

Prioritizing Self-Care and Relaxation:

Self-care and relaxation are essential for maintaining your overall well-being.

Self-Care Activities: Identify activities that help you relax and recharge. This might include reading, taking baths, listening to music, or engaging in a hobby. Make self-care a regular part of your routine, not just something you do when you are feeling overwhelmed. Regular self-care can prevent burnout and keep you feeling balanced.

Relaxation Techniques: Explore relaxation techniques like progressive muscle relaxation, guided imagery, or aromatherapy. These can help reduce stress and improve your mood. Experiment to find what works best for you and incorporate it into your daily routine.

Unplug Regularly: Take breaks from screens and social media to give your mind a rest. Spending time outdoors, practicing mindfulness, or engaging in face-to-face interactions can be refreshing and rejuvenating. Digital detoxes can help you feel more present and less overwhelmed.

Maintaining your health and well-being is a multifaceted approach that involves taking care of both your physical and mental health, finding a balance between various aspects of your life, and prioritizing self-care. By incorporating these practices into your daily routine, you can enhance your university experience, perform better academically, and enjoy a more fulfilling and balanced life. Remember, your well-being is the foundation for your success, so take the time to invest in yourself and build healthy habits that will support you throughout your university journey and beyond.

Chapter 4 Conclusion

Key Strategies for Academic and Social Integration

As we wrap up this chapter, let us revisit some of the most impactful strategies for making your academic and social integration as smooth and rewarding as possible. Think of these as your toolkit for success.

Understanding the Academic System: Grasping the differences between your home and host country's education systems is crucial. Be proactive in learning about course structures, grading scales, and key academic dates. This knowledge will help you navigate your studies more efficiently and meet academic expectations. Do not be shy about asking questions—your professors and academic advisors are there to help.

Engaging with Professors and Academic Staff: Building strong relationships with your professors and academic mentors can open doors to numerous opportunities. Attend office hours, participate in class discussions, and seek feedback to enhance your learning experience. Do not underestimate the value of academic mentorship and networking within your field. Remember, professors are not just there to teach but also to guide and support you.

Effective Study Habits and Time Management: Developing effective study habits and mastering time management are critical for academic success. Use active learning techniques, join study groups, and take advantage of campus resources like libraries and tutoring services. Balancing your study schedule with social activities ensures a well-rounded experience. Find what works best for you—everyone has a unique learning style.

Navigating Campus Life: Familiarize yourself with campus facilities, student services, and opportunities for involvement. Utilize resources like academic advising, mental health support, and accessibility services to navigate your university experience smoothly. Get involved in student organizations and take advantage of recreational facilities to enrich your campus life. The more you explore, the more at home you will feel.

Social Integration and Building Relationships: Making friends and building a diverse network can enhance your international experience. Join clubs, participate in social events, and be open to new cultural experiences. Understanding and adapting to cultural norms, improving communication skills, and overcoming culture shock are essential for building strong, meaningful relationships. Be open, be curious, and be yourself.

Extracurricular Activities and Hobbies: Exploring interests and participating in extracurricular activities can significantly enrich your university experience. Whether it is joining a sports team, engaging in creative pursuits, or exploring new hobbies, these activities provide a balance to academic life and contribute to personal growth. Do not be afraid to try something new—you might discover a hidden talent or passion.

Networking and Professional Development: Actively engage in networking opportunities and focus on professional development. Utilize career services, attend career fairs, and build a strong LinkedIn profile. Seek internships and work experiences that align with your career goals, and build professional relationships with professors, alumni, and industry professionals. Networking is not just about finding a job—it is about building a support system for your career.

Maintaining Health and Wellbeing: Prioritize your physical and mental health to ensure a balanced and fulfilling university experience. Engage in regular exercise, maintain a healthy diet, and utilize medical services when needed. Recognize signs of stress and seek mental health support. Practice mindfulness and stress management techniques to maintain mental clarity and resilience. Remember, taking care of yourself is the first step to achieving your goals.

Encouragement to Actively Engage and Make the Most of the International Experience

Your time as an international student is a unique opportunity for personal and academic growth. Embrace every aspect of this journey with an open mind and a proactive attitude. Engage actively in your studies, build meaningful relationships, and immerse yourself in the local culture. Each experience, whether challenging or rewarding, contributes to your overall development and shapes your perspective.

Imagine the stories you will have to tell, the friendships you will forge, and the personal growth you will experience. Embrace the ups and downs—they are all part of the adventure. This is your chance to explore new horizons, learn from diverse perspectives, and make lasting memories.

Tips for Maintaining Balance and Achieving Success

As you navigate your international experience, keep these final tips in mind to maintain balance and achieve success:

- **Set Realistic Goals**: Establish clear, achievable goals for both your academic and personal life. Regularly review and adjust these goals as needed. Small, consistent steps can lead to significant progress.
- **Stay Organized**: Use planners, digital calendars, and to-do lists to keep track of your commitments and deadlines. Staying organized helps reduce stress and increases productivity. Find a system that works for you and stick to it.
- **Prioritize Self-Care**: Make self-care a priority by engaging in activities that help you relax and recharge. Regularly check in with yourself to ensure you are maintaining a healthy balance. Self-care is not selfish—it is essential.
- **Seek Support When Needed**: Do not hesitate to reach out for help, whether it is academic support, mental health services, or advice from mentors. Utilizing available resources can significantly enhance your experience. Remember, asking for help is a sign of strength, not weakness.
- **Embrace Flexibility**: Be adaptable and open to change. Embracing flexibility allows you to navigate unexpected challenges and make the most of new opportunities. Sometimes the best experiences come from the unplanned moments.
- **Enjoy the Journey**: Lastly, remember to enjoy your time as an international student. Celebrate your achievements, learn from your experiences, and make the most of every moment. This is a once-in-a-lifetime opportunity—savor it.

By following these strategies and tips, you can successfully integrate into your new academic and social environment, achieving a fulfilling and memorable international experience. Take each day as it comes, embrace the new experiences, and always remember that this journey is shaping you in ways you might not even realize yet. Enjoy every moment and make it count!

Chapter 4 Review:

Summary of Key Concepts

In this chapter, we explored the essential strategies for successfully integrating into the academic and social life at your host university. Key areas of focus included understanding the academic system, building relationships with professors and academic staff, developing effective study habits and time management skills, navigating campus life, integrating socially, exploring extracurricular activities, networking for professional development, and maintaining health and wellbeing. These strategies are designed to help you thrive academically and socially during your international experience.

Review Questions

Multiple Choice Questions

1. Which of the following is a key strategy for adapting to a new academic system?
    - a) Ignoring the differences between your home and host academic systems
    - b) Understanding the grading scales and course structures
    - c) Avoiding interaction with academic advisors
    - d) Skipping orientation sessions
2. What is an effective way to build relationships with professors in a new academic environment?
    - a) Avoiding office hours
    - b) Showing genuine interest in their research
    - c) Not participating in class discussions
    - d) Only interacting with them through emails

Short Answer Questions

1. Describe two effective time management techniques that can help balance academic responsibilities and social activities.
2. How can joining student organizations and clubs enhance your social integration during your international experience?

Reflective Questions

1. What are the main differences between your home country's academic system and that of your host university? How do you plan to adapt to these differences?
2. Reflect on a time when you successfully managed your academic workload and social life. What strategies did you use, and how can you apply them during your international journey?

Application-Based Questions

1. Create a weekly schedule that includes your academic commitments, extracurricular activities, and time for self-care. Explain how this schedule will help you maintain a balanced life.
2. Identify three key resources or services provided by your host university that you plan to use. Describe how each resource will support your academic and personal growth.

Invitation to Reflective Exercises

To further deepen your understanding and application of the concepts covered in this chapter, we encourage you to complete the reflective exercises in the companion workbook, " Reflective Exercises: The International Experiences Guide Workbook." These exercises are designed to help you internalize the content, apply it to your personal situation, and enhance your overall international experience.

{ 5 }

Cultural Immersion and Adaptation

Embarking on an international program is more than just an academic pursuit—it is a cultural adventure. Immersing yourself in the local culture is a pivotal aspect of the international experience, offering invaluable lessons that extend far beyond the classroom. This chapter is your guide to navigating and embracing the cultural journey that awaits you.

Importance of Cultural Immersion for a Holistic International Experience:

Cultural immersion is about actively engaging with the customs, traditions, and daily life of your host country. Think of it as stepping out of your comfort zone and diving into a world of new experiences. This immersion allows you to gain a deeper understanding of the local way of life, fostering a more meaningful and memorable international experience. By immersing yourself in the local culture, you will develop a greater appreciation for diversity and enhance your intercultural competence—skills that are highly valued in our increasingly globalized world.

Imagine walking through bustling markets, trying exotic foods, and participating in local festivals. These experiences are not just about sightseeing; they are opportunities to live and breathe the culture, making your stay abroad truly enriching. You will find that the connections you make and the stories you gather will stay with you long after your international program ends.

Overview of the Benefits and Challenges of Cultural Adaptation:

Cultural adaptation is a journey filled with both rewards and challenges. On one hand, it offers numerous benefits, including personal growth, increased cultural awareness, and the development of new perspectives. You will learn to navigate different social norms, communicate more effectively across cultures, and appreciate the richness of your host country's heritage.

For instance, you might find yourself learning a new language, adopting local customs, or even developing a taste for dishes you never imagined trying. These experiences can broaden your horizons and make you more adaptable and empathetic.

On the other hand, this journey may also present challenges such as culture shock, language barriers, and the occasional feeling of isolation. It is perfectly normal to feel overwhelmed at times. Understanding that these challenges are a natural part of the adaptation process can help you approach them with patience and resilience. Remember, every challenge you overcome is a step towards deeper integration and understanding.

Encouragement to Embrace and Learn from Cultural Differences:

Embracing cultural differences is a transformative aspect of your international experience. It involves being open-minded, curious, and respectful towards new customs and viewpoints. By actively participating in cultural activities, trying local cuisines, and engaging with the community, you will not only gain a deeper understanding of your host culture but also grow as an individual.

Think about it—each cultural difference you encounter is a chance to learn something new and exciting. Maybe it is a different way of greeting people, unique holiday traditions, or a novel approach to problem-solving. Learning from these differences can expand your worldview, challenge your preconceptions, and foster a sense of empathy and global citizenship.

Imagine attending a local festival and dancing to traditional music or sitting down with a host family for a home-cooked meal. These moments create lasting memories and deepen your connection to the culture. They also teach you to appreciate the beauty of diversity and the common threads that unite us all.

Remember, the goal of cultural immersion is not to become an expert in your host culture, but to appreciate and learn from it. This chapter will guide you through the various aspects of cultural immersion and adaptation, offering practical tips and insights to help you make the most of this enriching journey. Embrace the adventure, be open to new experiences, and allow yourself to grow through the process of cultural adaptation.

So, get ready to dive in! Whether you are exploring ancient temples, learning a new language, or making friends from different backgrounds, each experience will contribute to your growth and understanding. The world is waiting—let us embark on this cultural adventure together!

5.1 Understanding Cultural Differences

Cultural Awareness

Defining Culture and Its Impact on Behavior and Perceptions:

Culture can be thought of as the shared values, norms, traditions, and customs that influence the way a group of people think, behave, and interact. It shapes our worldviews, our reactions to events, and our interactions with others. Recognizing the impact of culture on behavior and perceptions is crucial for understanding and adapting to a new environment. For instance, what might be considered polite in one culture could be seen as rude in another. Being aware of these differences helps you navigate social situations more effectively.

Imagine you are in a new country and someone hands you a gift. In some cultures, you might open it right away to show your appreciation. In others, it is polite to wait and open it later. These small nuances are shaped by deep-rooted cultural norms and understanding them can make your interactions smoother and more meaningful.

Recognizing and Respecting Cultural Diversity:

Respecting cultural diversity means acknowledging and valuing the differences between cultures. It is about appreciating the uniqueness of each culture and being open to learning from them. This respect can foster mutual understanding and harmonious relationships. When you respect cultural diversity, you are more likely to form meaningful connections and avoid misunderstandings. For example, learning a few phrases in the local language or showing interest in local customs can go a long way in building rapport.

Think about meeting someone from a different background. Showing curiosity about their traditions or trying their favorite local dish can spark conversations and build bridges. It is these little gestures that show you are interested and respectful, paving the way for deeper connections.

Common Cultural Dimensions:

Individualism vs. Collectivism: In individualistic cultures, people prioritize personal goals and individual rights. In collectivist cultures, the focus is on group goals and community well-being. Understanding where your host culture falls on this spectrum can help you navigate social expectations. For instance, in a collectivist society, you might notice decisions are often made with family or group consensus in mind.

High-Context vs. Low-Context Communication: High-context cultures rely heavily on non-verbal cues and the context of communication, while low-context cultures depend more on explicit verbal communication.

Being aware of this can improve your communication effectiveness. Imagine trying to understand a subtle hint versus a direct statement; each culture has its own way of conveying messages.

Power Distance: This dimension measures the acceptance of unequal power distribution in a society. High power distance cultures have clear hierarchical structures, while low power distance cultures strive for equality and accessible authority figures. This can affect how you address professors or interact with local authorities.

Uncertainty Avoidance: Cultures with high uncertainty avoidance prefer clear rules and stability, while those with low uncertainty avoidance are more comfortable with ambiguity and change. Knowing this can help you adapt to local norms and expectations.

Researching Your Host Culture

Historical Background and Significant Cultural Events:

Understanding the historical context of your host country can provide valuable insights into its present-day culture. Research major historical events, influential figures, and cultural milestones. This knowledge will not only enrich your experience but also show locals that you respect and appreciate their history.

Imagine walking through a historic site and knowing the story behind it. This context can deepen your appreciation and make your visit more memorable. Plus, locals will appreciate your effort to learn about their history.

Key Cultural Norms and Social Etiquette:

Familiarize yourself with the everyday social norms and etiquette of your host country. Learn about acceptable behavior in various social settings, such as greetings, dining etiquette, and public behavior. This preparation can help you avoid unintentional faux pas and demonstrate your willingness to adapt and integrate.

For example, in some cultures, it is common to greet everyone in a room, while in others, a simple nod might suffice. Understanding these nuances can make your interactions smoother and more respectful.

Major Holidays, Traditions, and Customs:

Get to know the important holidays, traditions, and customs of your host country. Participate in local celebrations and festivals to experience the culture firsthand. This involvement can be a great way to immerse yourself in the local way of life and create lasting memories.

Imagine joining a local festival, trying traditional foods, and participating in cultural dances. These experiences not only enrich your stay but also help you connect with locals on a deeper level.

Anecdotes and Insights
Navigating Cultural Differences- Elena's Story

Student Perspective: "When I first arrived in Spain, I was excited but also nervous about the cultural differences. One of the biggest adjustments was understanding the concept of 'siesta.' Shops and businesses closed for several hours in the afternoon, and it initially felt like my day was being disrupted. However, I soon realized this was a valuable time to relax and recharge, which made my evenings more enjoyable and productive. Adapting to this new rhythm helped me appreciate the local lifestyle and integrate better into the community." – Elena, Spain International Student

Expert Insight: Adapting to different cultural norms and routines, like the siesta in Spain, can be challenging but also enriching. Embrace these differences as opportunities to learn and grow. Understanding and respecting local customs not only helps you fit in better but also allows you to experience the culture more authentically. Take time to observe and participate in local practices, and you will find that these adjustments can enhance your overall experience.

5.2 Language and Communication

Improving Language Skills

Strategies for Language Learning:

Classes: Enroll in language classes offered by your university or local community centers. Structured learning can provide a strong foundation and clear progression. It is a great way to meet other learners and practice in a supportive environment.

Self-Study: Use textbooks, online courses, and language learning apps to practice on your own. Consistent practice is key to improvement. Set aside time each day to review vocabulary, practice grammar, and immerse yourself in the language.

Language Exchange Partners: Find a language exchange partner who wants to learn your language. This mutual exchange can enhance your speaking skills and provide cultural insights. It is also a fun way to make new friends and learn about each other's cultures.

Utilizing Language Learning Apps and Online Resources:

Apps like Duolingo, Babbel, and Rosetta Stone can make language learning interactive and fun. Online resources such as YouTube tutorials, language blogs, and forums can also offer additional practice and tips.

Imagine turning language learning into a game. These apps often have gamified elements that make learning more engaging and less of a chore. Plus, you can practice anytime, anywhere.

Practicing Speaking with Locals and Fellow Students:

Engage in conversations with locals and fellow students as much as possible. Practice makes perfect, and real-life interactions can significantly improve your fluency and confidence. Do not be afraid to make mistakes—locals will appreciate your effort to learn their language.

Picture yourself at a local café, chatting with the barista or having a conversation with classmates. These real-world interactions can boost your language skills and make you feel more integrated into the community.

Non-Verbal Communication

Understanding Body Language, Gestures, and Facial Expressions:

Non-verbal communication can vary widely between cultures. Some gestures that are positive in one culture might be offensive in another. Pay attention to body language, facial expressions, and gestures to ensure your non-verbal cues align with local norms.

Imagine being in a country where nodding means no and shaking your head means yes. Understanding these differences can prevent misunderstandings and enhance your communication.

Recognizing and Respecting Personal Space and Touch:

Different cultures have different norms regarding personal space and physical touch. In some cultures, close physical proximity is common, while in others, it is reserved for close relationships. Understanding these norms can help you avoid uncomfortable situations and show respect for others' boundaries.

Think about how close you stand to someone while talking. In some places, close proximity is a sign of friendliness, while in others, it might be seen as intrusive.

Eye Contact, Tone of Voice, and Other Non-Verbal Cues:

Eye contact and tone of voice are crucial components of communication. In some cultures, direct eye contact is a sign of confidence and honesty, while in others, it can be seen as disrespectful. Similarly, the tone of voice can convey different emotions and intentions. Being mindful of these cues can enhance your interactions and help you communicate more effectively.

Imagine trying to convey sincerity or empathy through your tone of voice. These subtle elements can significantly impact how your message is received.

Overcoming Language Barriers

Techniques for Effective Communication Despite Language Differences:

Simplify Your Language: Use simple sentences and avoid slang or idiomatic expressions. Clear and concise language is easier to understand. Imagine explaining something to a child or someone who is just learning your language—keep it straightforward and clear.

Use Visual Aids: Gestures, pictures, and written notes can help convey your message when words fail. Sometimes a simple drawing or pointing to an object can bridge the gap.

Patience and Persistence: Do not get frustrated if communication is challenging. Be patient and keep trying. Your effort to communicate despite the barriers will be appreciated.

Asking for Clarification and Repeating Key Information:

If you are unsure about what someone said, do not hesitate to ask for clarification. Repeating key information back to the speaker can ensure mutual understanding and prevent miscommunication.

Imagine confirming directions by repeating them back: "So, I turn left at the next street, right?" This technique ensures you have understood correctly.

Using Translation Tools and Language Apps:

Translation apps like Google Translate can be invaluable for bridging language gaps. Use these tools to assist with difficult conversations but try to rely on them less as your language skills improve.

Think of these tools as your backup plan. They are incredibly helpful in a pinch but aim to build your skills so you can communicate independently.

Anecdotes and Insights
Overcoming Language Barriers- Max's Story
Student Perspective: "In Japan, the language barrier was initially overwhelming. I knew basic Japanese, but conversations often went beyond my comprehension. I decided to join a language exchange group where I helped locals practice English while they helped me with Japanese. This not only improved my language skills but also led to meaningful friendships. One memorable experience was learning to write calligraphy with my language partner, which deepened my appreciation for Japanese culture." – Max, Japan International Student

Expert Insight: Overcoming language barriers is a common challenge for international students. Joining language exchange groups is an effective way to improve your language skills while building connections. Practice regularly, be patient with yourself, and do not be afraid to make mistakes. Immersing yourself in cultural activities related to the language, like calligraphy in Japan, can also enhance your learning experience and foster a deeper connection with the culture.

By understanding and respecting cultural differences, improving your language skills, and mastering both verbal and non-verbal communication, you will enhance your cultural immersion and make your international experience more rewarding. Embrace the challenges as opportunities for growth and enjoy the rich tapestry of experiences that come with living in a new culture. Each interaction, each new word learned, and each cultural norm understood will make your journey richer and more fulfilling.

5.3 Social Etiquette and Norms

Social Customs

Greeting Rituals and Forms of Address:

Greetings vary widely from culture to culture and knowing the appropriate way to greet some-one can set a positive tone for your interactions. In some cultures, a firm handshake is standard, while in others, a bow or a cheek kiss is customary. Addressing people correctly—using titles and last names versus first names—can also be important.

Imagine you have just landed in a new country and are meeting your host family or new friends for the first time. In Japan, a slight bow shows respect and politeness. In contrast, in many European countries, a light kiss on the cheek or a firm handshake is more common. These small gestures can make a big difference in how you are perceived. Understanding these nuances can help you make a good first impression and build rapport quickly.

Dining Etiquette and Table Manners:

Dining customs can be one of the most intricate aspects of cultural norms. This includes knowing how to use utensils, when to start eating, and what behaviors are considered polite or impolite at the table.

Picture yourself at a dinner table in Italy. It is common to use bread to mop up the sauce from your plate—a practice called "fare la scarpetta," which shows appreciation for the meal. In contrast, in some Asian cultures, it is polite to leave a bit of food on your plate to show that you are satisfied. Understanding these customs, like how to use chopsticks properly in China or Japan, can enhance your dining experience and show respect for your hosts.

Gift-Giving Traditions and Expectations:

Gift-giving is a significant cultural ritual in many societies, with specific traditions and expectations surrounding it. The type of gift, the way it is wrapped, and the timing of giving it can all carry important meanings.

Imagine you are invited to a Japanese home for dinner. Bringing a small gift, like sweets or a souvenir from your home country, wrapped beautifully, shows your gratitude and respect. In contrast, in Western cultures, gifts are often opened immediately, while in some Eastern cultures, it is customary to open them later. Being aware of these traditions can help you navigate social occasions smoothly and respectfully.

Behavioral Norms

Public Behavior and Social Interactions:

Behavior that is acceptable in public can vary greatly between cultures. This includes how loudly you speak, your body language, and how you interact with others in public spaces.

Consider walking through a market in Thailand, where maintaining a calm and quiet demeanor is respectful. In contrast, in Mediterranean cultures, animated conversations and expressive gestures are the norm. Understanding these differences can help you avoid awkward situations and integrate more seamlessly into your new environment.

Understanding and Adhering to Dress Codes:

Dress codes can reflect cultural values and social norms. What is considered appropriate attire in one culture may be viewed differently in another. This applies to both everyday clothing and attire for specific events or places, like religious sites.

Imagine visiting a temple in Thailand, where covering your shoulders and knees is a sign of respect. In contrast, casual attire might be acceptable in most settings in the United States. Adhering to these dress codes shows respect for local customs and can help you feel more comfortable and accepted.

Respecting Privacy and Personal Boundaries:

Personal space and privacy expectations can differ dramatically across cultures. Understanding these norms can help you respect others' boundaries and avoid uncomfortable situations.

Think about how close you stand to someone while talking. In many Western cultures, there is a significant emphasis on personal space, and people might feel uncomfortable if you stand too close. In contrast, in some Middle Eastern and Latin American cultures, closer physical proximity during conversations is common and seen as a sign of warmth and engagement.

Taboos and Sensitive Topics

Identifying Topics to Avoid in Conversation:

Every culture has topics that are considered sensitive or inappropriate for casual conversation. These might include personal finances, political opinions, or even certain family matters.

For instance, discussing salary or income might be a normal part of conversation in some cultures but considered impolite or intrusive in others. Being aware of these taboos can help you steer clear of potential faux pas and maintain positive interactions.

Navigating Political, Religious, and Cultural Sensitivities:

Politics, religion, and cultural practices can be deeply personal and sensitive subjects. It is important to approach these topics with caution and respect.

Imagine you are at a dinner party in India, and the topic of religion comes up. Instead of expressing strong opinions, listening respectfully, and showing curiosity without judgment can help you navigate these conversations gracefully. If such topics do come up, listening respectfully, and avoiding confrontation can help maintain harmonious relationships.

Responding to Cultural Misunderstandings Gracefully:

Despite your best efforts, misunderstandings are bound to happen when you are immersed in a new culture. How you respond to these situations can make a big difference.

Apologize sincerely if you have unintentionally offended someone and ask for guidance on how to avoid similar issues in the future. For example, if you accidentally use an inappropriate gesture, a genuine apology and willingness to learn will show respect and humility. Showing a willingness to learn and adapt demonstrates respect and humility.

5.4 Building Cultural Competence

Cultural Sensitivity

Developing Empathy and an Open-Minded Attitude:

Cultural sensitivity begins with empathy and openness. Putting yourself in others' shoes and being open to different ways of thinking and living can help you connect more deeply with people from other cultures.

Think about how you would feel if someone misunderstood or dismissed your cultural practices. Approach new cultures with the same respect and curiosity you would hope for yourself. This mindset can help you appreciate the beauty and diversity of different cultures and foster genuine connections.

Avoiding Stereotypes and Generalizations: It is easy to fall into the trap of stereotyping when you encounter new cultures. Avoid making assumptions based on limited experiences or media portrayals. Instead, focus on getting to know individuals and understanding their unique perspectives.

For example, not all French people eat croissants daily, and not all Australians are surfers. Recognizing the diversity within cultures helps you form more accurate and respectful perceptions. Engaging in conversations and asking open-ended questions can reveal the rich complexities of different cultures.

Reflecting on Your Own Cultural Biases and Perspectives:

We all have biases shaped by our cultural backgrounds. Reflecting on these biases and understanding how they influence your perceptions and interactions is a crucial step toward cultural competence.

Consider how your upbringing has shaped your views on work, family, and social interactions. Being aware of your biases can help you approach other cultures with greater sensitivity and understanding. This self-awareness can lead to more meaningful and respectful interactions with people from different backgrounds.

Cultural Adaptation

Stages of Cultural Adjustment:

Cultural adjustment typically follows several stages:

- **Honeymoon**: Initial excitement and fascination with the new culture.
- **Negotiation**: Challenges and frustrations as cultural differences become more apparent.
- **Adjustment**: Gradual adaptation and finding ways to navigate the new culture.
- **Mastery**: Feeling comfortable and integrated into the new environment.

Recognizing these stages can help you manage your expectations and emotions as you adapt to your host culture. Understanding that it is normal to experience ups and downs can provide comfort and perspective during challenging times.

Strategies for Coping with Culture Shock:

Culture shock is a common experience for many international students. Strategies for coping include:

Staying connected with support networks: Friends, family, and fellow students can provide emotional support. Keeping in touch with loved ones can offer a sense of stability and comfort.

Maintaining familiar routines: Keeping some aspects of your daily life consistent can provide a sense of stability. Whether it is a morning workout or a weekly phone call, routines can anchor you.

Engaging in local activities: Actively participating in cultural events and social activities can help you acclimate. Join local clubs, attend community events, and explore your new surroundings.

Tips for Integrating into the Local Culture:

Integration is about actively engaging with the local culture and community. Here are some tips:

- **Learn the language**: Even basic language skills can go a long way in helping you connect with locals. Simple phrases like "hello," "thank you," and "please" can open doors.
- **Participate in community events**: Attend local festivals, volunteer, or join clubs to meet people and learn more about the culture. Immersing yourself in community activities can create lasting memories and friendships.
- **Show curiosity and respect**: Ask questions, express genuine interest, and respect cultural norms and practices. Demonstrating respect and a willingness to learn can foster positive interactions.

Intercultural Skills

Active Listening and Effective Cross-Cultural Communication:

Active listening involves fully concentrating, understanding, and responding thoughtfully during conversations. In cross-cultural contexts, this means being attentive to both verbal and non-verbal cues.

For instance, nodding and maintaining eye contact can show you are engaged and respectful. Paraphrasing and asking clarifying questions can help ensure mutual understanding. Active listening can also reveal underlying cultural nuances that might not be immediately apparent.

Building Intercultural Relationships and Networks:

Forming relationships across cultures requires effort and openness. Be proactive in meeting new people and building a diverse network.

Attend cultural exchange events, join international student organizations, and seek out opportunities to connect with people from different backgrounds. These relationships can provide valuable support and enrich your international experience. Engaging with a diverse network can also enhance your global perspective and foster lifelong friendships.

Leveraging Cultural Diversity for Personal and Academic Growth:

Cultural diversity can be a powerful catalyst for personal and academic growth. Exposure to different perspectives can enhance your critical thinking, creativity, and problem-solving skills.

Embrace opportunities to collaborate with people from diverse backgrounds in academic projects or social activities. This not only broadens your horizons but also prepares you for working in global environments. Leveraging cultural diversity can lead to innovative ideas and solutions, enriching both your personal and professional life.

By understanding social etiquette and norms, building cultural competence, and developing intercultural skills, you can navigate your international experience with confidence and grace. Embrace the differences, learn from them, and allow yourself to grow through this incredible journey of cultural immersion and adaptation. Each interaction, each new word learned, and each cultural norm understood will make your journey richer and more fulfilling.

5.5 Participating in Local Culture

Engaging in Community Activities

Volunteering and Community Service Opportunities:

Volunteering is a fantastic way to immerse yourself in the local culture while making a positive impact. Look for community service opportunities that align with your interests and skills. This could involve teaching English, helping at a local food bank, or participating in environmental conservation efforts. Volunteering not only allows you to give back to the community but also provides a platform to meet new people and understand local issues more deeply.

Imagine spending your weekends teaching English to children or helping to organize a community event. These experiences can be incredibly rewarding and offer a unique insight into the daily lives and challenges of local residents. Plus, volunteering often opens doors to friendships and networks that might not be available through other activities. You might find yourself invited to local gatherings or special events, deepening your connection to the community.

Joining Local Clubs, Organizations, and Interest Groups:

Engaging with local clubs and organizations can significantly enhance your cultural immersion. Whether it is joining a sports team, a book club, or a special interest group, these organizations provide structured environments where you can meet locals and other international students with similar interests.

For instance, if you love hiking, joining a local hiking club can introduce you to beautiful trails and natural landscapes while fostering connections with people who share your passion. If you are interested in art, a local arts and crafts group can help you explore traditional and contemporary art forms. These groups often organize regular events, outings, and activities that can help you feel more integrated and engaged with your host community. You might also discover new hobbies and interests through these interactions.

Attending Local Events, Festivals, and Cultural Celebrations:

Local events and festivals are a window into the heart of a culture. They showcase the traditions, values, and social life of the community. Make it a point to attend these events, whether it is a national holiday celebration, a local fair, or a cultural festival.

Imagine the vibrant colors, music, and dances of a local festival. These events are not just about entertainment; they are opportunities to learn about the history and significance behind the celebrations. Engage with locals, ask questions, and participate in the festivities. Your active participation will not only enrich your cultural experience but also show your appreciation and respect for the host culture. You might even find yourself learning traditional dances or songs, adding a personal touch to your cultural immersion.

Anecdotes and Insights

Participating in Local Festivals- Priya's Story

Student Perspective: "Attending the Holi festival in India was one of the most unforgettable experiences of my exchange. The vibrant colors, music, and joyful atmosphere were unlike anything I had ever seen. Initially, I was hesitant to participate fully because I did not know the customs. However, my host family encouraged me to join in, explaining the significance of the festival. By the end of the day, I was covered in colors and filled with a sense of belonging and happiness." – Priya, India International Student

Expert Insight: Participating in local festivals and cultural events is a fantastic way to immerse yourself in the host culture. These events provide insights into the community's values, traditions, and social life. Do not hesitate to join in and experience these moments fully. Ask locals about the significance of the celebrations and follow their lead to ensure respectful participation. Such experiences can create lasting memories and a deeper appreciation for the culture.

Experiencing Local Traditions

Participating in Traditional Ceremonies and Practices:

Traditional ceremonies and practices are integral to understanding a culture's identity. These might include religious ceremonies, seasonal festivals, or important life events like weddings and funerals. Participate in these traditions when invited and approach them with respect and curiosity.

For example, attending a traditional tea ceremony in Japan can provide a profound understanding of Japanese aesthetics and values such as harmony, respect, purity, and tranquility.

Participating in these practices allows you to experience the culture's depth and significance first-hand. You might also gain insights into the local way of life and the importance placed on these traditions.

Learning About Local Arts, Music, and Dance:

Art, music, and dance are powerful expressions of culture. Take the time to learn about and experience the local arts scene. Visit galleries and museums, attend concerts and dance performances, and, if possible, take part in workshops or classes.

Imagine learning a traditional dance or attending a music festival that features local artists. These activities provide a sensory-rich experience that can deepen your appreciation of the host culture's artistic expressions. Engaging with the arts also offers a fun and interactive way to connect with locals and other students. You might even try your hand at creating traditional crafts or learning to play a local musical instrument.

Trying Local Cuisine and Cooking Traditional Dishes:

Food is a central part of any culture. Trying local cuisine is one of the most enjoyable ways to immerse yourself in the culture of your host country. Visit local markets, dine at traditional restaurants, and do not shy away from trying street food.

Imagine the aromas and flavors of a bustling market, where you can taste fresh, local ingredients. Take a cooking class to learn how to prepare traditional dishes. This not only enhances your culinary skills but also gives you a deeper understanding of the culture's food traditions and history. Sharing meals with locals can also be a wonderful way to bond and create lasting memories. You might even host a cooking night with friends to share your newfound culinary skills.

Travel and Exploration

Visiting Historical Sites, Museums, and Cultural Landmarks:

Exploring historical sites, museums, and cultural landmarks offers a tangible connection to the past and present of your host country. These visits can provide context and depth to your understanding of the culture.

Imagine standing in awe before ancient ruins, walking through historic neighborhoods, or exploring interactive exhibits in a museum. Each site tells a story and adds a layer to your cultural immersion. Museums and landmarks often provide guided tours and informational materials that can enrich your experience. You might even participate in a scavenger hunt or educational activity that makes learning about history fun and engaging.

Exploring Natural Attractions and Outdoor Activities:

Natural attractions offer a different perspective on the host country's culture and lifestyle. From national parks to local hiking trails, engaging in outdoor activities can provide a refreshing break from academic life and a chance to see the natural beauty of your host country.

Picture yourself hiking through lush forests, exploring stunning coastlines, or even joining a local group for a weekend camping trip. These experiences can reveal the country's natural heritage and biodiversity. Outdoor activities are also great ways to meet people who share an interest in nature and adventure. You might discover hidden gems like secluded beaches or mountain viewpoints that locals' treasure.

Planning Trips to Neighboring Cities and Regions:

Expand your cultural immersion by planning trips to neighboring cities and regions. Each area may have its own unique customs, dialects, and traditions. Traveling allows you to see the diversity within the host country and broaden your cultural understanding.

Imagine taking a weekend trip to a nearby town, exploring local markets, historic sites, and scenic landscapes. These short trips can offer a deeper appreciation for the regional variations and local specialties. Whether it is a bustling city or a quaint village, each place you visit adds to your cultural tapestry. You might even make friends with fellow travelers and exchange tips on must-see destinations. By actively participating in local culture, you will create a rich and rewarding exchange experience. Embrace every opportunity to engage with the community, learn from the traditions, and explore the beauty of your host country. Your openness and enthusiasm will not only enhance your personal growth but also leave a positive impact on the people you meet along the way. Dive into the local culture with curiosity and excitement, and let each new experience shape your journey.

5.6 Handling Cultural Challenges

Dealing with Cultural Misunderstandings

Recognizing Common Sources of Cultural Misunderstandings:

Cultural misunderstandings often stem from differences in communication styles, social norms, and expectations. These misunderstandings can pop up in everyday interactions, like interpreting gestures, tones of voice, or social cues. Being aware of these potential pitfalls can help you navigate them more effectively.

Imagine you are at a dinner party, and you think everyone's silence means disinterest. In reality, they might be showing respect by listening intently without interrupting. In some cultures, maintaining direct eye contact is a sign of confidence and honesty, while in others, it might be perceived as confrontational or disrespectful. Understanding these nuances can help you anticipate and avoid misunderstandings.

Strategies for Resolving Misunderstandings Respectfully:

When cultural misunderstandings occur, handling them with patience and respect is key. Here are some strategies:

Stay Calm: Take a deep breath and stay calm. Reacting with frustration or anger can escalate the situation.

Seek Clarification: Politely ask for clarification. Phrases like "I'm sorry, I didn't understand that" or "Can you please explain what you mean?" can be helpful.

Apologize and Explain: If you realize you have made a mistake, apologize sincerely and explain your perspective. A simple apology can go a long way in resolving tensions.

Learn and Adapt: Use the experience as a learning opportunity. Reflect on what happened and how you can avoid similar misunderstandings in the future.

Imagine you are at a social gathering and accidentally use a gesture that is considered rude in the host culture. Instead of feeling embarrassed or defensive, you calmly apologize and explain that you were unaware of the cultural significance. This approach shows respect and a willingness to learn, which can help mend any unintentional offense.

Learning from Mistakes and Growing from Experiences:

Every cultural misstep is an opportunity to learn and grow. Instead of dwelling on mistakes, focus on how you can use the experience to deepen your cultural understanding and improve your interactions.

For instance, if you mistakenly address someone incorrectly, take note of the appropriate titles and forms of address for future interactions. Reflecting on these experiences helps you build cultural competence and resilience, making you more adept at navigating diverse cultural landscapes.

Managing Homesickness and Loneliness

Recognizing Signs of Homesickness and Loneliness:

Homesickness and loneliness are common feelings for international students. You might miss your family, friends, familiar surroundings, or even the comfort of speaking your native language. Recognizing these feelings early on is crucial for managing them effectively.

Signs of homesickness can include a persistent longing for home, feeling isolated, difficulty concentrating, or a lack of motivation. Understanding these signs allows you to take proactive steps to address them.

Strategies for Staying Connected with Home While Engaging Locally:

Balancing the connection with your home culture and engaging with your host culture is essential for managing homesickness. Here are some strategies:

Regular Communication: Stay in touch with family and friends through calls, video chats, and social media. Regular contact can provide emotional support and a sense of continuity.

Create Familiar Comforts: Incorporate elements of your home culture into your daily life, such as cooking traditional meals, celebrating your holidays, or listening to music from home.

Engage Locally: Participate in local activities, join clubs, and attend events to build a sense of belonging in your new environment. Making new friends and creating new routines can help you feel more connected and less isolated.

Imagine setting up a weekly video call with your family and preparing a favorite dish from home to share with new friends. These activities can provide comfort and help bridge the gap between your home and host cultures.

Seeking Support from Friends, Mentors, and Counselors:

Do not hesitate to seek support if you are feeling homesick or lonely. Friends, mentors, and counselors can offer valuable advice and emotional support.

Friends and Peers: Sharing your feelings with friends who are also international students can be comforting, as they likely understand what you are going through.

Mentors: Academic or cultural mentors can provide guidance and support, helping you navigate challenges and integrate into the community.

Counselors: Many institutions offer counseling services for students. Professional counselors can help you develop coping strategies and provide a safe space to discuss your feelings.

Imagine talking to a counselor who helps you develop a plan for managing homesickness, including setting goals for engaging with your host culture and maintaining connections with home.

Anecdotes and Insights

Dealing with Homesickness- Carlos' Story

Student Perspective: "During my first few months in Germany, I struggled with homesickness. Everything felt foreign, and I missed my family and friends. To cope, I started cooking my favorite dishes from home and invited my new friends to join me. Sharing my culture with them helped me feel more connected and less isolated. It also sparked their interest in my background, leading to interesting cultural exchanges." – Carlos, Germany International Student

Expert Insight: Homesickness is a natural part of the international experience. Finding ways to incorporate elements of your home culture, such as cooking familiar dishes, can provide comfort and ease feelings of loneliness. Sharing these aspects with new friends not only helps you feel more at home but also fosters mutual cultural understanding and appreciation. Stay connected with loved ones through regular communication and seek out supportive communities within your host country.

Balancing Dual Identities

Navigating the Balance Between Your Home Culture and Host Culture:

Living in a new country often involves balancing your home culture with the norms and values of your host culture. This balance can be challenging but also enriching, as it allows you to develop a more nuanced identity.

Think of yourself as a cultural bridge, bringing together the best of both worlds. Embrace the aspects of your home culture that are important to you while being open to adopting new practices and perspectives from your host culture.

Maintaining Your Cultural Identity While Adapting to New Norms:

It is important to stay true to your cultural identity while adapting to new norms. Celebrate your heritage and share it with others, whether through food, traditions, or stories.

For example, you might host a cultural night where you share traditional dishes and customs with your new friends. This not only helps you stay connected to your roots but also fosters cultural exchange and understanding.

Celebrating Your Unique Cultural Blend:

Embrace the unique cultural blend that comes from living abroad. Your experiences in both your home and host cultures can enrich your worldview and personal growth.

Think of yourself as a cultural ambassador, sharing insights from your home culture while learning from and contributing to your host culture. Celebrate the diversity within yourself and recognize the value of your multicultural experiences.

Imagine reflecting on how your experiences abroad have broadened your perspectives, making you more adaptable and culturally aware. This self-awareness can enhance your personal and professional life, equipping you with skills that are highly valued in today's globalized world.

By handling cultural challenges with resilience and an open mind, you can turn potential obstacles into opportunities for growth. Embrace the journey of cultural adaptation and use each experience to deepen your understanding and enrich your international experience. Your ability to navigate these challenges will not only enhance your time abroad but also prepare you for future cross-cultural interactions and global citizenship.

Anecdotes and Insights

Embracing Cultural Blend- Amina's Story

Student Perspective: "In South Korea, I found myself constantly balancing my Nigerian heritage with the local culture. At first, I felt like I had to choose one over the other, but over time, I learned to celebrate both. I organized a cultural night where I shared Nigerian food, music, and dance with my Korean friends. They loved it, and it became a tradition. Embracing my cultural blend made my international experience richer and more fulfilling." – Amina, South Korea International Student

Expert Insight: Balancing your home culture with your host culture can be challenging but rewarding. Embrace your unique cultural blend and find ways to share it with others. Organizing cultural events or simply sharing aspects of your heritage with new friends can enrich your experience and those around you. Celebrating your dual identity helps you maintain a connection to your roots while adapting to new cultural norms, creating a more inclusive and diverse environment.

5.7 Enhancing Your Cultural Experience

Cultural Reflection

Reflecting on Your Cultural Experiences and Learning:

Taking time to reflect on your cultural experiences is crucial for deepening your understanding and appreciation of your journey. Reflection allows you to process what you have learned, identify personal growth, and recognize any challenges you have overcome. This can be as simple as pausing to think about how a particular event or interaction made you feel and what you learned from it.

Picture this: you are sitting in a cozy café, sipping on a local favorite, and thinking back to a festival you attended. The vibrant colors, the music, the food – each element offering a glimpse into the host culture's soul. Reflect on what surprised you, what you enjoyed, and what you found challenging. This practice not only enhances your cultural awareness but also solidifies your memories and lessons learned. It is like piecing together a beautiful mosaic of your experiences.

Keeping a Journal or Blog to Document Your Journey:

Documenting your experiences through a journal or blog can be a rewarding way to capture your journey. Writing regularly helps you articulate your thoughts and feelings, creating a personal record of your time abroad that you can look back on in the future.

Imagine starting a blog where you share your daily adventures, cultural observations, and personal reflections. Not only does this provide a creative outlet, but it also allows friends and family to follow along with your journey. You might even inspire others to embark on their own cultural adventures. Plus, a journal or blog serves as a time capsule, preserving your experiences and growth.

Sharing Your Experiences with Others Through Presentations or Discussions:

Sharing your experiences with others can deepen your understanding and foster cultural exchange. Whether it is through formal presentations, informal discussions, or social media, talking about your journey helps to process your experiences and educate others.

Picture this: you are giving a presentation to a group of new international students, sharing your challenges and triumphs, and offering tips for navigating cultural differences. This not only reinforces your learning but also provides valuable insights for others embarking on similar journeys. Sharing your story can be a powerful way to connect with others and build a supportive community.

Personal Growth

Developing Resilience and Adaptability:

Living abroad challenges you in ways that can significantly build your resilience and adaptability. You will encounter situations that require you to think on your feet, adapt to new circumstances, and bounce back from setbacks.

Think about a time when you had to navigate a complex situation, like finding your way in a new city or handling a language barrier. Each challenge you overcome strengthens your ability to adapt and thrive in
diverse environments. These experiences cultivate a mindset that is open to change and capable of handling unexpected challenges with grace. It is like developing a superpower for flexibility and resilience.

Enhancing Problem-Solving and Critical Thinking Skills:

Cultural immersion often presents unique problems that require creative solutions. Navigating these situations can sharpen your problem-solving and critical thinking skills, as you learn to view challenges from different perspectives and develop innovative approaches to overcome them.

Imagine dealing with a logistical issue, like organizing a trip in a foreign country where you do not speak the language fluently. This experience forces you to think critically, use available resources, and come up with effective solutions. These skills are not only valuable during your international experience but also highly sought after in academic and professional settings. You will find that you are not just thinking outside the box – you are expanding the box itself.

Building Confidence and Independence:

Living in a new culture independently helps you build self-confidence and a sense of independence. Every time you successfully navigate a new experience, from ordering food in a foreign language to making new friends, your confidence grows.

Reflect on the first time you successfully navigated the public transportation system in your host city. Each small victory builds your confidence, showing you that you are capable of handling the unknown and thriving in new environments. This newfound independence is a significant personal achievement that will benefit you long after your international program ends. It is like a series of small wins that add up to a major boost in your self-assurance.

Future Opportunities

Leveraging Your Cultural Experiences for Academic and Career Growth:

Your cultural experiences can be a powerful asset in your academic and career pursuits. Highlighting your ability to adapt to new environments, work with diverse teams, and navigate cross-cultural challenges can set you apart in job applications and academic endeavors.

Consider how you can incorporate your cultural experiences into your resume or academic portfolio. For example, emphasizing your participation in international projects, language skills, and the personal growth you have achieved can demonstrate your unique qualifications to potential employers or academic programs. These experiences are like gold stars on your CV, showcasing your global competence.

Continuing Cultural Engagement After Returning Home:

Your cultural journey does not have to end when you return home. Continue engaging with different cultures by joining international clubs, attending cultural events, and staying connected with the friends you made abroad.

Imagine joining a local cultural organization or volunteering with international student groups at your home institution. These activities allow you to continue learning about different cultures, maintain your language skills, and stay connected to the global community. You can also share your experiences with others, fostering cultural awareness and appreciation in your community. It is a way to keep the cultural fire burning brightly.

Networking with International Communities and Alumni:

Building and maintaining a network of international contacts can open doors to future opportunities. Stay in touch with the people you met during your international journey and participate in alumni networks and international organizations.

Consider attending alumni events, joining professional associations with an international focus, or participating in online forums and social media groups. These networks can provide valuable support, information, and opportunities for personal and professional growth. Whether it is finding a job abroad, collaborating on international projects, or simply sharing experiences, your international network can be a lifelong asset. It is like having a global safety net and a treasure trove of opportunities.

By reflecting on your cultural experiences, focusing on personal growth, and leveraging your newfound skills and insights, you can enhance your international experience and set the stage for future opportunities. Embrace the journey of cultural immersion, and let each experience shape you into a more adaptable, confident, and globally minded individual. Dive into the local culture with curiosity and excitement, and let each new experience shape your journey.

Chapter 5 Conclusion

Importance of Cultural Immersion and Adaptation

Cultural immersion and adaptation are at the heart of any international experience. They are not just about living in a new country; they involve actively engaging with and understanding the host culture. By diving into the local customs, traditions, and daily life, you open yourself up to a richer, more meaningful experience that can profoundly impact your personal and academic life.

Think back to everything we have covered in this chapter: understanding cultural differences, participating in local traditions, and building cultural competence. Each of these elements plays a crucial role in helping you thrive in a new environment. They help you develop a broader world-view, enhance your empathy, and equip you with invaluable skills to navigate diverse settings.

Encouragement to Embrace and Learn from Cultural Experiences

Embrace every moment of your cultural journey with enthusiasm and an open mind. Each interaction, whether it is a casual chat with a local, attending a traditional festival, or working through a cultural misunderstanding, is an opportunity to learn and grow. These experiences not only make your time abroad more enjoyable but also leave a lasting impact on your personal development.

Picture your cultural experiences as a vibrant tapestry, with each thread representing a unique encounter or lesson learned. The more threads you weave into your tapestry, the more colorful and complex it becomes. Do not shy away from challenges or differences; instead, approach them with curiosity and a desire to understand.

Final Thoughts on Making the Most of Your Cultural Journey

As you continue your international program, remember that the journey is just as important as the destination. The skills, insights, and relationships you build along the way will shape you into a more resilient, adaptable, and culturally aware individual. Here are a few final tips to help you make the most of your cultural journey:

Stay Open-Minded: Be willing to step out of your comfort zone and try new things. Whether it is tasting an unfamiliar dish, joining in a local celebration, or picking up new social customs, these experiences will broaden your horizons. Think of each new experience as an adventure that enriches your understanding of the world.

Reflect Regularly: Take time to reflect on your experiences. Keeping a journal or discussing your thoughts with friends can help you process and appreciate your journey. Writing down your thoughts can also provide a valuable record of your growth and learning over time.

Engage Actively: Dive into community activities, volunteer, and build connections with locals. The more you engage, the more enriched your experience will be. Do not just be a spectator—become an active participant in your host culture.

Seek Support When Needed: Do not hesitate to seek support from friends, mentors, or counselors if you face challenges. Acknowledging when you need help and taking steps to address any difficulties is crucial for your well-being and success. Remember, everyone faces challenges, and reaching out for support is a sign of strength, not weakness.

In conclusion, your time as an international student is a unique and transformative period filled with opportunities for growth and learning. Embrace it fully, cherish the memories you create, and let every experience contribute to your personal and cultural development. Your journey is not just about adapting to a new culture but about letting that culture become a part of who you are.

As you weave the threads of your experiences into your life's tapestry, you will find that each new interaction and adventure adds depth and richness to your story. So, go out there, explore with an open heart and mind, and make the most of this incredible journey. The world is waiting for you, and the possibilities are endless.

Chapter 5 Review

Summary

Chapter 5 explored the importance of cultural immersion and adaptation in enriching your international experience. We discussed understanding cultural differences, improving language skills, participating in local traditions, managing homesickness, balancing dual identities, and enhancing your overall cultural journey. By embracing these aspects, you can navigate cultural challenges with confidence and grow personally and academically.

Review Questions

Short Answer:

1. What are three key benefits of engaging in local festivals and traditions?
2. Describe one strategy you can use to overcome language barriers in your host country.
3. How can maintaining elements of your home culture help you manage homesickness?
4. What are the stages of cultural adjustment, and how can understanding them help you cope with culture shock?
5. Explain the importance of balancing your home culture with your host culture.

Multiple Choice:

1. Which of the following is NOT a recommended strategy for improving language skills?

a. Joining a language exchange group
b. Avoiding conversations with locals to prevent mistakes
c. Using language learning apps and online resources
d. Practicing speaking with fellow students

2. What is a benefit of keeping a journal or blog during your international program?

a. It helps you memorize local customs

b. It provides a creative outlet and records your experiences

c. It ensures you never forget to attend class

d. It guarantees you will make local friends

True or False:

- **True or False:** Participating in local community activities can help you build a sense of belonging in your host country.
- **True or False:** Avoiding local customs and traditions is the best way to prevent cultural misunderstandings.

Reflective Question:

Reflect on a recent cultural experience during your international program. What did you learn from it, and how did it influence your understanding of your host culture?

Invitation to Further Reflection

To further explore and internalize the concepts discussed in this chapter, we invite you to complete the exercises and questions in the companion "Reflective Exercises: The International Experiences Guide Workbook." These activities are designed to deepen your learning, apply the knowledge to your personal situation, and enhance your overall cultural experience.

By reviewing the key points and reflecting on your experiences, you will be better prepared to embrace and navigate the cultural immersion and adaptation process. Remember, every cultural challenge is an opportunity for growth and learning. Embrace your journey with an open mind and a curious heart, and let each experience enrich your understanding and appreciation of the diverse world around you.

{ 6 }

Health and Wellbeing

Introduction

Embarking on an international journey is an exciting adventure, filled with new experiences, learning opportunities, and personal growth. Amidst all the excitement, it is crucial to remember the importance of maintaining your health and wellbeing. Being in a new environment can be both exhilarating and challenging, and taking care of yourself is essential to making the most of your time abroad.

Maintaining health and wellbeing during your international adventure involves more than just avoiding illness; it encompasses physical, mental, and emotional wellness. This chapter will guide you through key areas to focus on, providing strategies to ensure you stay healthy, happy, and balanced throughout your journey.

Importance of Maintaining Health and Wellbeing During Your International Program

Your health and wellbeing are foundational to a successful and fulfilling international experience. When you feel good physically and mentally, you can fully engage with your new environment, participate in activities, and build meaningful relationships. Neglecting your health can lead to increased stress, illness, and overall dissatisfaction, which can overshadow the incredible opportunities your international program has to offer.

Overview of Key Areas to Focus on for Overall Wellness

Maintaining your health and wellbeing involves several key areas, each contributing to your overall sense of wellness:

Physical Health: This includes regular exercise, balanced nutrition, and adequate sleep. Physical health impacts your energy levels, immune system, and ability to handle the physical demands of everyday activities.

Mental Health: Mental wellness involves managing stress, maintaining a positive outlook, and seeking help when needed. Mental health is just as important as physical health, affecting your ability to cope with challenges and enjoy your experiences.

Emotional Wellbeing: Emotional health encompasses understanding and managing your emotions, building resilience, and maintaining strong social connections. Emotional wellbeing influences how you handle change, build relationships, and navigate the highs and lows of living abroad.

Preventative Health Measures: This involves staying up to date with vaccinations, understanding local health risks, and knowing how to access medical care if needed. Preventative health measures help you avoid illnesses and manage any health issues that arise.

Work-Life Balance: Balancing your academic, social, and personal life is crucial for sustained wellbeing. Overcommitting in one area can lead to burnout, while a balanced approach allows you to thrive in all aspects of your international program.

Encouragement to Prioritize Self-Care and Seek Support When Needed

Prioritizing self-care is not a luxury; it is a necessity. It means making conscious choices that contribute to your health and happiness, whether that is taking time to relax, eating nutritious meals, or setting boundaries to avoid overcommitting. Self-care looks different for everyone, so find what works best for you and make it a regular part of your routine.

Remember, it is okay to seek support when needed. Whether you are feeling homesick, overwhelmed, or just need someone to talk to, reaching out for help is a sign of strength. Utilize the resources available to you, such as counseling services, health centers, and peer support groups. Building a support network can provide comfort and guidance, helping you navigate the challenges of your international experience.

In this chapter, we will delve into practical strategies and tips for maintaining your health and wellbeing across these key areas. By prioritizing your wellness, you will be better equipped to fully embrace your international experience, making it a rewarding and transformative journey.

6.1 Physical Health

Maintaining your physical health is fundamental to ensuring a successful and enjoyable international experience. Your well-being impacts every aspect of your life abroad, from your academic performance to your social interactions. This section provides practical advice on accessing healthcare, taking preventive health measures, and adopting a healthy lifestyle to keep you thriving during your time abroad.

Healthcare Access

Registering with Local Health Services and Finding a Primary Care Physician:

One of the first steps after arriving in your host country should be registering with local health services. This ensures you have access to medical care when needed. Start by finding a primary care physician (PCP) or general practitioner (GP) who can provide routine care and refer you to specialists if necessary. Your host institution or local student services can usually provide a list of recommended doctors.

When choosing a physician, consider factors such as language proficiency, location, and availability. Do not hesitate to ask for recommendations from other students or your host institution. Having a reliable PCP will give you peace of mind and a go-to person for health concerns.

Imagine being in a new country and needing medical advice or treatment. Having a primary care physician, you can trust will make these situations much less stressful. It is like having a safety net; you know who to call when you need help, whether it is for a minor illness or something more serious.

Understanding How to Use Your Health Insurance Abroad:

Understanding your health insurance coverage is crucial. Whether you have insurance through your home country, a plan provided by your host institution, or a local policy, know the details of your coverage. Familiarize yourself with what services are covered, how to submit claims, and any out-of-pocket costs you might incur.

Keep a copy of your insurance policy and important contact numbers handy. In case of emergencies, knowing how to navigate your insurance can save time and reduce stress.

Think of health insurance as a tool. You need to know how to use it properly to get the most benefit from it. Spend some time reading through your policy, understanding the process for claims, and noting any specific requirements. This preparation will pay off if you need to use your insurance.

Knowing the Locations of Nearby Hospitals, Clinics, and Pharmacies:

Take the time to locate nearby hospitals, clinics, and pharmacies soon after you arrive. Knowing where to go in case of an emergency or for routine medical needs is essential. Your host institution can provide information about the closest and most reliable healthcare facilities.

Create a list of these locations along with their contact details and keep it accessible. This list should include 24-hour emergency services, pharmacies that accept your insurance, and clinics offering specialized care if needed.

Knowing the nearest hospital or pharmacy can save precious time in an emergency. Imagine it is late at night, and you suddenly need medical assistance or medication. Having a list of nearby facilities and their contact information can make a significant difference in how quickly you receive help.

Anecdotes and Insights

Navigating Healthcare Abroad- Anna's Story

Student Perspective: "When I first arrived in Germany, I was overwhelmed by the idea of navigating a completely different healthcare system. I remember feeling a bit lost when I needed to see a doctor for a persistent cold. Luckily, my university had a comprehensive orientation program that included a session on healthcare. They provided a list of local doctors who spoke English and explained how to use my health insurance. The first visit was still nerve-wracking but knowing that I had support and resources made a huge difference." – Anna, German International Student

Expert Insight: Navigating a new healthcare system can be daunting, but many universities offer resources to help international students. Take advantage of orientation sessions and information packets. It is also a good idea to familiarize yourself with local healthcare facilities and how to access them before you actually need them. Always carry your insurance card and a list of important contacts in case of emergencies.

Preventive Health Measures

Staying Up to Date with Vaccinations and Medical Check-Ups:

Preventive healthcare is your first line of defense against illness. Ensure you are up to date with all necessary vaccinations before departing and keep a record of them. Some countries require specific vaccinations for entry, so check these requirements well in advance.

Regular medical check-ups are also important. Schedule a health check before you leave and consider periodic visits to a local physician to monitor your health. Preventive care can help detect potential health issues early, making them easier to manage.

Vaccinations and regular check-ups act as a shield, protecting you from many health issues. It is like building a fortress around your health – the stronger your defenses, the less likely you are to face serious health problems.

Understanding Common Illnesses and Health Risks in Your Host Country:

Different regions have different health risks. Research common illnesses and health hazards in your host country. For instance, some areas might have a higher incidence of mosquito-borne diseases, while others may have pollution-related health concerns.

Stay informed about seasonal health risks such as flu outbreaks or heatwaves. Local health authorities and your host institution can provide valuable information and tips on how to protect yourself.

Being informed about local health risks is like having a map in a foreign land – it guides you in avoiding pitfalls and navigating your environment safely. Knowledge is power, especially when it comes to your health.

Practicing Good Hygiene and Safety Measures to Prevent Illness:

Good hygiene practices are vital in preventing illness. Wash your hands regularly with soap and water, especially before eating and after using the restroom. Carry hand sanitizer for times when soap and water are not available.

Be mindful of food and water safety. In some regions, it is advisable to drink bottled or filtered water and avoid raw or undercooked foods. Pay attention to safety warnings about local hazards and follow guidelines to minimize risk.

Think of hygiene practices as your everyday armor – simple actions like washing your hands can protect you from a host of illnesses. It is a small effort with significant impact on your health.

Healthy Living

Maintaining a Balanced Diet with Local and Familiar Foods:

Eating a balanced diet is essential for maintaining your energy levels and overall health. Explore local cuisine to enjoy new foods, but also make sure to include familiar foods from your home country to ensure a balanced intake of nutrients.

Visit local markets and grocery stores to find fresh produce and healthy ingredients. If you have dietary restrictions or preferences, plan ahead to ensure you have access to suitable food options.

Imagine your body as a finely tuned machine – it needs the right fuel to run efficiently. A balanced diet provides the nutrients you need to stay energized and healthy. Embrace the local cuisine while maintaining a balance that suits your nutritional needs.

Importance of Regular Physical Activity and Exercise:

Staying active is crucial for your physical health and mental well-being. Incorporate regular exercise into your routine, whether it is jogging, cycling, attending a local gym, or participating in sports. Many universities offer fitness facilities and recreational activities for students.

Consider joining a local sports club or fitness class to stay active and meet new people. Physical activity helps reduce stress, improve mood, and maintain a healthy body.

Exercise is like a daily boost for your body and mind. It keeps you fit, lifts your spirits, and helps you cope with stress. Find activities you enjoy and make them a regular part of your routine.

Getting Adequate Sleep and Managing Fatigue:

Adequate sleep is fundamental to your overall health. Establish a regular sleep schedule that allows you to get 7-9 hours of sleep per night. Create a relaxing bedtime routine to help you unwind and ensure your sleeping environment is comfortable and conducive to rest.

Managing fatigue is also important. If you feel tired, listen to your body and rest. Balancing academics, social activities, and personal time is key to preventing burnout.

Think of sleep as the foundation of your health – it restores your body and mind, preparing you for the day ahead. Prioritizing sleep and managing fatigue ensures you are always at your best, ready to take on new challenges.

By focusing on these areas of physical health, you can ensure you are in the best possible shape to enjoy and make the most of your international experience. Taking proactive steps to maintain your health will help you stay energized, engaged, and ready to embrace all the opportunities your time abroad offers.

6.2 Mental Health

Maintaining your mental health is just as important as caring for your physical health, especially during an international adventure. The new experiences and challenges can sometimes lead to stress, anxiety, or feelings of homesickness. This section provides insights on recognizing mental health issues, accessing resources, and developing coping strategies to support your mental well-being.

Recognizing Mental Health Issues

Identifying Signs of Stress, Anxiety, and Depression:

Living in a new country can be both exciting and overwhelming. It is normal to feel a range of emotions, but it is important to recognize when these feelings may indicate a mental health issue. Signs of stress, anxiety, and depression can include:

- Persistent sadness or low mood
- Feelings of hopelessness or helplessness
- Excessive worry or fear
- Irritability or anger
- Difficulty concentrating
- Changes in sleep patterns or appetite

- Loss of interest in activities you once enjoyed

If you notice these symptoms persisting for more than a few weeks, it is important to seek help. Think of your mental health like a barometer for your overall well-being. Just as you would address physical symptoms of illness, it is crucial to attend to these emotional signs. Early intervention can make a significant difference in your experience and recovery.

Understanding the Impact of Cultural Adjustment on Mental Health:

Cultural adjustment can significantly impact your mental health. The process of adapting to a new culture, often referred to as "culture shock," can include stages such as the honeymoon phase, frustration, adjustment, and acceptance. During the frustration phase, you might feel anxious or depressed as you navigate language barriers, unfamiliar social norms, and new academic expectations.

Recognizing that these feelings are a normal part of the adjustment process can help you manage them more effectively. Understanding that it is okay to struggle and seek support can make the transition smoother.

Think of cultural adjustment as climbing a mountain. The ascent may be steep and challenging, but reaching the summit offers a rewarding view. Understanding the stages of this climb helps you prepare for and navigate the journey.

Acknowledging Homesickness and Its Effects:

Homesickness is a common experience for international students. Missing familiar places, people, and routines can lead to feelings of sadness and isolation. It is important to acknowledge these feelings rather than suppress them. Homesickness can affect your mood, sleep, and overall well-being, so finding ways to cope is essential.

Imagine homesickness as waves in the ocean. They may be strong at times, but with the right strategies, you can ride them out and find calmer waters. Recognizing and addressing homesickness early helps prevent it from overwhelming you.

Mental Health Resources

Accessing Counseling and Psychological Services at Your Host Institution:

Most universities offer counseling and psychological services specifically designed to support students. These services can provide individual counseling, group therapy, workshops, and stress management resources. Do not hesitate to make an appointment if you are struggling; these professionals are there to help you navigate your emotions and challenges.

Think of these services as your mental health toolkit. Just as you would use tools to fix a physical issue, these resources help you address emotional and psychological concerns effectively. Making use of them can significantly enhance your well-being.

Anecdotes and Insights
Maintaining Mental Health- Mark's Story

Student Perspective: "During my semester in Japan, I experienced a lot of stress adjusting to the academic demands and cultural differences. I started feeling anxious and homesick, which affected my sleep and overall well-being. I decided to visit the counseling center at my university, and it was one of the best decisions I made. The counselor helped me develop strategies to manage my stress and anxiety, and I also joined a mindfulness workshop that was really beneficial." – Mark, Japanese International Student

Expert Insight: It is common for international students to experience stress and homesickness. Seeking help from a counseling center can provide valuable support. Universities often offer various mental health resources, including counseling, workshops, and peer support groups. Mindfulness and relaxation techniques, such as deep breathing and meditation, can also help manage stress and improve mental well-being.

Finding Local Mental Health Professionals and Support Groups:

In addition to on-campus resources, consider finding local mental health professionals or support groups. Look for therapists who specialize in working with international students or those familiar with cultural adjustment issues. Support groups can also provide a sense of community and shared understanding.

Imagine finding a local therapist or support group as establishing a lifeline. These connections offer targeted support and understanding, helping you navigate the complexities of living abroad. You are not alone—many have walked this path before you and can offer valuable insights.

Utilizing Online Resources and Helplines:

Online resources and helplines can be invaluable, especially if you are uncomfortable seeking in-person help initially. Websites and apps offer guided meditation, mindfulness exercises, and cognitive-behavioral techniques. Helplines provide immediate support and can connect you with local resources.

Think of online resources as your virtual support system. They offer flexibility and anonymity, making it easier to access help when you need it. These tools are available 24/7, providing continuous support regardless of time or location.

Coping Strategies

Practicing Mindfulness and Relaxation Techniques:

Mindfulness and relaxation techniques can significantly reduce stress and anxiety. Practices such as meditation, deep breathing exercises, and yoga can help calm your mind and improve your mental clarity. Consider setting aside a few minutes each day to practice mindfulness.

Apps like Headspace and Calm offer guided sessions tailored to various needs, whether it is managing stress or improving sleep. These practices help ground you in the present moment, making it easier to handle challenging situations.

Imagine mindfulness as pressing the pause button in your busy life. It allows you to step back, breathe, and regain control over your thoughts and emotions. Regular practice can transform how you respond to stress and improve your overall mental health.

Developing a Routine That Includes Self-Care Activities:

Creating a daily routine that incorporates self-care activities is crucial. This can include physical exercise, hobbies, and relaxation techniques. Having a consistent routine can provide a sense of stability and normalcy amidst the changes you are experiencing.

Include activities that bring you joy and relaxation, whether it is reading, cooking, listening to music, or spending time outdoors. Balance is key—make sure your routine includes time for rest and leisure, not just academics and responsibilities.

Think of your routine as a blueprint for well-being. It structures your day, ensuring you allocate time for essential activities that nurture your body and mind. A well-balanced routine acts as a foundation for maintaining mental health.

Seeking Social Support from Friends, Family, and Mentors:

Building a support network is essential for maintaining mental health. Stay connected with friends and family back home through regular calls or video chats. Developing friendships with fellow students and seeking out mentors at your host institution can provide a sense of belonging and support.

Do not hesitate to reach out to those around you when you are feeling down. Sharing your experiences and emotions with trusted individuals can provide comfort and perspective. Remember, seeking help is a sign of strength, not weakness.

Imagine your support network as your personal safety net. They catch you when you fall, offer encouragement, and help you navigate tough times. Cultivating these relationships provides emotional resilience and a sense of community, crucial for mental well-being.

By focusing on these areas of mental health, you can ensure you are in the best possible shape to enjoy and make the most of your international experience. Taking proactive steps to maintain your mental well-being will help you stay energized, engaged, and ready to embrace all the opportunities your time abroad offers.

6.3 Maintaining a Healthy Lifestyle

Maintaining a healthy lifestyle is essential for your overall well-being, especially when navigating the exciting yet demanding experience of living abroad. This section offers practical advice on nutrition, exercise, and sleep hygiene to help you stay healthy and energized throughout your international journey.

Nutrition and Diet

Adapting to Local Cuisine While Maintaining a Balanced Diet:

One of the joys of living abroad is exploring new cuisines. However, it is important to balance trying local foods with maintaining a nutritious diet. Start by familiarizing yourself with the local cuisine and identifying healthy options. Look for dishes that include a variety of vegetables, lean proteins, and whole grains.

Eating out can be fun, but also make time to cook at home. This allows you to control the ingredients and ensure your meals are balanced. Try to incorporate local ingredients into your cooking to blend familiarity with new flavors. For example, if you are in Italy, enjoy the fresh produce and delicious pastas, but balance it with plenty of vegetables and lean proteins.

Think of your diet as a puzzle – the local cuisine pieces add flavor and excitement, while familiar foods ensure you get all the nutrients you need. Enjoy the culinary adventure but keep an eye on balance.

Cooking at Home and Finding Healthy Food Options:

Cooking at home is a great way to maintain a healthy diet. Visit local markets and grocery stores to find fresh, seasonal produce. Experiment with new recipes that combine local ingredients with familiar foods from home. If you are unsure where to start, look for simple recipes online or ask locals for recommendations.

Finding healthy food options when dining out can be challenging, but not impossible. Opt for grilled rather than fried foods and ask for sauces and dressings on the side. Do not hesitate to ask restaurant staff about the ingredients and preparation methods to make healthier choices.

Imagine your kitchen as your health lab. Experimenting with local ingredients while maintaining a balance ensures you enjoy the best of both worlds – taste and nutrition.

Managing Dietary Restrictions and Allergies in a New Environment:

If you have dietary restrictions or allergies, navigating a new food landscape can be daunting. Before you go, learn the local terms for your dietary needs and practice explaining them in the local language. This will help you communicate effectively with restaurant staff and avoid any misunderstandings.

Carry a card that clearly states your dietary restrictions or allergies in the local language. This can be a lifesaver in situations where language barriers exist. Additionally, research local restaurants and food stores that cater to your dietary needs to ensure you have access to safe and healthy options.

Think of managing dietary restrictions as a treasure hunt. With the right tools and information, you can find delicious and safe food options wherever you go.

Exercise and Fitness

Exploring Local Gyms, Sports Clubs, and Fitness Centers:

Staying active is crucial for both physical and mental health. Explore the local gyms, sports clubs, and fitness centers available in your area. Many universities offer fitness facilities and classes that you can join. Look for options that interest you, whether it is yoga, dance, swimming, or weightlifting.

Joining a local sports club can also be a great way to stay fit and meet new people. Whether you enjoy soccer, basketball, or even martial arts, participating in group activities can make exercise more enjoyable and help you build a social network.

Think of local gyms and sports clubs as your fitness playground. Exploring these options not only keeps you fit but also helps you connect with the local community.

Anecdotes and Insights
Staying Active and Fit- David's Story
Student Perspective: "During my exchange in Australia, I struggled to maintain my fitness routine. Back home, I was used to going to the gym regularly, but in Sydney, I did not have a membership. I discovered that my university had excellent sports facilities, and I also started running along the beautiful coastal paths. Joining a local soccer team not only kept me active but also helped me make new friends." – David, Australian International Student

Expert Insight: Staying active is essential for both physical and mental health. Many universities offer sports facilities and fitness classes that are either free or discounted for students. Exploring outdoor activities such as hiking, running, or joining local sports teams can help you stay fit while also integrating into the local community. Finding activities, you enjoy will make it easier to maintain a regular fitness routine.

Incorporating Physical Activity into Your Daily Routine:

You do not need a gym membership to stay active. Incorporate physical activity into your daily routine by walking or cycling instead of taking public transportation. Explore your new city on foot to discover hidden gems while staying active.

Take advantage of any green spaces or parks for jogging, hiking, or outdoor workouts. Simple changes like taking the stairs instead of the elevator can also make a big difference. The key is to find activities that you enjoy and make them a regular part of your routine.

Imagine your daily routine as a canvas – physical activities add vibrant colors, making your day more dynamic and enjoyable.

Participating in Outdoor Activities and Sports:

Your host country may offer unique outdoor activities and sports that are new to you. Take this opportunity to try something different, whether it is skiing in the Alps, surfing in Australia, or hiking in the Rockies. Outdoor activities not only keep you fit but also allow you to explore and appreciate the natural beauty of your host country.

Look for community events or outdoor fitness classes. These are often less formal and can be a fun way to stay active while socializing with locals.

Think of outdoor activities as your adventure field. They offer a chance to stay fit, explore new places, and meet people in a relaxed and fun setting.

Sleep Hygiene

Establishing a Regular Sleep Schedule:

Maintaining a regular sleep schedule is fundamental to your health. Aim for 7-9 hours of sleep each night and try to go to bed and wake up at the same time every day, even on weekends. This consistency helps regulate your internal clock and improve the quality of your sleep.

If you find it difficult to fall asleep, establish a relaxing bedtime routine. This could include activities like reading, listening to calming music, or practicing mindfulness or meditation. Avoid screens and caffeine close to bedtime, as they can interfere with your sleep.

Think of your sleep schedule as the foundation of your day. A consistent routine helps ensure you wake up refreshed and ready to tackle new challenges.

Creating a Sleep-Friendly Environment:

Your sleep environment plays a crucial role in the quality of your sleep. Make sure your bedroom is comfortable, quiet, and dark. Invest in a good mattress and pillows if possible. Use blackout curtains or an eye mask to block out light and consider using earplugs or a white noise machine to drown out any disruptive sounds.

Keep your room cool and well-ventilated. A clutter-free space can also promote relaxation and help you unwind after a busy day.

Imagine your bedroom as your personal sanctuary. Creating a peaceful environment ensures you get the restful sleep you need to stay healthy and energized.

Managing Jet Lag and Adjusting to Time Zone Changes:

Jet lag can be a significant challenge when traveling to a new time zone. To minimize its effects, try to gradually adjust your sleep schedule a few days before you leave. Once you arrive, spend time outside in natural light to help reset your internal clock.

Stay hydrated and avoid alcohol and caffeine, as they can disrupt your sleep patterns. If needed, take short naps to help you adjust, but avoid long naps that can interfere with night-time sleep.

Think of managing jet lag as fine-tuning your internal clock. With the right strategies, you can quickly adjust and get back to a healthy sleep routine.

Anecdotes and Insights
Managing Sleep and Jet Lag- Claire's Story

Student Perspective: "Arriving in Canada from France, the jet lag hit me hard. My sleep schedule was completely off, and it affected my concentration and mood. I researched ways to adjust and found that sticking to a regular sleep schedule and getting plenty of natural light during the day helped a lot. It took about a week, but gradually, my body clock adjusted, and I started feeling more like myself." – Claire, Canadian International Student

Expert Insight: Jet lag can significantly disrupt your sleep and overall well-being. To manage it, try to adjust your sleep schedule gradually before your departure. Once you arrive, expose yourself to natural light, especially in the morning, to help reset your internal clock. Avoid heavy meals and caffeine close to bedtime and stick to a consistent sleep routine to help your body adjust more quickly.

By focusing on these areas of maintaining a healthy lifestyle, you can ensure you are in the best possible shape to enjoy and make the most of your international experience. Taking pro-active steps to maintain your nutrition, fitness, and sleep will help you stay energized, engaged, and ready to embrace all the opportunities your time abroad offers.

6.4 Social Wellbeing

Maintaining social wellbeing is a key component of a successful and fulfilling international experience. Building strong social connections, balancing your social and academic life, and engaging with the local culture can significantly enhance your overall wellbeing. This section provides practical advice on creating a support network, balancing your responsibilities, and immersing yourself in the local culture.

Building a Support Network

Making New Friends and Forming Meaningful Connections:

One of the most rewarding aspects of studying abroad is meeting new people and forming lasting friendships. Start by reaching out to your classmates, attending social events, and joining study groups. Do not be afraid to introduce yourself and show genuine interest in getting to know others.

Making new friends can sometimes feel daunting but remember that many of your peers are in the same situation and are also looking to build connections. Be open, approachable, and willing to step out of your comfort zone. Shared experiences, such as exploring the city or trying new activities together, can quickly turn acquaintances into close friends.

Joining Student Organizations, Clubs, and Social Groups:

Joining student organizations and clubs is a great way to meet people with similar interests. Whether it is a sports team, a cultural club, or an academic society, these groups provide opportunities to socialize, learn, and grow outside the classroom.

Look for clubs that match your hobbies or areas of interest. Participating in club activities can help you develop new skills, build a sense of community, and create a support network. Many universities offer a wide range of organizations, so there is likely something for everyone.

Maintaining Relationships with Family and Friends Back Home:

While it is important to immerse yourself in your new environment, maintaining connections with family and friends back home is equally vital. Regular communication through calls, video chats, and social media can help reduce feelings of homesickness and provide emotional support.

Schedule regular check-ins to stay updated on each other's lives and share your experiences abroad. Balancing your new friendships with maintaining old ones can create a strong support system that spans across continents.

Balancing Social and Academic Life

Finding a Healthy Balance Between Social Activities and Academic Responsibilities:

Balancing social life and academic responsibilities can be challenging but is crucial for your overall wellbeing. Plan your schedule to include time for both study and social activities. Prioritize your tasks and set realistic goals to ensure you are meeting academic deadlines while still enjoying your time with friends.

Using a planner or digital calendar can help you manage your time effectively. Block out periods for study, attending classes, and completing assignments, as well as time for relaxation and socializing. A balanced approach prevents burnout and ensures you make the most of your international experience.

Setting Boundaries and Managing Your Time Effectively:

Setting boundaries is essential to maintaining a healthy balance. Learn to say no when necessary and prioritize activities that align with your goals and values. If you are feeling overwhelmed, take a step back and reassess your commitments.

Effective time management involves not just scheduling but also sticking to your plans. Avoid overcommitting by being selective about the events and activities you participate in. Focus on quality over quantity to ensure your engagements are meaningful and fulfilling.

Prioritizing Activities That Contribute to Your Wellbeing:

Choose activities that contribute positively to your physical, mental, and emotional wellbeing. This might include joining a fitness class, participating in cultural events, or simply spending time with friends in a relaxed setting.

Recognize the importance of downtime and self-care. Engaging in activities that relax and rejuvenate you, such as reading, hiking, or practicing mindfulness, can help you maintain a balanced and healthy lifestyle.

Cultural Engagement

Participating in Local Traditions, Festivals, and Events:

Engaging in local traditions and festivals is an enriching way to immerse yourself in the culture of your host country. Attend public celebrations, religious festivals, and cultural events to learn more about the local customs and practices.

Participating in these events not only enhances your understanding of the culture but also helps you feel more connected to the community. Be curious, respectful, and take the opportunity to ask questions and share in the local experiences.

Engaging with the Local Community Through Volunteering and Service:

Volunteering is a meaningful way to give back to your host community and gain a deeper understanding of its social fabric. Look for local volunteer opportunities that align with your interests and skills. This could involve teaching, environmental conservation, or helping at community events.

Volunteering allows you to connect with locals, make a positive impact, and develop a sense of belonging. It also provides valuable experiences that can enhance your personal growth and resume.

Learning and Respecting Cultural Norms and Practices:

Respecting cultural norms and practices is essential for positive social interactions and integration. Take the time to learn about the social etiquette, communication styles, and cultural values of your host country.

Be mindful of behaviors that might be considered rude or inappropriate. Showing respect for local customs demonstrates your willingness to adapt and can help you build stronger relationships with locals. Engage with an open mind and a respectful attitude to foster mutual understanding and respect.

By focusing on these aspects of social wellbeing, you can create a supportive and enriching environment during your international experience. Building strong connections, balancing your responsibilities, and engaging with the local culture will enhance your overall experience, helping you to thrive both academically and personally. Taking proactive steps to maintain your social wellbeing will ensure that you are fully equipped to enjoy and make the most of your time abroad.

6.5 Managing Stress and Building Resilience

Adjusting to a new country and academic environment can be exciting but also stressful. Managing stress and building resilience are crucial for maintaining your mental and physical health during your international program. This section provides practical strategies for stress management, resilience building, and accessing professional support to help you thrive abroad.

Stress Management Techniques

Identifying Common Sources of Stress for International Students:

Understanding the common stressors, you might encounter can help you prepare and manage them effectively. Typical sources of stress for international students include academic pressure, cultural adjustment, language barriers, homesickness, and social integration. Recognizing these stressors early allows you to take proactive steps to mitigate their impact.

Imagine these stressors as obstacles on a path. Knowing where they are helps you navigate around them more effectively. Awareness is the first step towards effective stress management.

Practicing Relaxation Techniques Such as Deep Breathing, Meditation, and Yoga:

Incorporating relaxation techniques into your daily routine can significantly reduce stress levels. Deep breathing exercises, meditation, and yoga are proven methods to calm the mind and relax the body. Even just a few minutes a day can make a big difference.

Deep breathing helps to oxygenate your blood and calm your nervous system. Meditation, on the other hand, helps to clear your mind of clutter and refocus on the present. Yoga combines physical movement with breath control, promoting both physical and mental well-being.

Consider setting aside time each day for these practices. Apps like Headspace or Calm can guide you through meditation and breathing exercises, while local yoga classes or online tutorials can help you get started with yoga.

Using Time Management and Organizational Skills to Reduce Stress:

Effective time management and organizational skills are essential for reducing stress. Start by creating a study schedule that balances academic responsibilities with personal time. Use planners or digital calendars to keep track of deadlines, assignments, and social activities.

Break tasks into smaller, manageable steps to avoid feeling overwhelmed. Prioritize tasks by importance and deadline and tackle them one at a time. This approach helps you stay organized and reduces the likelihood of last-minute stress.

Think of time management as a map for your day. It helps you allocate your time wisely, ensuring that you have enough for both work and relaxation.

Building Resilience

Developing a Positive Mindset and Coping Skills:

Building resilience starts with developing a positive mindset. Embrace challenges as opportunities for growth and maintain a hopeful outlook even in difficult situations. Positive self-talk and affirmations can reinforce a resilient mindset.

Coping skills are essential for handling stress and adversity. Techniques such as problem-solving, seeking social support, and practicing self-care can enhance your ability to bounce back from setbacks. Remember that resilience is not about avoiding stress but managing it effectively and learning from it.

Imagine resilience as a muscle that strengthens with use. Each challenge you face and overcome adds to your resilience, making you stronger and more adaptable.

Learning from Challenges and Setbacks:

Every challenge presents a learning opportunity. Reflect on setbacks and consider what you can learn from them. This might involve developing new skills, gaining insights into your strengths and weaknesses, or discovering new ways to approach problems.

By viewing setbacks as learning experiences, you can transform them into steppingstones for personal growth. Keep a journal to document your experiences and reflect on your progress over time.

Think of challenges as tests that reveal your growth areas. Each test prepares you better for the next, gradually building your resilience and problem-solving skills.

Seeking Opportunities for Personal Growth and Development:

Actively seek out opportunities that promote personal growth. This could include participating in workshops, joining clubs, taking on new responsibilities, or pursuing hobbies and interests. Each new experience contributes to your development and resilience.

Volunteering, internships, and leadership roles offer valuable experiences that enhance your skills and confidence. Embrace these opportunities as they come, and do not shy away from stepping out of your comfort zone.

Consider personal growth opportunities as nutrients for your resilience. They provide the experiences and skills needed to thrive in diverse situations.

Professional Support

Knowing When to Seek Help from Mental Health Professionals:

It is important to recognize when professional help is needed. If you experience persistent feelings of sadness, anxiety, or stress that interfere with your daily life, consider seeking help from a mental health professional. They can provide support, counseling, and strategies tailored to your needs.

Think of seeking professional help as a proactive step, much like visiting a doctor for physical health issues. Mental health is equally important, and professional support can make a significant difference.

Accessing Resources Provided by Your Host Institution:

Your host institution likely offers a range of resources to support your mental health and well-being. These might include counseling services, wellness workshops, peer support groups, and stress management programs. Take advantage of these resources to help manage stress and build resilience.

Familiarize yourself with the available services and do not hesitate to use them when needed. These resources are designed to support you and enhance your international experience.

Consider these resources as tools in your resilience toolkit. They provide practical support and guidance, helping you navigate challenges more effectively.

Connecting with Mentors and Advisors for Guidance:

Mentors and advisors can offer valuable guidance and support. Connect with academic advisors, faculty members, or professional mentors who can provide insights and advice based on their experience. They can help you navigate academic challenges, career planning, and personal development.

Building relationships with mentors adds another layer of support to your network. They can provide perspective, encouragement, and practical advice to help you succeed.

Think of mentors as your personal coaches. They offer guidance and support, helping you build resilience and achieve your goals.

By focusing on these areas of stress management and resilience building, you can enhance your ability to handle the challenges of studying abroad. Taking proactive steps to manage stress and build resilience will help you stay balanced, focused, and ready to make the most of your international experience.

6.6 Safety and Security

Ensuring your safety and security while studying abroad is paramount. Understanding local safety concerns, being prepared for emergencies, and complying with legal regulations can help you navigate your new environment with confidence. This section provides practical advice on personal safety, emergency preparedness, and legal compliance to ensure a secure and worry-free international experience.

Personal Safety

Understanding Local Safety Concerns and Precautions:

Each city and country has its own unique safety concerns. Before you arrive, research the local safety issues specific to your host city. Understand areas to avoid, common types of crime, and typical safety precautions locals take.

For instance, in some cities, pickpocketing may be a common issue, so it is wise to keep your belongings secure and be cautious in crowded places. In other areas, specific neighborhoods might be known for higher crime rates, so knowing where to go and where to avoid is crucial.

Staying Informed About the Political and Social Climate:

Stay updated on the political and social climate of your host country. Changes in government policies, protests, or social unrest can impact your safety. Follow local news sources and stay connected with your host institution for timely updates.

Engage with locals to gain insights into the current atmosphere and learn about any potential risks. Being informed allows you to make safer decisions about where to go and what activities to engage in.

Practicing Situational Awareness and Personal Safety Measures:

Situational awareness involves being aware of your surroundings and understanding what is normal or unusual. This skill can help you identify and avoid potential threats. Pay attention to the people around you, the environment, and any sudden changes that might indicate a safety concern.

Some practical personal safety measures include:

- Avoiding walking alone at night, especially in unfamiliar areas
- Keeping your valuables secure and out of sight
- Using reputable transportation options
- Trusting your instincts and leaving situations that feel unsafe

Emergency Preparedness

Knowing Emergency Contact Numbers and Procedures:

Familiarize yourself with local emergency contact numbers, such as those for police, fire, and medical services. Keep these numbers easily accessible on your phone and written down in case of an emergency.

Learn the emergency procedures specific to your host institution and residence. Know where to go and whom to contact in case of an emergency. Many universities provide emergency contact cards or apps with essential information.

Creating a Personal Safety Plan and Emergency Kit:

Having a personal safety plan can help you respond quickly and effectively in an emergency. This plan should include:

- Emergency contact information for local friends, family, and your host institution
- A designated meeting place if communication is disrupted
- A list of important documents and items to take if you need to evacuate

Create an emergency kit with essentials such as:

- A first-aid kit
- Copies of important documents (passport, visa, insurance)
- Basic supplies like water, snacks, a flashlight, and batteries
- Any necessary medications

Staying Connected with Your Host Institution's Emergency Services:

Your host institution likely has dedicated emergency services and protocols. Stay connected with these services by attending orientation sessions, signing up for emergency alerts, and keeping their contact information handy.

Regularly check in with your institution's international office, especially if there are any safety concerns or emergencies in the area. They can provide support and guidance tailored to international students.

Legal and Regulatory Compliance

Understanding Visa and Immigration Regulations:

Complying with visa and immigration regulations is essential for maintaining your legal status in your host country. Ensure you understand the terms of your visa, including work restrictions, study requirements, and expiration dates.

Stay informed about any changes in immigration policies that may affect you. Keep copies of all your visa documents and carry them with you when traveling within or outside the host country.

Knowing Your Rights and Responsibilities as an International Student:

As an international student, you have specific rights and responsibilities. Familiarize yourself with these to avoid any legal issues. This includes understanding your right to fair treatment, access to education, and legal protections.

Know the rules regarding academic integrity, housing, and conduct both on and off-campus. Adhering to these rules ensures a smooth and successful stay in your host country.

Complying with Local Laws and Regulations:

Respecting and complying with local laws is crucial for your safety and legal standing. This includes understanding local traffic laws, drinking age regulations, and any specific cultural norms that may have legal implications.

Avoid behaviors that could lead to legal trouble, such as illegal drug use or engaging in activities without proper permits. Being aware of and following local laws demonstrates respect for your host country and ensures a trouble-free experience.

6.7 Health Insurance and Medical Care

Access to healthcare and understanding your health insurance are vital aspects of living abroad. This section provides detailed guidance on how to navigate health insurance, access medical services, and ensure you receive the care you need.

Understanding Your Health Insurance

Coverage Details and Limitations of Your Health Insurance Plan:

Before you depart, thoroughly review your health insurance plan to understand what is covered and what is not. Coverage may include medical emergencies, routine check-ups, prescription medications, and specialist visits. Some plans might also cover mental health services and dental care.

Be aware of any limitations, such as exclusions for pre-existing conditions, coverage caps, or specific network requirements. Understanding these details helps you avoid unexpected costs and ensures you know when to seek additional coverage if necessary.

How to File Claims and Seek Reimbursements:

Filing claims and seeking reimbursements can vary depending on your insurance provider. Familiarize yourself with the process before you need to use it. Typically, this involves submitting receipts, medical reports, and other documentation.

Keep copies of all medical documents, receipts, and correspondence with healthcare providers. Some insurance companies have online portals or apps that make submitting claims easier. Knowing how to navigate this process ensures you receive the benefits you are entitled to.

Knowing What to Do in Case of a Medical Emergency:

In a medical emergency, knowing the steps to take can save crucial time. Immediately contact local emergency services for urgent medical needs. Inform your host institution and follow their emergency protocols.

Carry an emergency card with essential information, such as allergies, medical conditions, and emergency contacts. This can help healthcare providers give you the best possible care quickly.

Accessing Medical Services

Finding and Visiting Doctors, Dentists, and Specialists:

Finding reliable healthcare providers is crucial for maintaining your health. Start by asking your host institution for recommendations. They often have lists of trusted doctors, dentists, and specialists who work with international students.

When visiting a new healthcare provider, bring any medical records and a list of current medications. This helps them understand your health history and provide appropriate care.

Understanding the Local Healthcare System and Procedures:

Healthcare systems vary widely between countries. Take the time to understand how the local system works, including how to make appointments, the typical wait times, and any necessary paperwork.

Learn about the cost of medical services and whether payment is required upfront or can be billed to your insurance. Familiarize yourself with local pharmacies and how to get prescriptions filled.

Utilizing Telehealth Services if Available:

Telehealth services have become increasingly popular and can be a convenient way to access medical care. Check if your insurance plan covers telehealth appointments and find out which providers offer these services.

Telehealth can be particularly useful for routine check-ups, mental health consultations, and follow-up appointments. It offers flexibility and reduces the need for in-person visits, which can be especially beneficial if you live far from medical facilities.

By focusing on these aspects of safety, security, and healthcare, you can ensure a secure and healthy international experience. Taking proactive steps to understand local safety concerns, being prepared for emergencies, and navigating the healthcare system will help you stay safe and well during your time abroad. This comprehensive approach allows you to fully embrace your international experience with confidence and peace of mind.

6.8 Substance Use and Abuse

Maintaining a healthy and balanced lifestyle is crucial during your time abroad, and this includes being aware of the risks associated with alcohol and drug use. Understanding the potential dangers, recognizing signs of abuse, and knowing where to find support and resources can help you make informed decisions and seek help if needed. This section provides valuable insights and practical advice on substance use and abuse.

Awareness and Education

Understanding the Risks Associated with Alcohol and Drug Use:

Alcohol and drug use can have serious consequences on your health, academic performance, and overall well-being. It is important to understand these risks, which can include physical health problems, mental health issues, addiction, and legal consequences.

For example, excessive alcohol consumption can lead to liver disease, cardiovascular problems, and impaired judgment, which increases the risk of accidents and injuries. Drug use, depending on the substance, can have a range of harmful effects, including dependency, cognitive impairment, and severe health complications.

Imagine alcohol and drugs as obstacles on your path. They may seem harmless or fun at first, but they can trip you up and lead to significant problems down the line. Awareness of these risks helps you navigate your choices more carefully.

Recognizing Signs of Substance Abuse:

Recognizing the signs of substance abuse in yourself or others is crucial for early intervention and support. Common signs of substance abuse include:

- Changes in behavior or personality
- Neglecting responsibilities and declining academic performance
- Withdrawal from social activities and isolation
- Physical symptoms such as unexplained weight loss, changes in sleep patterns, or poor hygiene
- Increased tolerance and frequent use of alcohol or drugs

- Engaging in risky behaviors, such as driving under the influence

Being aware of these signs allows you to take action if you or someone you know may be struggling with substance abuse. Think of these signs as warning signals. Ignoring them can lead to more severe problems but addressing them early can prevent further harm.

Anecdotes and Insights
Recognizing and Seeking Help for Substance Use- Luis' Story

Student Perspective: "I didn't realize how much my occasional drinking had escalated until I missed a couple of classes and felt increasingly disconnected from my studies and friends. It was a wake-up call when one of my friends expressed concern. I reached out to the student health center and found support groups and counseling. Addressing the issue head-on helped me regain control and focus on my academic and personal goals." – Luis, U.S. International Student

Expert Insight: Substance use can become problematic if not addressed early. Recognizing the signs of substance abuse and seeking help is crucial. Most universities provide confidential counseling services and support groups. If you or someone you know is struggling with substance use, do not hesitate to reach out for help. Maintaining a healthy and balanced lifestyle is key to a successful international experience.

Accessing Educational Resources on Substance Use:

Educational resources can provide valuable information on the effects of substance use and strategies for prevention and harm reduction. Many universities offer workshops, seminars, and online resources to educate students about the risks of alcohol and drug use.

Take advantage of these resources to increase your knowledge and awareness. Understanding the facts about substance use empowers you to make safer choices and support others who may be at risk.

Imagine these resources as your personal guidebook. They offer essential information and tools to help you navigate the challenges of substance use and make informed decisions.

Support and Resources

Seeking Help for Substance Abuse Issues:

If you or someone you know is struggling with substance abuse, seeking help is a crucial step towards recovery. Most universities offer confidential counseling services where you can speak with a professional about your concerns. These counselors can provide support, guidance, and referrals to specialized treatment programs if needed.

Do not hesitate to reach out for help. Acknowledging the problem and seeking assistance is a sign of strength and a vital step towards healing and recovery. Think of seeking help as putting on your life jacket. It keeps you afloat and helps you navigate the turbulent waters of substance abuse.

Finding Support Groups and Counseling Services:

Support groups can provide a sense of community and understanding for those dealing with substance abuse. Groups like Alcoholics Anonymous (AA) or Narcotics Anonymous (NA) offer peer support and a structured program for recovery.

In addition to support groups, individual counseling can be highly beneficial. Professional counselors can help you develop coping strategies, address underlying issues, and create a plan for maintaining sobriety.

Research local support groups and counseling services in your host city. Your university's health center or international office can also provide information and referrals. Imagine these support networks as your team. They provide encouragement, understanding, and practical advice to help you stay on track.

Encouraging a Healthy and Balanced Lifestyle:

Maintaining a healthy and balanced lifestyle can help prevent substance abuse and support overall well-being. Engage in activities that promote physical, mental, and emotional health. This includes regular exercise, a nutritious diet, adequate sleep, and meaningful social connections.

Participate in hobbies and activities that you enjoy, whether it is sports, arts, or volunteering. These positive outlets can provide fulfillment and reduce the likelihood of turning to substances for comfort or escape.

Cultivating a balanced lifestyle acts as a protective factor against the temptation of substance use. It fosters resilience and helps you manage stress in healthy ways.

Imagine your lifestyle as the foundation of a strong, resilient house. The more balanced and healthier your daily activities, the more robust your structure against the storms of life.

By focusing on these aspects of substance use and abuse, you can ensure a safer and healthier international experience. Understanding the risks, recognizing signs of abuse, and knowing where to find support will help you navigate this important aspect of your life abroad with confidence and responsibility. Taking proactive steps to maintain your health and well-being will enable you to make the most of your time abroad while staying safe and healthy.

Chapter 6 Conclusion

Maintaining health and wellbeing during your international experience is crucial for making the most of your time abroad. As we wrap up Chapter 6, let us recap the key points covered, offer some encouragement to prioritize self-care, and provide final tips for ensuring a healthy and successful international journey.

Key Points for Maintaining Health and Wellbeing

Throughout this chapter, we have explored various aspects of health and wellbeing that are essential for your international experience. Here is a quick recap of the key points:

Physical Health: Accessing healthcare, staying updated with vaccinations, and practicing good hygiene are fundamental. Ensure you maintain a balanced diet, engage in regular exercise, and get adequate sleep to keep your body in top shape.

Mental Health: Recognize the signs of stress and mental health issues and make use of available mental health resources. Practice relaxation techniques, establish a supportive social network, and maintain a positive mindset to cope with the challenges of living abroad.

Healthy Lifestyle: Balance local cuisine with a nutritious diet, find ways to stay physically active, and establish good sleep hygiene. Incorporating these habits into your daily routine will support your overall health and energy levels.

Social Wellbeing: Build a strong support network by making new friends, joining clubs, and maintaining connections with loved ones back home. Balance your social life with academic responsibilities and engage with the local culture to enrich your experience.

Managing Stress and Building Resilience: Identify stressors and practice effective stress management techniques. Develop resilience through a positive mindset, learning from setbacks, and seeking opportunities for growth. Do not hesitate to seek professional support when needed.

Safety and Security: Stay informed about local safety concerns, be prepared for emergencies, and comply with legal and regulatory requirements. Understanding and respecting local laws will help you stay safe and avoid legal issues.

Substance Use and Abuse: Be aware of the risks associated with alcohol and drug use, recognize signs of abuse, and seek help if needed. Engage in activities that promote a healthy and balanced lifestyle to prevent substance abuse.

Encouragement to Prioritize Self-Care and Seek Support When Needed

Living abroad presents unique challenges and opportunities. Prioritizing self-care is essential to navigating these experiences successfully. Self-care is not just about occasional pampering; it is about maintaining a daily routine that supports your physical, mental, and emotional health.

Remember, seeking support is a sign of strength, not weakness. Whether it is talking to a friend, reaching out to a counselor, or using university resources, getting help when needed can make a significant difference in your wellbeing. Surround yourself with a supportive network and do not hesitate to lean on them during tough times.

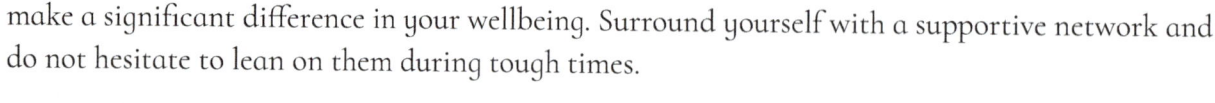

Tips for a Healthy and Successful International Experience

- **Stay Informed**: Regularly update yourself on local health, safety, and legal information. Knowledge is your first line of defense against potential issues.
- **Create a Routine**: Establish a balanced routine that includes study, exercise, social activities, and relaxation. A structured day helps manage time and reduces stress.
- **Engage with the Local Community**: Participate in cultural events, volunteer, and explore your surroundings. This not only enriches your experience but also helps you integrate into your new environment.
- **Practice Mindfulness**: Stay present and mindful of your experiences. Reflecting on your journey helps you appreciate the growth and learning that comes with living abroad.
- **Stay Connected**: Maintain regular communication with family and friends back home. Their support can provide comfort and stability amidst the changes you are experiencing.
- **Be Proactive About Health**: Regularly check in with your physical and mental health. Do not wait for problems to escalate before seeking help.
- **Enjoy the Journey**: Finally, remember to enjoy the journey. Embrace the challenges and cherish the memories. Your time abroad is a unique chapter in your life, filled with opportunities for growth, learning, and adventure.

By prioritizing your health and wellbeing, you set a strong foundation for a successful and enriching international experience. Take proactive steps to care for yourself, seek support when needed, and make the most of this incredible opportunity. Here is to a healthy, happy, and memorable journey abroad!

Chapter 6 Review

Summary of Key Points

Chapter 6 covered essential aspects of maintaining health and wellbeing during your international experience. We explored navigating healthcare systems abroad, maintaining physical and mental health, balancing nutrition and exercise, building social networks, managing stress, and ensuring personal safety and security. Understanding these elements will help you create a supportive environment for your overall well-being.

Review Questions

Short Answer:

- What are three key steps you should take to familiarize yourself with the healthcare system in your host country?
- Name two strategies you can use to manage stress and maintain mental health while studying abroad.
- What are the benefits of cooking your own meals and balancing local cuisine with a healthy diet?

Which of the following is NOT a recommended practice for managing jet lag?

a) Gradually adjusting your sleep schedule before departure
b) Exposing yourself to natural light during the day
c) Drinking caffeinated beverages before bedtime
d) Avoiding heavy meals before sleep

When seeking help for substance abuse, which resource is typically available at most universities?

a) Confidential counseling services
b) Online shopping discounts
c) Free travel vouchers
d) Sports equipment rental

True/False:
True or False: Regular physical activity can help reduce stress and improve mental well-being.

True or False: It is important to understand local laws and safety concerns to ensure personal security while abroad.

Reflective Question:
Reflect on your current health and wellbeing routines. How might these need to change to adapt to your new environment, and what steps can you take to ensure you maintain a balanced and healthy lifestyle?

Case Study:

Read the following scenario and answer the questions: *Jessica has recently arrived in her host country and is feeling overwhelmed with the academic workload and cultural adjustments. She finds herself staying up late to finish assignments and is beginning to feel anxious and fatigued.*

- What strategies can Jessica use to manage her stress and improve her mental health?
- How can Jessica balance her academic responsibilities with self-care practices?

Invitation to Reflective Exercises

To further explore the concepts discussed in this chapter and apply them to your personal situation, we invite you to complete the exercises in the companion workbook, "Reflective Exercises: The International Experiences Guide Workbook." These exercises will help you internalize the content, develop personalized strategies for maintaining health and wellbeing, and enhance your overall international experience.

Engage with these review questions to reinforce your understanding of the key points covered in Chapter 6. Remember, maintaining your health and wellbeing is essential for a successful and enjoyable international experience. Prioritize self-care, seek support when needed, and make the most of this incredible opportunity to grow and learn in a new environment.

{ 7 }

Career Development and Networking

Introduction

Your international experience is not only an opportunity for personal growth and cultural immersion but also a pivotal moment for career development and networking. As an international student, you are uniquely positioned to enhance your professional skills, expand your network, and make valuable connections that can significantly influence your future career path. This chapter will guide you through the various opportunities available to you and provide practical advice on how to leverage your international experience for career advancement.

Importance of Career Development During Your International Program

Participating in an international program offers more than just academic enrichment; it presents a unique platform to develop and refine your career goals. Engaging in career development activities while abroad can help you:

Gain International Experience: Employers value international experience as it demonstrates your ability to adapt, navigate diverse cultures, and work effectively in global environments.

Enhance Your Resume: The skills and experiences you acquire during your international program can make your resume stand out. Highlighting your adaptability, problem-solving abilities, and cross-cultural communication skills can give you a competitive edge.

Build a Global Network: Networking with peers, professors, and professionals in your host country can open doors to new opportunities, provide mentorship, and create lasting connections that benefit your career.

Overview of Opportunities to Enhance Your Professional Growth

There are numerous opportunities to enhance your professional growth during your international program. Here are some key areas to focus on:

Internships and Work Experience: Many universities and organizations offer internship programs for international students. These internships can provide practical experience in your field of study and help you build relevant skills.

Career Services and Workshops: Utilize the career services offered by your host institution. Attend workshops on resume writing, interview skills, and job search strategies to better prepare yourself for the job market.

Professional Organizations and Clubs: Join professional organizations, student clubs, and industry-specific groups. These platforms offer networking opportunities, industry insights, and the chance to participate in events and conferences.

Mentorship Programs: Seek out mentorship programs that pair you with experienced professionals in your field. A mentor can provide valuable advice, guidance, and support as you navigate your career path.

Encouragement to Leverage International Experience for Career Advancement

Your international experience is a powerful tool that can significantly enhance your career prospects. Here are some ways to leverage this experience for career advancement:

Highlight Your International Experience: On your resume and in interviews, emphasize your international experience and the skills you developed. Discuss specific projects or challenges you faced and how you overcame them.

Develop a Professional Online Presence: Use platforms like LinkedIn to connect with professionals you meet during your international program. Share your experiences and insights to build your personal brand and showcase your expertise.

Seek Out Networking Events: Attend networking events, industry conferences, and career fairs both during and after your international program. These events are excellent opportunities to meet potential employers and industry leaders.

Stay in Touch with Connections: Maintain relationships with the people you meet abroad. Regularly update them on your career progress and seek their advice and support when needed.

Embracing career development and networking opportunities during your international program can significantly impact your future career success. By actively engaging in professional growth activities, building a global network, and leveraging your international experience, you can position yourself as a highly competitive candidate in the global job market. Remember, your international experience is not just an academic journey but also a crucial step in shaping your professional future. Take advantage of every opportunity to learn, grow, and connect, and you will see the benefits in your career for years to come.

7.1 Setting Career Goals

Setting clear career goals is a crucial step in leveraging your international experience for professional growth. By identifying your aspirations, creating a detailed career plan, and setting actionable objectives, you can make the most of your time abroad and ensure that your efforts align with your long-term ambitions. Let us dive into how you can do this in a way that is both practical and inspiring.

Identifying Career Aspirations

Reflecting on Your Interests and Strengths:

Start by taking some time to reflect on what truly excites you and where your natural talents lie. Think about the activities and subjects that light you up and the environments where you thrive. Ask yourself:

- What topics or activities make me lose track of time?
- What skills do people often compliment me on?
- In what kind of work environment do I feel most productive and happy?

Consider keeping a journal to jot down your thoughts. Sometimes, talking with friends, family, or mentors can provide new perspectives and help you see your strengths and interests more clearly.

Researching Potential Career Paths and Industries:

Once you have a better sense of your interests and strengths, it is time to explore how they might translate into a career. Dive into resources like:

- Your university's career services and advisors, who can provide personalized guidance.
- Online career exploration tools, such as O*NET or My Next Move, offer detailed job descriptions and career paths.
- Professional organizations and industry publications, which can give you insights into various fields.

Do not just look at job titles—explore what people in those roles actually do day-to-day, the skills they use, and the paths they took to get there.

Setting Short-Term and Long-Term Career Goals:

With your research and reflections in hand, start setting goals. Short-term goals could be things you want to achieve within the next year, such as securing an internship or mastering a new skill. Long-term goals are your broader ambitions, like becoming a project manager or starting your own business.

Write these goals down and keep them visible—on your desk, as a phone background, or in your planner. This constant reminder will keep you focused and motivated.

Creating a Career Plan

Mapping Out Steps to Achieve Your Career Goals:

Think of your career plan as a roadmap to your future. Break down your long-term goals into smaller, actionable steps. For instance:

- If you want to become a marketing manager, start by gaining relevant experience through internships.
- Enroll in courses or online certifications that build your marketing knowledge and skills.

Create a timeline for these steps. Set specific deadlines to keep yourself accountable and on track.

Identifying Skills and Experiences Needed for Your Desired Career:

Take a close look at the skills and experiences required for your chosen career path. Compare this with what you currently possess and identify any gaps. Consider:

Technical skills: coding, data analysis, or graphic design.

Soft skills: such as communication, leadership, or teamwork.

Industry knowledge: understanding market trends, key players, and essential tools.

Use your time abroad to fill these gaps. Seek out internships, part-time jobs, or volunteer opportunities that allow you to develop these skills. Your host institution may also offer relevant workshops or courses.

Setting Actionable and Measurable Objectives:

Your objectives should be SMART: Specific, Measurable, Achievable, Relevant, and Time-bound. For example, instead of setting a vague goal like "Get better at networking," try "Attend three networking events this semester and connect with at least five new people at each event."

Writing down these objectives and reviewing them regularly can help keep you focused. Adjust them as needed to stay aligned with your evolving career goals and the opportunities that arise.

Setting career goals and creating a detailed plan are essential steps in making the most of your international experience for professional growth. Reflect on your interests and strengths, research potential career paths, and set both short-term and long-term goals to guide you. By mapping out the steps needed to achieve your goals, identifying the necessary skills and experiences, and setting actionable objectives, you can navigate your journey with clarity and purpose.

Remember, your career plan is a living document. Regularly review and update your goals and objectives to stay aligned with your aspirations and the ever-changing job market. This proactive approach will not only help you make the most of your time abroad but also position you for long-term success in your chosen field. Embrace the journey, take advantage of the opportunities that come your way, and watch your career aspirations come to life.

7.2 Building Professional Skills

Building professional skills during your international journey is an excellent way to enhance your career prospects. Both soft skills and technical skills are crucial for success in today's job market. This section will provide you with practical strategies to develop these skills through coursework, extracurricular activities, and hands-on experience.

Developing Soft Skills

Importance of Communication, Teamwork, and Problem-Solving Skills:

Soft skills are the interpersonal attributes you need to succeed in the workplace. These include communication, teamwork, and problem-solving abilities, which are highly valued by employers across all industries. Developing these skills can help you navigate professional environments, collaborate effectively with colleagues, and solve complex problems.

Communication: Effective communication is key to expressing ideas clearly, listening to others, and facilitating discussions. It encompasses verbal, non-verbal, and written communication.

Teamwork: Being able to work well with others is crucial. Teamwork involves collaboration, understanding different perspectives, and working towards common goals.

Problem-Solving: The ability to analyze situations, identify problems, and develop practical solutions is essential in any job.

Strategies for Improving These Skills Through Coursework and Extracurricular Activities:

- **Join Clubs and Organizations**: Participating in student clubs, societies, or professional organizations can provide numerous opportunities to practice communication and teamwork. Look for roles that require you to coordinate events, lead projects, or manage teams.

- **Group Projects**: Engage actively in group projects and assignments. These are excellent opportunities to enhance teamwork and problem-solving skills. Take on different roles within the group to broaden your experience.
- **Public Speaking**: Take advantage of opportunities to practice public speaking, such as presentations in class or joining a debate club. This can significantly improve your verbal communication and confidence.
- **Volunteering**: Volunteer for community service projects or campus events. These activities often require teamwork and problem-solving, providing a practical way to develop these skills.

Practicing Leadership and Time Management:

Seek Leadership Roles: Aim for leadership positions within clubs, organizations, or group projects. Leadership roles help you develop skills in decision-making, delegation, and conflict resolution.

Time Management Workshops: Attend workshops or seminars on time management. Learning to prioritize tasks, set deadlines, and manage your time efficiently is crucial for balancing academics, work, and social activities.

Use Organizational Tools: Utilize tools like planners, calendars, and task management apps to organize your schedule. Setting clear goals and breaking tasks into manageable steps can help you stay on track and meet deadlines.

Enhancing Technical Skills

Identifying Key Technical Skills Relevant to Your Field:

Technical skills are specific abilities and knowledge required to perform certain tasks. These can range from computer programming and data analysis to design and engineering. Identifying the key technical skills needed in your field is the first step to enhancing them.

Research Job Requirements: Look at job postings and descriptions in your field to identify commonly required technical skills.

Consult with Mentors: Talk to professors, industry professionals, and career advisors to get insights into the essential technical skills for your career path.

Taking Advantage of Workshops, Online Courses, and Certifications:

University Workshops: Many universities offer workshops and seminars on various technical skills. These are often free or discounted for students.

Online Learning Platforms: Websites like Coursera, edX, Udacity, and LinkedIn Learning offer a wide range of courses on technical subjects. Look for courses that offer certificates upon completion.

Professional Certifications: Pursue industry-recognized certifications that can enhance your resume and demonstrate your expertise to potential employers.

Gaining Hands-On Experience Through Projects and Internships:

Class Projects: Engage deeply in class projects that allow you to apply technical skills. Choose projects that challenge you to learn new technologies or methodologies.

Internships: Seek internships that provide practical experience in your field. Internships are invaluable for applying classroom knowledge to real-world situations and gaining industry insights.

Personal Projects: Work on personal projects or join open-source initiatives. These experiences not only enhance your technical skills but also show your initiative and passion for the field.

Developing both soft and technical skills is essential for building a successful career. By actively seeking opportunities to enhance these skills through coursework, extracurricular activities, and hands-on experiences, you can significantly boost your employability and professional growth. Embrace the challenges and opportunities that come your way during your international adventure and use them as steppingstones to build a robust skill set that will serve you well in your future career. Remember, the more you invest in developing these skills now, the more prepared you will be to excel in the professional world.

7.3 Networking and Professional Relationships

Networking and building professional relationships are critical components of career development. During your international program, you will have countless opportunities to expand your professional network, connect with industry experts, and form meaningful relationships that can support your career aspirations. This section will guide you through the basics of networking, strategies for building relationships, and the importance of mentorship.

Networking Basics

Understanding the Importance of Networking in Career Development:

Networking is the art of building and nurturing professional relationships. It is not just about collecting business cards or connecting on LinkedIn; it is about creating genuine connections that can lead to mutual support and opportunities. Effective networking can:

Open doors to job opportunities and internships.

Provide insights into industry trends and best practices.

Offer support and advice from experienced professionals.

Identifying Opportunities to Network (Events, Conferences, Seminars):

To build a robust network, you need to put yourself in situations where you can meet and connect with others. Here are some opportunities to consider:

Events and Conferences: Attend industry-specific conferences, workshops, and seminars. These events are perfect for meeting professionals and learning about the latest trends in your field.

University Functions: Participate in networking events organized by your host institution, such as career fairs, alumni gatherings, and guest lectures.

Professional Organizations: Join local chapters of professional organizations related to your field. These groups often host regular meetings and networking events.

Anecdotes and Insights

Networking at Career Fairs- Priya's Story

Student Perspective: "Attending a career fair at my host university in Canada was a game-changer for me. I was able to meet potential employers, learn about different companies, and understand what skills are in demand. Through the connections I made, I secured several interviews and eventually landed a job offer. Networking at these events opened doors I never thought possible." – Priya, Indian International Student

Expert Insight: Career fairs are excellent opportunities to expand your professional network and explore job opportunities. Prepare in advance by researching companies, updating your resume, and practicing your pitch. During the event, be confident, ask insightful questions, and follow up with the contacts you make.

Building a Diverse Professional Network:

A diverse network includes connections from various industries, backgrounds, and levels of experience. This diversity can provide a wealth of perspectives and opportunities. Here is how to build a diverse network:

Be Open-Minded: Engage with people from different fields and with varying levels of experience. Each connection can offer unique insights.

Attend Various Events: Do not limit yourself to events strictly related to your field. Broader events can provide unexpected connections and opportunities.

Stay Active Online: Participate in online forums, webinars, and social media groups relevant to your interests and career goals.

Building Relationships

Strategies for Initiating and Maintaining Professional Relationships:

Initiating and maintaining professional relationships requires effort and genuine interest. Here are some strategies:

Be Genuine: Show genuine interest in others. Ask questions about their experiences, career paths, and challenges.

Follow Up: After meeting someone, follow up with a personalized message or email. Mention something specific you discussed to show you were paying attention.

Stay in Touch: Keep in regular contact with your connections. Share relevant articles, congratulate them on achievements, and check in periodically.

Effective Communication and Follow-Up Techniques:

Good communication is key to maintaining professional relationships. Here are some tips:

Be Clear and Concise: Whether in person or via email, communicate your points clearly and concisely.

Listen Actively: Show that you value others' input by listening actively and responding thoughtfully.

Timely Follow-Up: After an initial meeting or conversation, follow up within a few days to reinforce the connection.

Leveraging Social Media Platforms like LinkedIn for Professional Networking:

LinkedIn is a powerful tool for building and maintaining your professional network. Here is how to make the most of it:

Complete Your Profile: Ensure your LinkedIn profile is complete and professional. Include a professional photo, detailed work experience, and a compelling summary.

Connect Strategically: Send personalized connection requests to people you meet at events, colleagues, and industry leaders.

Engage Regularly: Share industry-related content, comment on others' posts, and participate in LinkedIn groups to stay active and visible.

Mentorship

Finding and Approaching Potential Mentors:

A mentor can provide invaluable guidance and support. Here is how to find and approach potential mentors:

Identify Suitable Candidates: Look for individuals who have experience in your field and whose career path you admire.

Make the Ask: Reach out with a respectful and thoughtful message. Explain why you are seeking their mentorship and how you believe they can help you grow.

Be Patient and Persistent: Building a mentor-mentee relationship takes time. Be patient and follow up if you do not receive an immediate response.

Benefits of Having a Mentor for Career Guidance and Support:

Mentors can offer a range of benefits:

Guidance and Advice: They provide insights into industry trends, career paths, and skill development.

Networking Opportunities: Mentors can introduce you to their professional network.

Support and Encouragement: They offer emotional support and encouragement, helping you navigate challenges and setbacks.

How to Make the Most of a Mentorship Relationship:

To fully benefit from a mentorship relationship, you need to be proactive and engaged:

Set Clear Goals: Establish what you hope to achieve from the mentorship and discuss these goals with your mentor.

Be Prepared: Come to meetings prepared with questions and updates on your progress.

Show Appreciation: Acknowledge your mentor's time and effort. A simple thank you can go a long way in maintaining a positive relationship.

Anecdotes and Insights

The Impact of Mentorship- Carlos' Story

Student Perspective: "I was fortunate to find a mentor during my exchange in Australia. My mentor, a seasoned professional in my field, provided invaluable guidance and support. We discussed my career goals, and she helped me navigate the job market. Her insights and encouragement were instrumental in my securing a post-graduation job in Sydney." – Carlos, Brazilian International Student

Expert Insight: Finding a mentor can significantly impact your career development. Mentors offer guidance, support, and networking opportunities. To find a mentor, look for professionals you admire, reach out with a clear purpose, and be open to their feedback and advice. Maintain regular communication and show appreciation for their time and effort.

Networking and building professional relationships are vital for your career development. By understanding the importance of networking, identifying opportunities to connect with others, and actively building and maintaining these relationships, you can significantly enhance your career prospects. Additionally, finding a mentor can provide invaluable guidance and support, helping you navigate your career path with confidence. Embrace these opportunities during your international experience and watch your professional network and career grow.

7.4 Gaining Work Experience

Gaining work experience during your international program is an invaluable way to enhance your career prospects. Whether through internships, part-time jobs, or volunteering, practical experience helps you apply what you have learned in the classroom to real-world situations. This section will guide you on how to find and make the most of these opportunities.

Internships

Finding and Applying for Internships in Your Host Country:

Internships are a great way to gain hands-on experience in your field of study. Here is how to find and apply for them:

Research Opportunities: Start by researching companies and organizations in your host country that offer internships. Use online job boards, your university's career services, and professional networks like LinkedIn.

Tailor Your Application: Customize your resume and cover letter for each internship application. Highlight relevant skills and experiences and explain why you are interested in that particular organization.

Prepare for Interviews: Practice common interview questions and research the company beforehand. Be ready to discuss how your skills and experiences make you a good fit for the role.

Balancing Internship Responsibilities with Academic Commitments:

Managing an internship alongside your studies can be challenging but rewarding. Here are some tips:

Create a Schedule: Use a planner or digital calendar to organize your time. Allocate specific blocks for classes, study time, and internship work.

Set Priorities: Determine which tasks are most important and focus on completing them first. Do not hesitate to communicate with your professors and internship supervisor if you need adjustments.

Stay Organized: Keep track of deadlines and assignments for both your academic and internship responsibilities. Staying organized will help you manage your workload effectively.

Anecdotes and Insights

Balancing Work and Study- Mei's Story

Student Perspective: "During my exchange in the United States, I took on a part-time job at a local bookstore. Balancing work and study was challenging, but it taught me essential time management skills. The experience also helped me develop customer service skills and build a local network. This balance of work and study enriched my international experience and prepared me for future career challenges." – Mei, Chinese International Student

Expert Insight: Balancing work and study requires effective time management and prioritization. Create a schedule that allocates time for classes, study, and work. Communicate with your employer about your academic commitments and seek flexible work arrangements if necessary. This balance not only helps you financially but also enhances your resume with practical experience.

Making the Most of Your Internship Experience for Career Growth:

Your internship is an opportunity to learn and grow. Make the most of it by:

Taking Initiative: Volunteer for projects, ask questions, and seek out learning opportunities. Show your enthusiasm and willingness to go beyond basic tasks.

Building Relationships: Network with colleagues and supervisors. These connections can provide valuable advice, mentorship, and future job opportunities.

Reflecting on Your Experience: After your internship, take time to reflect on what you learned. Consider how the experience has influenced your career goals and what skills you need to develop further.

Anecdotes and Insights

The Value of Internships Abroad- Akira's Story

Student Perspective: "During my international program in Germany, I secured an internship with a local tech startup. Initially, I was overwhelmed by the language barrier and the new work culture. However, this experience turned out to be incredibly enriching. Not only did I improve my technical skills, but I also learned how to navigate a multicultural work environment. This internship helped me realize the importance of adaptability and cultural sensitivity in professional settings." – Akira, Japanese International Student

Expert Insight: Internships abroad can significantly enhance your career prospects. They provide hands-on experience in your field, improve your adaptability, and help you develop a global perspective. To maximize your internship experience, immerse yourself in the local culture, seek feedback, and be proactive in taking on new challenges.

Part-Time Jobs and Work-Study

Exploring Opportunities for Part-Time Work on and Off-Campus:

Part-time jobs can provide additional income and work experience. How to find them:

Campus Jobs: Check your university's job board for on-campus opportunities such as research assistant positions, library jobs, or administrative roles.

Off-Campus Jobs: Look for part-time work in local businesses, such as retail, hospitality, or tutoring. Websites like Indeed and local classifieds can be useful.

Networking: Ask professors, classmates, and career services about available opportunities. Sometimes jobs are not advertised and are filled through word-of-mouth.

Understanding Work-Study Programs and Eligibility:

Work-study programs offer part-time jobs to students with financial need. Here is what you need to know:

Eligibility: Check if you qualify for work-study through your host institution. Financial aid offices can provide information on eligibility and application processes.

Job Types: Work-study jobs often align with your academic interests or provide valuable skills. These roles can range from research positions to community service jobs.

Benefits: Work-study jobs can help you finance your education while gaining work experience. They often offer flexible hours that accommodate your class schedule.

Managing Work and Study Effectively:

Balancing work and study require good time management:

Set a Schedule: Plan your work hours around your class schedule. Make sure to leave enough time for studying and relaxation.

Communicate: Keep open communication with your employer and professors about your availability and any potential conflicts.

Self-Care: Do not forget to take care of yourself. Ensure you are getting enough sleep, eating well, and taking breaks to avoid burnout.

Volunteering and Community Service

Benefits of Volunteering for Skill Development and Networking:

Volunteering offers numerous benefits beyond just helping others:

Skill Development: Gain valuable skills such as leadership, teamwork, and project management. These skills are transferable to any career.

Networking: Meet new people, including professionals in your field. Volunteering can open doors to job opportunities and mentorship.

Personal Growth: Volunteering can be a fulfilling way to give back to the community and develop a sense of purpose.

Finding Volunteer Opportunities Related to Your Career Interests:

Look for volunteer opportunities that align with your career goals:

University Programs: Many universities have volunteer programs that connect students with local organizations.

Nonprofits and NGOs: Research local nonprofits and NGOs in your host country that align with your interests.

Online Platforms: Websites like VolunteerMatch and Idealist list volunteer opportunities around the world.

Making a Positive Impact in Your Host Community:

Engage with your host community through meaningful volunteer work:

Be Committed: Dedicate yourself to the volunteer work you choose. Your commitment will make a significant impact and reflect positively on you.

Be Respectful: Show respect for the community and its culture. Be open to learning and adapting to new environments.

Share Your Experience: Reflect on your volunteer experiences and share them with others. This can inspire more people to get involved and highlight the importance of community service.

7.5 Professional Development Resources

Developing your professional skills requires access to the right resources. Your host institution and various organizations offer numerous tools and opportunities to support your career growth.

Career Services

Utilizing Career Counseling and Job Placement Services at Your Host Institution:

Career services can be a valuable resource for finding jobs and internships:

Career Counseling: Schedule meetings with career advisors to discuss your career goals and receive personalized advice.

Job Placement: Use job placement services to find internships and part-time work opportunities. These services often have strong connections with local employers.

Workshops: Attend workshops on resume writing, interview preparation, and job search strategies to improve your skills.

Attending Career Fairs and Employer Information Sessions:

Career fairs and employer sessions are excellent for networking:

Career Fairs: Attend career fairs to meet potential employers, learn about job opportunities, and practice your networking skills.

Information Sessions: Go to employer information sessions to learn more about specific companies and industries. These sessions often provide insights into the hiring process and company culture.

Accessing Resume Writing and Interview Preparation Workshops:

Polish your resume and interview skills with professional guidance:

Resume Workshops: Participate in workshops to learn how to create a compelling resume that highlights your skills and experiences.

Interview Prep: Join mock interview sessions to practice answering common questions and receive feedback on your performance.

Professional Associations

Joining Professional Organizations and Student Chapters Related to Your Field:

Professional associations offer networking and learning opportunities:

Membership: Join relevant professional organizations to access resources, attend events, and network with industry professionals.

Student Chapters: Get involved with student chapters of professional organizations. These chapters often offer events, workshops, and mentoring programs tailored to students.

Participating in Association Events and Activities:

Engage actively with professional organizations:

Conferences and Seminars: Attend conferences and seminars to learn about the latest industry trends and connect with professionals.

Workshops and Webinars: Participate in workshops and webinars to develop new skills and knowledge.

Networking with Professionals and Staying Updated on Industry Trends:

Stay informed and connected:

Industry News: Follow industry publications and newsletters to stay updated on trends and developments.

Networking Events: Attend networking events to meet professionals and expand your contacts.

Online Resources

Leveraging Online Platforms for Job Searching and Networking:

Use online tools to find opportunities and connect with professionals:

Job Boards: Use job boards like LinkedIn, Indeed, and Glassdoor to search for internships and part-time jobs.

Networking Platforms: Connect with professionals and join industry groups on LinkedIn and other networking platforms.

Utilizing Online Learning Platforms for Continuous Skill Development:

Keep learning with online courses:

Learning Platforms: Websites like Coursera, Udemy, and Khan Academy offer courses on various topics. Look for courses that enhance your skills and knowledge.

Certifications: Earn certifications in your field to boost your resume and demonstrate your expertise.

Engaging with Professional Communities Through Forums and social media:

Join discussions and learn from others:

Forums: Participate in forums like Reddit and Stack Exchange to ask questions, share knowledge, and connect with peers.

Social Media: Follow industry leaders and join professional groups on social media platforms to stay engaged and informed.

Gaining work experience and utilizing professional development resources are vital steps in building a successful career. By seeking internships, part-time jobs, and volunteer opportunities, you can gain practical experience and develop valuable skills. Leveraging career services, joining professional associations, and using online resources will further enhance your career growth. Embrace these opportunities during your international program to build a strong foundation for your future career.

7.6 International Career Opportunities

The prospect of working internationally can be both exciting and daunting. It offers a unique chance to immerse yourself in different cultures, broaden your professional horizons, and develop a global perspective. In this section, we will explore how to navigate and prepare for an international career, from understanding global job markets to leveraging alumni networks.

Exploring Global Careers

Understanding the Benefits of Working Internationally:

Working abroad can significantly enhance your career in various ways:

Cultural Exposure: Experience diverse cultures, languages, and working environments, which can enrich your personal and professional life.

Career Advancement: Many multinational companies value international experience, and it can make you a more attractive candidate for leadership roles.

Network Expansion: Build a global network of contacts and friends, opening doors to opportunities worldwide.

Personal Growth: Living and working in a foreign country will challenge you to adapt and grow, developing resilience and problem-solving skills.

Researching Global Job Markets and Demand for Your Field:

Before embarking on an international career, it is crucial to understand where your skills are in demand:

Global Job Portals: Websites like LinkedIn, indeed, and Glassdoor often list international job openings. Use these platforms to research job markets.

Industry Reports: Look for industry-specific reports that detail job market trends and demand for professionals in your field.

Country-Specific Information: Research job markets in different countries. Consider factors like economic stability, industry growth, and unemployment rates.

Identifying Countries with Favorable Work Visa Policies for International Graduates:

Navigating work visas can be complex, but some countries have favorable policies for international graduates:

Research Visa Policies: Countries like Canada, Australia, and Germany often have work visa programs designed to attract skilled international graduates.

University Resources: Your host institution's career services may provide information on countries with favorable visa policies.

Government Websites: Visit government websites of the countries you are interested in to understand their visa requirements and application processes.

Preparing for an International Career

Developing Cross-Cultural Communication and Adaptability Skills:

To thrive in an international career, you must be able to communicate effectively across cultures and adapt to new environments:

Cultural Sensitivity Training: Participate in workshops or courses that focus on cross-cultural communication.

Adaptability Exercises: Engage in activities that push you out of your comfort zone, such as living in different regions or participating in diverse cultural events.

Learning Through Experience: Take every opportunity to interact with people from different backgrounds, whether through university clubs, community events, or travel.

Learning Additional Languages and Understanding Global Business Practices:

Being multilingual and understanding international business etiquette can give you a significant edge:

Language Courses: Enroll in language classes offered by your university or online platforms like Duolingo, Babbel, or Rosetta Stone.

Business Practices: Study global business practices and cultural norms. Books, webinars, and courses can provide valuable insights.

Practical Application: Practice your new language skills and business etiquette in real-world settings, such as internships or study abroad programs.

Building a Globally Competitive Resume and Cover Letter:

Tailor your resume and cover letter to appeal to international employers:

Highlight International Experience: Emphasize any international experience you have, such as study abroad, internships, or volunteer work.

Skills and Achievements: Focus on skills that are highly valued globally, such as language proficiency, cross-cultural communication, and adaptability.

Professional Format: Ensure your resume and cover letter follow the format and style preferred in the target country. Use resources like international resume guides and templates.

Alumni Networks

Connecting with Alumni from Your Host Institution and Home Country:

Alumni networks are valuable resources for career advice and job opportunities:

University Alumni Networks: Join alumni associations and participate in their events. Many universities have global chapters that can connect you with alumni in different countries.

LinkedIn: Use LinkedIn to find and connect with alumni from your host institution and home country. Reach out to them for advice and insights.

Mentorship Programs: Some alumni networks offer formal mentorship programs. Enroll in these programs to receive guidance from experienced professionals.

Leveraging Alumni Networks for Job Opportunities and Career Advice:

Tap into the wealth of knowledge and connections within alumni networks:

Informational Interviews: Conduct informational interviews with alumni working in your desired field or location. Ask about their career paths, challenges, and advice for job seekers.

Job Referrals: Alumni can often provide job referrals or alert you to job openings within their companies.

Career Guidance: Alumni can offer valuable advice on navigating the job market, preparing for interviews, and developing your career.

Anecdotes and Insights

Leveraging Alumni Networks- Lara's Story

Student Perspective: "Connecting with alumni from my host institution in France was incredibly beneficial. Through the alumni network, I met professionals who shared their experiences and offered advice. One alum even helped me secure an internship at their company. The alumni network provided a support system and valuable career opportunities." – Lara, South African International Student

Expert Insight: Alumni networks are powerful resources for career development. Engage with alumni through your university's alumni association, LinkedIn, and alumni events. Alumni can provide job leads, mentorship, and industry insights. Building and maintaining these connections can open doors and support your career growth.

Participating in Alumni Events and Mentoring Programs:

Engage actively with alumni networks to maximize your opportunities:

Alumni Events: Attend networking events, seminars, and workshops organized by alumni associations. These events are excellent opportunities to meet professionals and expand your network.

Mentoring Programs: Enroll in mentoring programs to receive personalized guidance from experienced alumni. A mentor can provide career advice, support, and valuable industry insights.

Stay Connected: Maintain regular contact with your alumni network. Share your achievements, seek advice, and offer support to others in the network.

Exploring international career opportunities can significantly enrich your professional journey. By understanding global job markets, preparing for an international career, and leveraging alumni networks, you can enhance your employability and career growth. Embrace the opportunities to work abroad, develop cross-cultural skills, and build a global network that will support your career aspirations.

Chapter 7 Conclusion

Career Development Strategies and Resources:

Throughout this chapter, we have explored a variety of strategies and resources to help you develop your career during your international program. We discussed the importance of setting clear career goals and creating a plan to achieve them. You learned about building both soft and technical skills through coursework, extracurricular activities, and hands-on experiences like internships and part-time jobs.

We also covered the essentials of networking and maintaining professional relationships. From attending career fairs to leveraging social media platforms like LinkedIn, these strategies can significantly expand your professional network. Furthermore, we emphasized the value of mentorship and how having a mentor can guide your career path and provide support.

We delved into gaining work experience through internships, part-time jobs, and volunteering, highlighting how each can enhance your resume and provide practical skills. Additionally, you discovered various professional development resources, including career services, professional associations, and online learning platforms, all designed to support your growth.

Finally, we explored international career opportunities, understanding the benefits of working abroad, preparing for an international career, and utilizing alumni networks for job opportunities and career advice.

Encouragement to Actively Pursue Career Growth During Your International Program:

Your international program is more than just an academic journey; it is a pivotal opportunity to advance your career. Actively pursue career growth by taking advantage of the numerous resources and opportunities available to you. Engage with your host institution's career services, attend networking events, and seek internships or part-time work to gain valuable experience.

Remember, building a successful career takes initiative and effort. Do not wait for opportunities to come to you – go out and find them. Participate in workshops, join professional organizations, and continuously seek ways to improve your skills. Every step you take towards your career development will pay off in the long run.

Tips for Leveraging Your International Experience for Professional Success:

- **Be Proactive**: Take charge of your career development. Identify your goals, make a plan, and take actionable steps towards achieving them.
- **Network Actively**: Build and maintain relationships with peers, professors, professionals, and alumni. Networking is key to uncovering job opportunities and gaining industry insights.

- **Gain Practical Experience**: Seek internships, part-time jobs, and volunteer opportunities. Practical experience not only enhances your resume but also provides you with valuable skills and insights.
- **Develop a Global Mindset**: Embrace the cultural diversity and unique experiences your exchange offers. Develop cross-cultural communication skills and adaptability, which are highly valued in the global job market.
- **Leverage Resources**: Utilize the resources available at your host institution and online. Attend career fairs, join professional associations, and make the most of learning platforms to continuously develop your skills.
- **Reflect and Adapt**: Regularly reflect on your experiences, learn from them, and adapt your strategies as needed. Stay flexible and open to new opportunities and challenges.

By following these tips and actively engaging in your career development, you can maximize the benefits of your international experience and set a strong foundation for your future professional success. Your journey is just beginning, and with the right mindset and strategies, you can achieve your career aspirations and make a significant impact in your chosen field.

Chapter 7 Review:

As you conclude this chapter, reflect on the key strategies and resources discussed to enhance your career development and networking during your international program. Use this review section to consolidate your understanding and prepare to apply these insights to your personal and professional growth.

Short Answer Questions:

What are the benefits of setting clear career goals during your international program?

List three strategies for developing soft skills that are essential for career success.

Why is networking important for career development, and what are two effective networking techniques?

Describe the role of mentorship in career development and provide one tip for finding a mentor.

What are the advantages of gaining work experience through internships, part-time jobs, or volunteering during your international program?

Multiple Choice Questions:

Which of the following is NOT a benefit of joining professional associations?

a) Networking with industry professionals
b) Accessing exclusive job listings
c) Guaranteed job placement
d) Staying updated on industry trends

Which platform is most commonly used for professional networking and job searching?

a) Facebook
b) Instagram
c) LinkedIn
d) Twitter

When preparing for an international career, which of the following skills is most important?

a) Technical skills only
b) Cross-cultural communication and adaptability
c) Local cuisine knowledge
d) Social media proficiency

True or False Questions:

True or False: Alumni networks can provide valuable job leads and mentorship opportunities.

True or False: It is unnecessary to tailor your resume and cover letter for different job applications.

True or False: Balancing work and study during your international program can help you develop time management skills.

Reflection Prompt:

Think about the career goals you have set for yourself. How can the experiences and opportunities during your international program help you achieve these goals? Reflect on specific actions you can take to build your professional skills, expand your network, and gain valuable work experience.

Invitation to Workbook:

To further deepen your understanding and apply the concepts from this chapter, turn to the companion "Reflective Exercises: The International Experiences Guide Workbook." This workbook provides engaging exercises and questions designed to help you internalize the content, reflect on your personal situation, and create a practical plan for your career development.

{ 8 }

Returning Home and Reintegrating

Introduction

Returning home after an international program can be as challenging and transformative as the experience of going abroad. It is crucial to plan for a smooth transition to ensure that you maximize the benefits of your time abroad and seamlessly reintegrate into your home environment. This chapter explores the importance of planning for this transition, addresses the challenges you may face, and highlights the opportunities that come with sharing and applying your international experiences.

Importance of Planning for a Smooth Transition Back Home

Transitioning back home requires thoughtful preparation. Just as you prepared to go abroad, returning home involves adjusting to familiar yet changed surroundings, reconnecting with family and friends, and reintegrating into your academic or professional life. Planning for this transition can help mitigate the reverse culture shock and make the adjustment process more manageable.

Consider setting aside time to reflect on your international experience and think about how it has changed you. What new skills and perspectives have you gained? How can these be applied to your life at home? By identifying these elements, you can create a clear plan for reintegrating into your home environment while leveraging the growth you have experienced.

Overview of Challenges and Opportunities Upon Returning

One of the main challenges students face when returning home is reverse culture shock. After adapting to a new culture and way of life, coming back to your familiar environment can feel unexpectedly alien. You might find it challenging to relate to those who have not shared your experience, and they may struggle to understand the changes you have undergone. Recognizing that these feelings are normal is the first step towards overcoming them.

On the flip side, returning home offers numerous opportunities. Your international program has likely equipped you with new skills, increased cultural awareness, and a broader worldview.

These attributes can set you apart in your academic and professional life. Use this transition period to reflect on your achievements and experiences abroad and consider how they can contribute to your future goals. Whether it is through applying for new positions, engaging in community service, or participating in alumni networks, there are many ways to harness the power of your international experience.

Encouragement to Apply and Share Your International Experiences

Your international program is a treasure trove of stories, lessons, and insights that can inspire and educate others. Sharing these experiences can reinforce your learning and help you stay connected to your host culture. Consider writing a blog, giving presentations, or participating in forums and discussion groups related to international education.

Applying the skills and knowledge you have gained is equally important. Reflect on how you can incorporate the adaptability, problem-solving skills, and cross-cultural communication abilities you have developed into your daily life. This might involve pursuing new academic interests, seeking out international career opportunities, or advocating for cultural awareness and diversity in your community.

By planning for your return, acknowledging the challenges, and seizing the opportunities, you can turn your transition into a powerful period of growth and reintegration. Embrace the changes, stay connected to your experiences, and continue to build on the foundation you have created during your time abroad.

8.1 Preparing for Departure

As your international program draws to a close, preparing for your departure is a crucial step to ensure a smooth transition back home. This period involves wrapping up academic and administrative tasks, saying goodbye to the friends and mentors you have made, and reflecting on the significant experiences you have had. By organizing these elements effectively, you can leave your host country with a sense of closure and readiness for the next chapter.

Finalizing Academic and Administrative Tasks

Completing academic requirements and final exams:

Ensure you have met all the academic requirements set by your host institution. This includes completing assignments, projects, and final exams. Check with your professors or academic advisors to confirm that all your coursework is up to date.

If you have any pending academic obligations, create a timeline to manage your study schedule and complete everything on time. Staying organized will help you avoid last-minute stress and ensure that you leave on a high note.

Returning library books and settling any outstanding fees:

Return all borrowed library books and materials before your departure. Libraries often have strict return policies, and any overlooked items can result in fines or holds on your student account.

Check for any outstanding fees or balances with the university, including tuition, housing, or miscellaneous charges. Settling these accounts promptly will prevent any issues with receiving your transcripts or other important documents.

Requesting transcripts and other academic documents:

Request your transcripts and any other necessary academic documents from your host institution. Make sure these documents are sent to both your home university and any future academic or professional institutions that may require them.

It is also wise to obtain extra copies for your personal records. These documents serve as a testament to your academic achievements abroad and may be needed for future applications or verifications.

Anecdotes and Insights

Finalizing Academic and Administrative Tasks- Sarah's Story

Student Perspective: "When I was nearing the end of my exchange in Germany, I realized there were several academic and administrative tasks I needed to complete. I had to return all library books, pay any outstanding fees, and ensure my transcript was sent to my home university. It felt overwhelming at first, but making a checklist really helped. I also scheduled meetings with my professors to discuss my final projects and exams. This proactive approach ensured I left on a positive note and with all my paperwork in order." – Sarah, German International Student

Expert Insight: Creating a detailed checklist of academic and administrative tasks before your departure can streamline the process and prevent last-minute stress. Schedule meetings with professors and academic advisors well in advance to address any outstanding issues. Ensure all borrowed materials are returned, and financial obligations are settled. Request your transcript early to avoid delays. Staying organized and proactive will make your departure smoother and ensure you leave with everything in order.

Saying Goodbye

Planning farewell events with friends, professors, and mentors:

Organize farewell events to celebrate and acknowledge the relationships you have built during your international journey. Whether it is a small gathering with close friends or a larger event with classmates and professors, these farewells provide a meaningful way to conclude your time abroad.

Use these gatherings to express your gratitude and appreciation for the support and friendship you have received. Farewell events are an opportunity to create lasting memories and leave a positive impression on those you have met.

Collecting contact information for future correspondence:

Ensure you exchange contact information with friends, professors, and mentors. Collecting email addresses, phone numbers, and social media handles will help you stay in touch and maintain these valuable connections.

Consider creating a digital address book or a shared document where everyone can input their contact details. This will make it easier to keep track of your network and continue communication once you return home.

Anecdotes and Insights
Saying Goodbye- Ken's Story

Student Perspective: "Saying goodbye to the friends I made in Japan was one of the hardest parts of my exchange. To make it memorable, we organized a small farewell party. We shared our favorite memories, exchanged contact information, and made promises to stay in touch. It was emotional, but it also provided closure. We created a group chat to stay connected, and it has been wonderful to see everyone's updates and maintain those friendships." – Ken, Japanese International Student

Expert Insight: Organizing farewell events can provide a sense of closure and celebration of the relationships you have built. Collect contact information and consider creating group chats or social media groups to stay connected. Reflecting on shared experiences and expressing gratitude can make goodbyes more meaningful and strengthen your ongoing connections. Remember, these friendships can continue to grow and provide support even after you return home.

Reflecting on your experiences and accomplishments:

Take some time to reflect on your international experience. Think about the challenges you overcame, the skills you developed, and the personal growth you experienced. Journaling or creating a scrapbook can be a rewarding way to capture these reflections.

Celebrate your accomplishments and recognize the hard work and dedication that went into making your international experience a success. Reflecting on your journey will help you appreciate the impact it has had on your personal and academic development.

By diligently finalizing your academic and administrative tasks, thoughtfully saying goodbye, and reflecting on your experiences, you can ensure a smooth and meaningful transition as you prepare to leave your host country. This preparation not only provides a sense of closure but also sets a positive tone for your return home, allowing you to carry forward the lessons and memories from your international program.

8.2 Reverse Culture Shock

Returning home after an extended period abroad can be an emotionally complex experience. While you might expect to feel a sense of relief and comfort in returning to familiar surroundings, many students face a phenomenon known as reverse culture shock. We will dive into understanding reverse culture shock, recognizing its symptoms, and discovering effective coping strategies to ease your transition back home.

Understanding Reverse Culture Shock

Defining reverse culture shock and its symptoms:

Reverse culture shock is the disorientation and discomfort you may feel upon returning to your home country after spending a significant amount of time abroad. Think of it as the flip side of the initial culture shock you experienced when you first arrived in your host country. It is like adjusting to a new environment all over again, but this time, it is your own home that feels unfamiliar.

Common symptoms include feelings of restlessness, frustration, alienation, and sadness. You might also experience a sense of loss or nostalgia for your host country and the lifestyle you adapted to there. It can be surprising to feel out of place in a setting that once felt completely natural.

Comparing it to initial culture shock experienced upon arrival:

Like initial culture shock, reverse culture shock involves adjusting to a new environment – in this case, your home environment, which now feels different. The familiarity of your surroundings can make these feelings even more unsettling because you expect to feel at home but find it challenging to readjust.

The phases of reverse culture shock mirror those of initial culture shock: an initial period of excitement to be home, followed by frustration and discomfort, and eventually leading to re-adjustment and reintegration. It is like a rollercoaster of emotions but knowing this can help you navigate the ups and downs.

Recognizing common challenges in readjusting to home culture:

You may find that friends and family are not as interested in your experiences abroad as you hoped. This can lead to feelings of isolation or being misunderstood. It can be frustrating when you are eager to share your stories, but others do not seem to share the same enthusiasm.

Daily routines, social norms, and even food and weather might seem strangely foreign or disappointing compared to what you became accustomed to abroad. It is almost as if you have developed a new normal and fitting back into the old one feels awkward.

There may be a sense of anticlimax or lack of direction as the excitement of new experiences is replaced by routine. The buzz of daily discoveries is replaced by the familiarity of old habits, and this can feel a bit like a letdown.

Anecdotes and Insights
Understanding Reverse Culture Shock- Alex's Story

Student Perspective: "Coming back home to the U.S. after a year in Spain was surprisingly difficult. I experienced reverse culture shock – everything felt familiar yet different. I missed the daily interactions and pace of life in Spain. It took time to readjust. Talking to friends who had similar experiences and being patient with myself really helped. I also found it helpful to stay engaged with Spanish culture, like cooking Spanish dishes and attending local cultural events." – Alex, Spanish International Student

Expert Insight: Reverse culture shock is a common experience for returning international students. It is important to recognize that it is a normal part of the re-entry process. Stay patient with yourself and seek support from friends, family, or fellow returnees who understand what you are going through. Engaging with aspects of your host culture, such as food, music, or language, can help ease the transition. Reflect on your growth and give yourself time to readjust.

Coping Strategies

Preparing mentally and emotionally for the transition:

Acknowledge that reverse culture shock is a normal part of the re-entry process. Understanding that these feelings are common can help you be more patient with yourself. Just as you allowed yourself time to adapt to a new culture, give yourself permission to readjust to your home environment.

Reflect on your time abroad and the changes you have experienced. Writing in a journal or talking with someone who has also studied abroad can help process these emotions and provide a sense of closure. This reflection can be incredibly grounding.

Keeping an open mind and staying patient with the process:

Give yourself time to readjust and be patient with the process. Just as it took time to adapt to a new culture abroad, it will take time to reintegrate into your home culture. Expecting instant comfort might set you up for frustration.

Maintain an open mind and embrace the changes in both your home environment and yourself. Recognize that both have evolved during your time away. This can be a period of rediscovery, both of your home and of yourself.

Seeking support from family, friends, and fellow returnees:

Share your experiences and feelings with friends and family but be prepared for varying levels of interest. Seek out fellow returnees or alumni who understand what you are going through. Their support and shared experiences can be invaluable. Sometimes, just knowing someone else gets it can make all the difference.

Engage in activities and groups that connect you with others who have studied abroad. Many universities offer re-entry programs or support groups that can help you navigate this transition. These groups can offer a sense of community and belonging.

Do not hesitate to seek professional help if you find that reverse culture shock is significantly impacting your well-being. Counselors and mental health professionals can provide strategies and support to help you cope. There is no shame in reaching out for help when you need it.

By understanding reverse culture shock and employing effective coping strategies, you can make your transition back home smoother and more manageable. Embrace the process as part of your overall growth from your international experience. The insights and resilience you gain will not only help you readjust but also enrich your future endeavors. Remember, the end of your international program is just the beginning of another exciting chapter in your life.

8.3 Reflecting on Your Experience

Reflecting on your international experience is a vital part of your journey. It allows you to assess your growth, document your achievements, and prepare to apply what you have learned in meaningful ways. This reflection will not only help you appreciate the value of your experience but also guide you in leveraging it for future success.

Self-Reflection

Assessing Personal Growth and Development During the International Experience:

Take some time to think about how you have changed since you first arrived in your host country. Consider the new perspectives you have gained, the skills you have developed, and the challenges you have overcome. How have these experiences shaped you as a person? Reflect on moments when you stepped out of your comfort zone and grew as a result.

Maybe you learned to navigate a new city, communicate in a different language, or adapt to unfamiliar cultural norms. Each of these experiences contributes to your personal growth and builds resilience.

Identifying New Skills, Knowledge, and Perspectives Gained:

Make a list of the skills and knowledge you acquired during your international journey. This could include language proficiency, cultural understanding, problem-solving abilities, and more. Think about how these new attributes can be applied in different areas of your life, both personally and professionally.

Did you pick up new study techniques or develop a stronger work ethic? These are valuable skills that can benefit you long after your international program ends.

Reflecting on Challenges Overcome and Lessons Learned:

Consider the difficulties you faced during your international adventures and how you managed to overcome them. What strategies did you use to navigate these challenges? Reflecting on these experiences can provide valuable lessons that will help you handle future obstacles with confidence and resilience.

Think about a particularly tough moment – maybe it was a cultural misunderstanding or a challenging academic project. How did you overcome it? What did you learn from the experience? These reflections can offer deep insights and prepare you for future challenges.

Documenting Your Journey

Keeping a Journal or Blog to Capture Your Experiences and Memories:

Maintaining a journal or blog is a great way to document your journey. Write about your daily experiences, significant moments, and personal reflections. This not only creates a keepsake of your time abroad but also helps you process and understand your experiences more deeply.

You do not have to be a professional writer to keep a journal. Just jot down your thoughts and feelings honestly. Over time, you will have a rich record of your international experiences that you can look back on and share with others.

Anecdotes and Insights

Reflecting on Your Experience- Emma's Story

Student Perspective: "One of the most rewarding parts of my exchange in Australia was reflecting on the personal growth I experienced. I kept a journal throughout my time there, documenting challenges, achievements, and memorable moments. Looking back at my entries after returning home, I could see how much I had changed and grown. This reflection helped me appreciate the journey and reinforced the skills and perspectives I gained." – Emma, Australian International Student

Expert Insight: Journaling is an excellent way to document your international experience and reflect on your personal growth. Reviewing your entries can provide valuable insights into your development and highlight the challenges you overcame. This reflection can reinforce the skills and perspectives you have gained, helping you integrate them into your future endeavors. Consider sharing your experiences through presentations or writing to inspire others and solidify your learning.

Creating a Portfolio of Academic and Extracurricular Achievements:

Compile a portfolio that showcases your academic and extracurricular accomplishments during your international program. Include projects, essays, photos, and any other evidence of your achievements. This portfolio can be a valuable resource for future academic or job applications.

Your portfolio is not just about what you did, but what you learned and how you grew. Be sure to highlight these aspects to show the full impact of your international experience.

Sharing Your Story Through Presentations, Articles, or social media:

Share your international story with others. Consider giving presentations at your home university, writing articles for student publications, or posting on social media. Sharing your experiences can inspire others and reinforce the value of your journey.

Do not be shy about sharing both the highs and the lows. Authentic stories resonate the most and can offer valuable lessons to others considering a similar path.

8.4 Applying Your International Experience

The skills and insights gained during your international program are powerful tools that can enhance your academic, professional, and personal life. Applying these experiences thoughtfully will help you stand out and succeed in various contexts.

Academic Applications

Leveraging your international experience in future academic pursuits:

Use your international experience to enrich your academic endeavors. Incorporate the knowledge and perspectives you gained into your coursework, discussions, and research. This will demonstrate your global awareness and critical thinking skills.

For example, if you studied environmental science abroad, bring those global perspectives into your projects and papers. How does environmental policy differ in your host country compared to your home country? Use your insights to deepen your academic work.

Enhancing your resume and academic profile with international experience:

Highlight your international experience on your resume and academic profile. Emphasize the skills and knowledge you acquired, such as language proficiency, cultural competence, and adaptability. These attributes are highly valued in academic and professional settings.

Be specific about what you did and learned. Instead of simply stating you studied abroad, mention specific projects, courses, and any accolades you received.

Using your experience in graduate school applications and research projects:

When applying to graduate school or proposing research projects, emphasize how your international experience has prepared you for advanced study. Discuss specific examples of how your time abroad has influenced your academic interests and goals.

Admissions committees love to see candidates who have taken initiative and expanded their horizons. Your international experience can set you apart as a proactive and globally minded applicant.

Professional Applications

Highlighting Your International Experience in Job Applications and Interviews:

In job applications and interviews, clearly articulate the value of your international experience. Explain how the skills and perspectives you gained make you a strong candidate. Use specific examples to illustrate your points and demonstrate your intercultural competence.

For instance, if you managed a team project while abroad, talk about how you navigated different working styles and cultural expectations. This shows your ability to adapt and lead in diverse environments.

Demonstrating Intercultural Competence and Adaptability to Employers:

Employers value candidates who can thrive in diverse environments. Showcase your ability to work effectively with people from different backgrounds, adapt to new situations, and solve problems creatively. These qualities are increasingly important in today's globalized workforce.

Mention any cross-cultural collaborations or initiatives you were involved in. Highlighting these experiences can demonstrate your ability to bring unique perspectives and solutions to the table.

Applying New Skills and Perspectives to Your Career Field:

Think about how the skills and knowledge you gained during your international journey can be applied to your career. Whether it is improved language skills, a deeper understanding of global markets, or enhanced problem-solving abilities, these attributes can give you a competitive edge.

Reflect on how your international experience has broadened your thinking and approach to your field. Use this expanded perspective to drive innovation and improvement in your professional life.

Anecdotes and Insights
Applying Your International Experience- Lucas' Story
Student Perspective: "During job interviews after my exchange in France, I made sure to highlight the skills I gained abroad. I talked about my adaptability, language skills, and cultural competence. Employers were impressed by my international experience and how I could bring a global perspective to the workplace. It definitely gave me an edge in the job market, and I secured a position at a multinational company." – Lucas, French International Student

Expert Insight: Your international experience is a valuable asset in the job market. Highlight the skills and perspectives you gained abroad, such as adaptability, intercultural communication, and problem-solving. Employers value candidates who can bring a global perspective and demonstrate cultural competence. Prepare specific examples of how your international experience has prepared you for professional challenges. This can significantly enhance your resume and interview performance.

Personal Applications

Integrating new habits and practices into your daily life:

Incorporate the positive habits and practices you developed during your international experience into your daily routine. This might include new approaches to time management, healthier eating habits, or regular exercise routines. These changes can enhance your overall well-being and productivity.

Perhaps you adopted a habit of taking daily walks or discovered a new favorite cuisine. Keep these positive changes going to maintain the benefits of your international experience.

Maintaining international friendships and networks:

Stay connected with the friends and networks you built during your international adventure. These relationships can provide ongoing support, opportunities for collaboration, and insights into different cultures. Use social media, email, and travel to maintain these connections.

Regular check-ins and visits can keep these relationships strong. These international friendships can also open doors for future travels and professional opportunities.

Continuing cultural engagement and learning:

Keep exploring and learning about different cultures. Attend cultural events, read books, watch films, and engage with diverse communities. Continuing your cultural engagement will enrich your life and keep the spirit of your international experience alive.

Join cultural clubs or language exchange groups in your home country. These activities can help you stay connected to the global perspectives you gained and continue your journey of cultural discovery.

By reflecting on your international experience and thoughtfully applying what you have learned, you can maximize the benefits of your time abroad. Embrace the changes and opportunities that come with returning home and let your international experience continue to shape your future in meaningful ways.

8.5 Staying Connected

One of the most rewarding aspects of an international program is the relationships you build and the connections you make. Staying connected with these international relationships and engaging with the global community can continue to enrich your life long after you have returned home. This section will provide strategies for maintaining those connections and staying involved with the global community.

Maintaining International Relationships

Keeping in touch with friends, mentors, and host families:

The friendships and connections you made during your international journey are invaluable. To maintain these relationships, make a conscious effort to stay in touch. Regular communication, even if it is just a quick message or video call, can help keep your relationships strong. Share updates about your life, ask about theirs, and keep the dialogue open.

Remember special occasions like birthdays and holidays. A simple gesture like sending a card, a thoughtful gift, or even a heartfelt message can go a long way in showing that you value and remember them. This personal touch helps sustain the emotional connection you built.

Your host family likely played a significant role in your international experience. Keep them updated on your life and let them know how much their support meant to you. This will help maintain a warm and lasting bond. Consider inviting them to visit your home country or plan a return visit to theirs.

Utilizing social media and Communication Apps to Stay Connected:

Social media platforms like Facebook, Instagram, and LinkedIn are great tools for keeping in touch with your international friends. Share updates, photos, and milestones to keep them informed about your life and stay updated on theirs. Commenting on their posts and engaging with their content shows that you still care about their lives.

Communication apps such as WhatsApp, Skype, and Zoom make it easy to have real-time conversations with your friends and mentors abroad. Schedule regular catchups to maintain those connections. Video calls can be especially meaningful, as they allow for more personal interaction.

Create group chats or online groups with fellow international students. This can be a fun way to reminisce about your shared experiences and support each other as you transition back to life at home. Sharing memories, photos, and future plans can help keep the group bonded.

Planning future visits or reunions:

If possible, plan future visits or reunions with your international friends. Having something to look forward to can help keep the connection alive and give you the opportunity to experience their culture more deeply. Plan these visits well in advance to ensure they fit into everyone's schedules.

Consider inviting your international friends to visit you in your home country. Hosting them can be a great way to share your culture and create new memories together. This reciprocal exchange can deepen your understanding of each other's backgrounds.

If visiting in person is not feasible, consider virtual reunions. Organize online meetups where you can all catch up and relive your international memories. Virtual game nights, movie watch parties, or themed discussion sessions can be great ways to stay connected and have fun together.

Engaging with the Global Community

Participating in alumni networks and international associations:

Join alumni networks and international associations related to your international program. These organizations often offer events, resources, and networking opportunities that can help you stay connected to the global community. Look for local chapters or virtual events to participate in.

Attend alumni gatherings and reunions. These events are excellent opportunities to reconnect with fellow international students and expand your professional network. They can also be a great source of inspiration and motivation as you hear about others' post-international journeys.

Volunteer to mentor new international students. Sharing your experiences and providing guidance can be incredibly rewarding and helps maintain your connection to the international community. Your insights can be invaluable to students who are just beginning their own international adventures.

Anecdotes and Insights
Staying Connected- Maria's Story

Student Perspective: "After returning from my exchange in Brazil, I made a conscious effort to stay connected with my friends and mentors there. We regularly catch up via video calls and social media. I also joined an alumni network, which has been a fantastic way to stay engaged with the global community. These connections have been invaluable, providing both personal support and professional opportunities." – Maria, Brazilian International Student

Expert Insight: Maintaining international connections is essential for both personal and professional growth. Utilize social media and communication apps to stay in touch with friends and mentors from your host country. Joining alumni networks and international associations can provide ongoing support and open doors to new opportunities. Regular communication and engagement with the global community can enrich your life and keep the spirit of your international adventure alive.

Attending Global Conferences and Cultural Events:

Look for global conferences, seminars, and cultural events related to your field of study or interests. These events provide opportunities to meet people from around the world, share ideas, and stay updated on global trends. They also offer a platform to showcase your own experiences and insights.

Attend cultural festivals and events in your home country that celebrate international traditions. This can help you stay connected to the cultures you experienced abroad and meet others with similar interests. Participating in these events can keep the excitement and curiosity of your international experience alive.

Participate in webinars and virtual conferences. Many organizations offer online events that make it easier to engage with the global community without the need for travel. These virtual platforms can be just as enriching and offer opportunities for networking and learning.

Joining Online Communities and Forums Related to Your Interests:

Online communities and forums are excellent platforms for staying connected with people who share your interests. Whether it is a professional network, a hobby group, or a cultural forum, these spaces provide a sense of belonging and continuous learning.

Engage actively in these communities by contributing to discussions, sharing resources, and offering support to others. This active participation can lead to meaningful connections and opportunities. It also helps you stay informed and engaged with the latest trends and developments in your areas of interest.

Use platforms like Reddit, Quora, and specialized forums to connect with people from around the world. These platforms offer diverse perspectives and can help you stay globally engaged. Participate in discussions, ask questions, and share your own experiences to enrich the community.

Staying connected with the people and communities you encountered during your international program can greatly enrich your post-exchange life. These relationships and networks provide ongoing support, opportunities, and a continuous connection to the global community. By maintaining these connections, you keep the spirit of your international experience alive and continue to grow from the lessons and experiences you gained abroad. Embrace these relationships as part of your lifelong journey of cultural discovery and global engagement.

8.6 Future Opportunities

Your international experience opens a world of opportunities for further education, international careers, and global citizenship. Leveraging the skills, networks, and perspectives you gained can lead to enriching future endeavors that continue to expand your horizons. This section will explore various paths you can take to build on your international experience.

Further Education Abroad

Exploring options for further studies in your host country or other international locations:

If you enjoyed your international experience, consider pursuing further studies in your host country or exploring other international education opportunities. Look into universities that offer programs in your field of interest and evaluate their academic reputation, faculty, and resources.

Many universities have strong international student support systems, including dedicated offices, counseling services, and cultural integration programs. These resources can help make your continued education abroad a positive and enriching experience.

Additionally, studying in a different educational system can expose you to new teaching methodologies, research opportunities, and academic networks, further broadening your academic and professional outlook.

Applying for Scholarships and Grants for International Education:

There are numerous scholarships and grants available for students wishing to study abroad. Research organizations, foundations, and universities that offer financial support for international students. Applying for these can significantly reduce the financial burden and make studying abroad more accessible.

Websites like ScholarshipPortal, DAAD (German Academic Exchange Service), and Fulbright offer extensive databases of funding opportunities. Start your search early to meet application deadlines and requirements.

Reach out to advisors and mentors for guidance on crafting compelling scholarship applications. Highlight your international experience, academic achievements, and future aspirations to strengthen your candidacy.

Considering International Programs for Graduate Studies:

Many universities offer international programs specifically for graduate students. These programs can provide unique opportunities to conduct research, gain advanced knowledge, and build international networks. Look for programs that align with your academic and professional goals.

Participating in a graduate international program can also enhance your resume, demonstrating your commitment to international collaboration and advanced study in your field.

Research the specific benefits and requirements of graduate international programs. Consider factors such as duration, academic focus, funding options, and the potential for professional development and networking.

International Careers

Pursuing job opportunities abroad or with multinational companies:

Your international experience has equipped you with valuable intercultural skills that are highly sought after by employers. Consider pursuing job opportunities abroad or with multinational companies that value global experience. Research job markets in countries of interest and identify industries that align with your skills and career goals.

Websites like LinkedIn, Glassdoor, and Indeed have international job listings. Tailor your resume to highlight your international experience, language skills, and cultural competencies.

Attend international job fairs and career events. These platforms provide direct access to recruiters from global companies and offer insights into the qualifications and experiences they seek.

Networking with professionals in your field globally:

Networking is crucial for career development, especially in a global context. Attend international conferences, join professional associations, and participate in webinars to connect with professionals in your field worldwide. These connections can lead to job opportunities, collaborations, and mentorship.

Utilize social media platforms like LinkedIn to build and maintain your professional network. Engage with industry leaders, participate in discussions, and share your insights to establish your presence in the global professional community.

Join online forums, attend virtual meetups, and participate in professional development workshops. These activities can help you stay informed about industry trends and connect with potential collaborators and mentors.

Preparing for long-term international assignments or relocations:

If you are interested in long-term international assignments or relocations, start preparing early. Research visa requirements, work permits, and the cultural landscape of potential host countries. Understanding these aspects will help you transition smoothly and adapt to a new environment.

Seek advice from professionals who have experience working abroad. They can provide valuable insights and tips on navigating the challenges and maximizing the opportunities of international assignments.

Consider language training, cultural orientation programs, and cross-cultural communication courses to enhance your readiness for living and working in a new country.

Volunteering and Global Citizenship

Engaging in international volunteer programs and initiatives:

Volunteering internationally is a great way to give back, gain new experiences, and continue your global engagement. Look for programs that align with your interests and skills. Organizations like Peace Corps, UN Volunteers, and Habitat for Humanity offer a range of opportunities.

Volunteering can also help you build a global network of like-minded individuals and organizations, further enhancing your personal and professional growth.

Reflect on your international experience to identify causes and communities you feel passionate about supporting. Volunteering in these areas can provide a deeper connection and a sense of purpose.

Promoting Global Awareness and Cultural Understanding in Your Community:

Share your international experiences to promote global awareness and cultural understanding within your local community. Give presentations at schools, community centers, or local organizations. Your stories and insights can inspire others to explore international opportunities and foster a more inclusive and globally minded community.

Organize cultural events, language exchange programs, or international food festivals to celebrate diversity and encourage cultural exchange. These activities can help bridge cultural gaps and build stronger community connections.

Collaborate with local cultural institutions, embassies, or international student organizations to create impactful events and initiatives that highlight global diversity and foster mutual understanding.

Becoming an Ambassador for International Programs and International Education:

Use your experience to advocate for international programs and international education. Volunteer to speak at information sessions, participate in mentorship programs, or join alumni associations. Your firsthand experience and enthusiasm can motivate others to pursue their own international adventures.

Stay involved with the international organizations that facilitated your experience. Your on-going support and involvement can help improve these programs and expand their reach to more students.

Consider writing articles, blog posts, or social media content that highlights the benefits of international programs. Sharing your journey can reach a wider audience and encourage more students to consider studying abroad.

By exploring these future opportunities, you can continue to build on the foundation of your international experience. Whether through further education, international careers, or global citizenship, these paths offer ways to deepen your understanding of the world, contribute to global communities, and achieve personal and professional growth. Embrace these opportunities and let your international experience guide you towards a future full of possibility and discovery.

Chapter 8 Conclusion

Key Points for a Successful Return and Reintegration

Returning home after an enriching international experience can be both exciting and challenging. It is essential to plan and prepare for this transition to ensure a smooth reintegration. Here is a detailed recap of the key points to remember:

Finalizing Academic and Administrative Tasks:

Ensure all academic requirements are completed, such as final exams, projects, and presentations. Do not leave any loose ends that could affect your grades or academic standing.

Return all borrowed materials, including library books and lab equipment. Clearing your records can prevent any future complications.

Settle any outstanding fees or fines to avoid holds on your account that could delay transcript requests or graduation.

Request transcripts and other necessary academic documents. These are crucial for your future educational or career pursuits. Make sure to have both physical and digital copies for your records.

Saying Goodbye:

Organize farewell events to bid adieu to friends, mentors, and host families. This is a great way to show appreciation and celebrate the relationships you have built.

Collect contact information, including social media handles, email addresses, and phone numbers. Keeping these connections alive can be beneficial both personally and professionally.

Reflect on your experiences and the growth you have achieved during your international journey. Take time to appreciate how far you have come and document these reflections through journaling or creating a photo album.

Understanding and Managing Reverse Culture Shock:

Be aware that returning home can trigger reverse culture shock, similar to what you may have experienced upon arrival in your host country. This can include feelings of disorientation, frustration, and even sadness.

Prepare mentally and emotionally for the transition. Understand that it is a normal part of the re-entry process.

Keep an open mind and stay patient with the process. Allow yourself time to readjust and do not rush the transition.

Seek support from family, friends, and fellow returnees. Sharing your experiences and feelings can provide comfort and insight.

Reflecting on Your Experience:

Assess your personal growth and development during the international program. Identify specific skills, knowledge, and perspectives you have gained.

Reflect on challenges you have overcome, and the lessons learned. This can help you appreciate your resilience and adaptability.

Document your journey through journals, blogs, or video diaries. These records can serve as a valuable reference for your future endeavors and a way to share your story with others.

Create a portfolio of academic and extracurricular achievements. Highlight significant projects, papers, and activities that showcase your experience.

Share your story through presentations, articles, or social media. Your insights can inspire others and contribute to the broader discourse on international education.

Applying Your International Experience:

Leverage your international experience in academic and professional contexts. Highlight your international experience in resumes, job applications, and interviews to demonstrate your intercultural competence and adaptability.

Use your experience to enhance your resume and academic profile. Highlight specific projects, skills, and accomplishments that are directly related to your time abroad.

Apply new skills and perspectives to your career field. Whether it is problem-solving techniques, language skills, or cultural insights, these can set you apart in your professional life.

Integrate new habits and practices into your daily life. Whether it is a new approach to studying, a fitness routine, or a culinary skill, continue to benefit from the habits you developed abroad.

Maintain international friendships and networks. These connections can provide ongoing support, opportunities, and a continuous connection to the global community.

Continue cultural engagement and learning. Stay curious and open to new experiences, even within your own country.

Staying Connected:

Maintain relationships with international friends, mentors, and host families. Regular communication and visits can keep these bonds strong.

Engage with the global community through alumni networks, international associations, and online forums. Participate in global events and continue your cultural engagement.

Join alumni networks and international associations related to your international program. These organizations often offer events, resources, and networking opportunities that can help you stay connected to the global community.

Attend alumni gatherings and reunions. These events are excellent opportunities to reconnect with fellow international students and expand your professional network. They can also be a great source of inspiration and motivation as you hear about others' post-exchange journeys.

Volunteer to mentor new international students. Sharing your experiences and providing guidance can be incredibly rewarding and helps maintain your connection to the international community. Your insights can be invaluable to students who are just beginning their own international adventures.

Exploring Future Opportunities:

Consider further education abroad, pursuing international careers, and engaging in global volunteer programs. Use your international experience as a foundation for continued personal and professional growth.

Research universities that offer programs in your field of interest and evaluate their academic reputation, faculty, and resources.

Apply for scholarships and grants for international education. There are numerous scholarships and grants available for students wishing to study abroad. Research organizations, foundations, and universities that offer financial support for international students. Applying for these can significantly reduce the financial burden and make studying abroad more accessible.

Join online forums, attend virtual meetups, and participate in professional development workshops. These activities can help you stay informed about industry trends and connect with potential collaborators and mentors.

Encouragement to Leverage Your International Experience for Future Growth

Your international experience is a significant milestone in your academic, professional, and personal development. Embrace the lessons learned and the relationships formed during your time abroad. These experiences have equipped you with unique skills and perspectives that will benefit you in various aspects of your life.

Embrace Continuous Learning: The journey of learning does not end with your return home. Continue to seek out opportunities for growth, whether through further education, professional development, or personal exploration.

Apply Global Perspectives: Use the intercultural insights and adaptability skills you have gained to navigate and excel in diverse environments. Your ability to understand and bridge cultural differences is an asset in today's interconnected world.

Network and Collaborate: Leverage the global network you have built. Collaborate on international projects, seek mentorship, and stay engaged with the global community. These connections can open doors to exciting opportunities and foster lifelong friendships.

Tips for Staying Connected and Continuing Your International Journey

- **Stay Engaged:** Keep in touch with your international network through regular communication and visits. Engage with global communities and participate in events that celebrate cultural diversity. This ongoing engagement will enrich your life and keep the spirit of your international adventure alive.
- **Share Your Experience:** Inspire others by sharing your international journey. Whether through presentations, writing, or social media, your story can encourage others to embark on their own international adventures. Sharing your experiences not only helps others but also reinforces your learning and reflections.
- **Plan for the Future:** Consider how you can continue your international journey. Whether through further studies, a career abroad, or volunteering, explore options that allow you to build on your international experience. Look for opportunities that align with your passions and goals, and do not be afraid to take bold steps toward new horizons.

Returning home marks the beginning of a new chapter in your international journey. By staying connected, leveraging your experiences, and continuously seeking growth opportunities, you can ensure that your international program remains a transformative part of your life. Embrace the future with the confidence and skills you have gained and continue to make a positive impact on the world around you. Remember, your international experience is not just a past event but a foundation for a lifelong journey of discovery and global engagement.

Chapter 8 Review:

Key Points
Preparing for Departure:
Finalize academic and administrative tasks.
Plan meaningful farewells and gather contact information.
Understanding Reverse Culture Shock:
Recognize symptoms and prepare for emotional challenges.
Utilize coping strategies and seek support.
Reflecting on Your Experience:
Engage in self-reflection and document your journey.
Share your experiences through various platforms.
Applying Your International Experience:
Leverage your international experience in academic and professional settings.
Highlight new skills and perspectives in resumes and interviews.
Staying Connected:
Maintain relationships with international contacts.
Engage in global communities and alumni networks.
Future Opportunities:
Explore further education abroad and international career options.
Participate in volunteer programs and promote global awareness.

Review Questions

Short Answer:

What are three key academic and administrative tasks you should complete before departing your host country?

Define reverse culture shock and list two common symptoms.

How can maintaining a journal or blog help you reflect on your international experience?

Multiple Choice:

Which of the following is a strategy for coping with reverse culture shock?

a) Isolating yourself from friends and family
b) Staying engaged with hobbies and interests from your host country
c) Ignoring the feelings and hoping they go away
d)Moving to a new city immediately

What is one way to apply your international experience in a professional setting?

A) Forgetting about it and moving on
B) Highlighting new skills in your resume and interviews
C) Only talking about it with friends
D) Refusing to discuss it in any job application

True/False:

True or False: Joining alumni networks can help you stay connected and explore new opportunities globally.

True or False: Reverse culture shock is less impactful than initial culture shock and does not require any coping strategies.

Reflective Questions:

Reflect on a specific challenge you overcame during your international journey. How has this experience prepared you for future academic or professional challenges?

Describe how you plan to stay connected with the friends and mentors you met during your international adventure. What steps will you take to maintain these relationships?

Invitation to Reflective Exercises

To further deepen your understanding and apply the concepts discussed in this chapter, we invite you to engage with the companion "Reflective Exercises: The International Experiences Guide Workbook." This workbook provides additional exercises and questions designed to help you reflect on your experiences, set actionable goals, and continue your journey of growth and learning.

{ 9 }

Conclusion: Embracing the Journey

Introduction

As we reach the conclusion of this comprehensive guide for international experiences, it is time to reflect on the journey you have taken through these pages. The path from preparing for your departure to returning home and reintegrating into your own culture is filled with challenges, growth, and profound experiences. This book has aimed to provide you with the knowledge, tools, and insights needed to navigate this journey successfully and make the most of your international experience.

Reflecting on the Journey

From the initial excitement of applying for an international program to the complex emotions of reverse culture shock upon returning home, each chapter has been designed to address specific stages and aspects of your international journey. You have learned how to prepare effectively, adapt to a new cultural environment, achieve academic success, and maintain your health and wellbeing. Additionally, the guide has provided strategies for career development, networking, and leveraging your international experience for future opportunities.

Each section of this book has been crafted to offer practical advice, real-life anecdotes, and actionable insights. The aim has been to equip you with a robust framework to support your journey, ensuring you are well-prepared to face challenges and seize opportunities. Reflecting on the content covered, consider how each chapter has contributed to your overall understanding and preparedness for an international adventure and program.

Acknowledging the Transformative Nature of the International Experience

An international experience is more than just an academic endeavor; it is a life-changing experience that shapes your worldview, enhances your personal and professional skills, and fosters lasting global connections. The transformative nature of this journey cannot be overstated. You have likely encountered diverse cultures, languages, and perspectives that have broadened your understanding of the world and your place in it.

Through these experiences, you have developed resilience, adaptability, and a greater appreciation for cultural diversity. These qualities will serve you well in both your personal and professional life. Embracing the changes within yourself and recognizing the growth you have undergone is crucial. Each challenge overcome, and each lesson learned contributes to the person you have become.

Encouragement to Embrace the Lessons Learned and the Growth Achieved

As you conclude your international journey, remember that the lessons learned, and the growth achieved are invaluable. Embrace these experiences as integral parts of your personal and professional development. The skills and insights gained during your time abroad will continue to benefit you long after your international program ends.

Take pride in your accomplishments and be open to sharing your experiences with others. Whether through storytelling, mentoring future international students, or engaging in global initiatives, your journey has the potential to inspire and impact others. Continue to seek opportunities for growth and learning, both locally and internationally.

In embracing the journey, you acknowledge the full spectrum of experiences – the highs and lows, the challenges, and triumphs. This holistic approach will not only enrich your life but also contribute positively to the global community. As you move forward, carry the spirit of curiosity, resilience, and cultural appreciation with you, and let these guide you in all your future endeavors.

Final Thoughts

Your journey as an international student is a remarkable chapter in your life. It is a testament to your courage, adaptability, and willingness to explore the unknown. As you reflect on your experiences and the knowledge gained, remember that this is just the beginning. The world is full of opportunities waiting to be discovered.

Embrace the journey, cherish the memories, and continue to grow. Your international experience is a powerful foundation upon which you can build a future filled with endless possibilities. Thank you for embarking on this journey with us, and we wish you all the best in your future adventures.

Key Themes

Preparation and Planning

Importance of Thorough Preparation for a Successful International Experience:

Your international journey starts long before you set foot in a new country. Thorough preparation is the foundation for a smooth and successful experience. It involves meticulous planning and an understanding of all necessary steps to ensure you are ready for the adventure ahead.

Key Steps in Travel Arrangements, Visas, and Financial Planning:

Travel Arrangements: Book your flights early to get the best deals and ensure you have all necessary documentation, such as your passport, visa, and any required health certificates.

Visas: Research the visa requirements for your host country, apply well in advance, and ensure you have all supporting documents ready.

Financial Planning: Budget for all aspects of your international journey, including tuition, accommodation, food, transportation, and personal expenses. Explore scholarships and part-time job opportunities to supplement your income.

Navigating Airports and Customs Smoothly:

Airport Procedures: Arrive early, use online check-in, and have your documents ready. Familiarize yourself with security and boarding processes.

Customs Procedures: Declare necessary items honestly, understand prohibited items, and be prepared for customs inspections.

Settling In and Adjusting

Finding and Securing Accommodation:

Types of Accommodation: Explore options such as university dormitories, private rentals, homestays, and shared housing. Each has its benefits and challenges.

Securing Accommodation: Understand application processes, required documentation, and how to avoid scams. Make sure to check safety measures of the place.

Navigating the New Environment and Managing Daily Life:

Campus Orientation: Attend orientation sessions, campus tours, and familiarize yourself with key locations like libraries and health services.

Local Transportation: Learn about public transit options, transportation passes, and student discounts. Consider biking or walking as alternatives.

Daily Life Management: Find local supermarkets, understand healthcare services, and set up a local bank account.

Building Social Connections and Integrating into Campus Life:

Making Friends: Join clubs, attend social events, and actively participate in campus activities.

Cultural Adjustment: Learn about local customs and social etiquette, overcome culture shock, and respect local norms.

Effective Communication: Improve your language skills through practice, classes, and language exchange programs.

Cultural Immersion and Adaptation

Understanding and Respecting Cultural Differences:

Cultural Awareness: Understand the impact of culture on behavior and perceptions. Respect and appreciate cultural diversity.

Researching Your Host Culture: Learn about historical background, key cultural norms, significant events, and customs.

Developing Language Skills and Effective Communication:

Language Learning: Utilize classes, self-study, and language exchange partners to improve proficiency. Use language learning apps and online resources.

Non-Verbal Communication: Understand local body language, gestures, and personal space norms. Recognize and respect these non-verbal cues.

Engaging with Local Traditions and Communities:

Community Activities: Volunteer, join local clubs, and attend cultural events to immerse yourself in the community.

Local Traditions: Participate in traditional ceremonies, learn about local arts and music, and try traditional foods.

Academic and Social Integration

Balancing Academic Responsibilities with Social Activities:

Academic Structure: Understand the education system, course registration process, and grading methods in your host country.

Effective Study Habits: Develop good study techniques, time management skills, and balance between academics and social life.

Building Professional Skills and Networking:

Professional Relationships: Network with professors, peers, and professionals. Utilize social media platforms for professional networking.
Mentorship: Seek out mentors for guidance and support in your academic and career pursuits.

Leveraging Resources for Academic Success and Personal Growth:

Study Resources: Use libraries, online databases, study groups, and academic support services.
Extracurricular Activities: Engage in clubs, sports, and creative pursuits to enhance your personal growth and build a diverse network.

Health and Wellbeing

Maintaining Physical and Mental Health:

Healthcare Access: Register with local health services, understand your health insurance, and know where to find medical help.
Preventive Measures: Stay up to date with vaccinations, practice good hygiene, and be aware of local health risks.

Building Resilience and Managing Stress:

Stress Management: Practice relaxation techniques, time management, and organizational skills to reduce stress.
Resilience: Develop a positive mindset, learn from challenges, and seek growth opportunities.

Ensuring Safety and Accessing Medical Care:

Personal Safety: Stay informed about local safety concerns, practice situational awareness, and know emergency procedures.
Emergency Preparedness: Have an emergency plan, know contact numbers, and stay connected with your host institution's services.

Career Development

Setting Career Goals and Gaining Relevant Experience:

Career Planning: Identify your career aspirations, create a career plan, and set actionable goals.

Skill Development: Enhance both soft and technical skills through coursework, workshops, and extracurricular activities.

Networking and Building Professional Relationships:

Networking: Attend events, join professional associations, and use social media for building a professional network.

Professional Relationships: Maintain and leverage these relationships for career growth.

Exploring International Career Opportunities:

Global Careers: Understand the benefits of working internationally, research global job markets, and identify countries with favorable visa policies.

International Preparation: Develop cross-cultural skills, learn new languages, and prepare a globally competitive resume.

Returning Home and Reintegrating

Preparing for Departure and Understanding Reverse Culture Shock:

Departure Preparation: Complete academic and administrative tasks, plan farewells, and gather contact information.

Reverse Culture Shock: Recognize symptoms, prepare emotionally, and seek support during the transition.

Reflecting on the International Experience and Applying Lessons Learned:

Self-Reflection: Assess personal growth, document your journey, and share your experiences.

Application: Leverage your experience in academic and professional settings, highlight skills in job applications, and maintain international networks.

Staying Connected with International Networks and Pursuing Future Opportunities:

Connections: Stay in touch with friends, mentors, and alumni networks. Engage in global communities and events.

Future Opportunities: Explore further education, international careers, and volunteer programs. Promote global awareness and cultural understanding in your community.

By reflecting on these key themes, you can appreciate the full spectrum of your international journey and the invaluable experiences it has brought into your life. This comprehensive understanding will empower you to continue growing, learning, and making meaningful contributions to your personal and professional worlds.

Embracing Lifelong Learning

Continued Cultural Engagement

Encouraging Ongoing Curiosity and Openness to New Cultures:

Your international experience is just the beginning of a lifelong journey of cultural discovery. Embrace an open mind and curiosity, always seeking to learn about new cultures and perspectives. This ongoing engagement will enrich your life and broaden your horizons.

Participating in Cultural Events and Global Initiatives:

Stay connected to the global community by participating in cultural events, festivals, and international initiatives. Join local cultural organizations, attend global conferences, and engage with international causes. These activities keep you connected to the world and allow you to continue learning and growing.

Staying Informed About International Issues and Developments:

Keep abreast of global news and issues. Understanding international affairs not only makes you a more informed global citizen but also helps you stay connected to the broader world. Read international news, follow global trends, and stay engaged with issues that impact different cultures and communities.

Global Citizenship

Understanding the Responsibilities of Being a Global Citizen:

Being a global citizen means recognizing your role and responsibilities in the interconnected world. Promote cultural understanding, respect, and empathy in your interactions. Advocate for global causes and contribute to the betterment of the international community.

Promoting Cultural Understanding and Respect in Your Community:

Take the lessons and insights gained from your international experience and share them within your local community. Promote cultural diversity, organize intercultural events, and educate others about the importance of global understanding. Your experiences can inspire others to embrace cultural differences and foster a more inclusive environment.

Advocating for International Education and Programs:

Support and advocate for international programs and international education. Share your positive experiences and the benefits of cultural exchange with others. Encourage students to participate in these programs and help them navigate the process. Your advocacy can contribute to the growth and success of future international students.

Lifelong Learning

Emphasizing the Importance of Continuous Learning and Growth:

Lifelong learning is a crucial aspect of personal and professional development. Embrace opportunities for further education, whether through formal studies, online courses, or self-directed learning. Stay curious and committed to expanding your knowledge and skills.

Seeking Opportunities for Further Education and Professional Development:

Look for opportunities to further your education and professional growth. Attend workshops, seminars, and conferences related to your field. Consider pursuing advanced degrees or certifications that align with your career goals. Continuous professional development keeps you competitive and adaptable in an ever-changing world.

Embracing New Challenges and Experiences with a Positive Mindset:

Approach new challenges and experiences with a positive attitude. Each new situation is an opportunity to learn and grow. Embrace change, take risks, and be willing to step out of your comfort zone. This mindset will help you navigate life's uncertainties and seize new opportunities.

Personal Growth and Transformation

Reflecting on Personal Growth

Recognizing the Changes and Developments in Yourself:

Take time to reflect on how you have grown and changed during your international journey. Identify the skills, attitudes, and perspectives you have developed. Recognize the personal achievements and milestones you have reached and appreciate the journey you have undertaken.

Celebrating Achievements and Milestones Reached During the International Journey:

Celebrate your successes, no matter how small. Whether it is mastering a new language, building meaningful relationships, or overcoming cultural challenges, each achievement is a testament to your resilience and adaptability. Take pride in your accomplishments and acknowledge the hard work you have put in.

Understanding How the Experience Has Shaped Your Perspectives and Future Goals:

Consider how your international experience has influenced your future aspirations and goals. Reflect on how your experiences have shaped your worldview and personal values. Use these insights to guide your future decisions and ambitions, both personally and professionally.

Applying Lessons Learned

Using the Skills and Knowledge Gained to Navigate Future Challenges:

Apply the skills and knowledge you have acquired during your international program to future endeavors. Whether it is problem-solving, cross-cultural communication, or resilience, these abilities will serve you well in various aspects of life. Use them to tackle new challenges with confidence.

Implementing New Habits and Practices in Daily Life:

Incorporate the positive habits and practices you developed abroad into your daily routine. Whether it is a new approach to time management, a healthier lifestyle, or improved study techniques, these practices can enhance your overall wellbeing and productivity.

Sharing Your Experiences and Insights with Others:

Share your journey and insights with others. Whether through storytelling, presentations, or mentoring, your experiences can inspire and educate those around you. By sharing your journey, you contribute to a culture of learning and mutual understanding.

Final Encouragement and Inspiration

Overcoming Challenges

Acknowledging That Challenges and Setbacks Are Part of the Journey:

Recognize that challenges and setbacks are a natural part of any journey. They are opportunities for growth and learning. Embrace them as part of your experience and use them to build resilience and adaptability.

Encouragement to View Obstacles as Opportunities for Growth:

Every obstacle is an opportunity to learn something new and grow stronger. Approach challenges with a positive mindset, seeking the lessons they offer. This perspective will help you overcome difficulties and emerge more capable and confident.

Strategies for Maintaining Resilience and a Positive Outlook:

Develop strategies to maintain your resilience and positivity. Practice mindfulness, seek support when needed, and stay connected to your goals and values. These strategies will help you stay grounded and focused, even in the face of adversity.

Maximizing the Experience

Encouragement to Make the Most of Every Opportunity During the International Adventure:

Make the most of every opportunity that comes your way. Be proactive, curious, and engaged. Whether it is academic, social, or cultural, seize every chance to learn and grow.

Advice on Staying Proactive and Engaged Throughout the Journey:

Stay proactive and engaged in all aspects of your international program. Attend events, join groups, and seek out new experiences. Your active participation will enrich your experience and open doors to new opportunities.

Reminders to Take Time to Appreciate and Enjoy the Experience:

Amidst all the activities and challenges, take time to appreciate and enjoy your international experience. Reflect on the moments of joy and wonder and savor the unique experiences. This appreciation will enhance your overall satisfaction and fulfillment.

Staying Connected and Looking Forward

Maintaining Relationships

Importance of Keeping in Touch with Friends and Contacts Made During the International Program:

Maintaining the relationships you formed during your international experience is crucial. These connections can provide support, opportunities, and lifelong friendships. Make an effort to stay in touch and nurture these relationships.

Strategies for Maintaining Long-Distance Relationships:

Use technology to stay connected with friends and contacts from your international program. Regular communication, virtual meetups, and visits can help maintain these bonds. Be proactive in reaching out and keeping the relationships alive.

Planning Reunions and Future Visits:

Plan reunions and future visits with your friends from the international program. These reunions can strengthen your bonds and provide new shared experiences. Keep the spirit of your international adventures alive through these gatherings.

Future Opportunities

Encouragement to Explore Further International Opportunities:

Your international experience is just the beginning. Explore further international opportunities, whether for education, career, or personal growth. The world is full of possibilities waiting to be discovered.

Information on Scholarships, Grants, and Programs for Continued Global Engagement:

Research scholarships, grants, and programs that support further international engagement. These resources can help you pursue additional studies, work, or volunteer opportunities abroad. Take advantage of these opportunities to continue your global journey.

Inspiration to Pursue International Careers or Further Education Abroad:

Consider pursuing an international career or further education abroad. These experiences can enhance your professional and personal growth, providing unique opportunities and perspectives. Let your international experience inspire you to seek new horizons and continue your journey of discovery.

Conclusion

Final Reflections on the Exchange Experience as a Life-Changing Journey

Reflecting on your international experience it becomes clear that this journey is far more than just an academic endeavor. It is a transformative adventure that reshapes your worldview, enhances your personal growth, and broadens your horizons. The challenges you faced, the cultures you immersed yourself in, and the people you met have all contributed to a rich tapestry of experiences that will stay with you for a lifetime. This journey has helped you develop resilience, adaptability, and a deeper understanding of the world and your place in it.

Acknowledgement of the Reader's Efforts and Achievements

Your commitment to this international journey has been remarkable. From preparing and planning to adapting and thriving in a new environment, your efforts have paved the way for numerous accomplishments. You have navigated new academic systems, formed meaningful relationships, and immersed yourself in a different culture. These achievements are a testament to your determination, courage, and open-mindedness. Celebrate these milestones and recognize the hard work and perseverance that made them possible.

Encouragement to Continue Embracing New Experiences and Challenges

As you move forward, let the lessons and experiences from your exchange guide you. Continue to seek out new challenges and embrace opportunities for growth. Whether it is further education, international careers, or personal adventures, the skills and insights you have gained will serve you well. Stay curious, keep an open mind, and remain committed to lifelong learning and exploration. The world is full of opportunities waiting to be discovered, and your international experience has prepared you to seize them with confidence.

Closing Thoughts on the Lasting Impact of the Exchange on Personal and Professional Growth

The impact of your international experience will resonate throughout your life. Professionally, the intercultural competence, adaptability, and global perspective you have developed will make you a valuable asset in any field. Personally, the friendships, memories, and growth you have experienced will continue to enrich your life. This journey has equipped you with the tools to navigate a complex, interconnected world and to contribute positively to global understanding and cooperation.

As you reflect on this journey, remember that it is just the beginning. The skills, knowledge, and experiences you have gained are a foundation upon which you can build a future full of promise and potential. Embrace this foundation, continue to grow, and let your international experience be a constant reminder of your ability to adapt, learn, and thrive in any environment.

Appendices and Additional Resources

Introduction to Appendices

As you reach the conclusion of this comprehensive guide, it is important to recognize that your journey as an international student is ongoing. The appendices and additional resources provided here are designed to serve as a continuous support system, offering practical tools, detailed information, and further guidance to help you navigate every aspect of your exchange experience.

Purpose of Including Appendices and Additional Resources

The purpose of including these appendices and additional resources is to offer you a consolidated collection of valuable information that complements the main content of this guide. While the chapters have covered a wide range of topics essential for your success, the appendices provide specific, actionable details and references that you can refer to whenever needed. This section is your go-to resource for detailed information, templates, checklists, and contacts that will aid you throughout your international journey.

Overview of the Types of Resources Provided

The appendices encompass a variety of resources tailored to different aspects of your exchange experience:

Practical Tools and Templates:

Budget planning worksheets

Sample packing lists

Academic planning templates

Cultural research checklists

Detailed Information:

Health and safety guidelines

Visa and immigration information

Local transportation guides

Accommodation tips and resources

Contacts and Support Networks:

Important contact numbers (embassies, consulates, local authorities)

University support services

International student organizations and clubs

Online communities and forums

Further Reading and Learning:

Recommended books and articles on cultural adaptation and global citizenship
Online courses and workshops for language learning and skill development
Websites and apps for travel, communication, and cultural exploration

Encouragement to Utilize These Resources for Further Support and Information

These appendices are crafted to provide you with continuous support and to be readily accessible whenever you need additional information or guidance. Whether you are preparing for departure, navigating daily life in a new country, or planning your return home, these resources are here to assist you. Make the most of the tools and information provided, and do not hesitate to explore the additional reading and learning opportunities to further enrich your experience.

Your journey as an international student is a dynamic and evolving adventure. By utilizing these resources, you can enhance your preparedness, stay informed, and find the support you need to thrive in your new environment. Embrace these tools as essential companions on your path to personal and academic growth, ensuring that you have the knowledge and resources to make the most of every opportunity that comes your way.

Appendix A: Pre-Departure Checklists

Travel Documents

Passport and Visa Requirements:

- **Passport:** Ensure your passport is valid for at least six months beyond your planned return date. Apply for a renewal if necessary.
- **Visa:** Research visa requirements for your host country. Apply for the appropriate student visa well in advance and follow the instructions provided by the host country's embassy or consulate.

Copies of Important Documents:

- Make multiple copies of important documents, including:
- Passport
- Visa
- Acceptance letter from the host institution
- Health insurance card and documents
- Emergency contact information
- Academic transcripts and course registration documents
- Travel itinerary and accommodation confirmation
- Store these copies in different locations (e.g., one set with you, one set in your luggage, one set left with family or friends).

Financial Preparation

Budget Planning:

- Create a detailed budget that includes:
    - Tuition and academic fees
    - Housing costs
    - Transportation expenses
    - Food and daily living expenses
    - Health insurance
    - Personal expenses (entertainment, travel, etc.)
- Use budget planning worksheets to organize your finances. (see our website for digital resources)

Budget Planning Worksheet Example

Expense Category	Estimated Cost	Actual Cost	Notes
Tuition and Academic Fees			
Housing			
Transportation			Include flights, local transit, etc.
Food and Daily Living			
Health Insurance			
Personal Expenses			Entertainment, travel, etc.
Total			

Securing Financial Aid and Scholarships:

- Apply for scholarships, grants, and financial aid early.
- Confirm the receipt and amount of any awards and understand the disbursement schedule.
- Investigate part-time job opportunities and work-study programs in your host country.

Setting Up Bank Accounts and Access to Funds:

- Open a bank account in your host country, if possible.
- Inform your home bank about your travel plans to avoid issues with international transactions.
- Set up online banking and consider a backup payment method (e.g., an international credit card).

Health and Safety

Vaccinations and Health Check-Ups:

- Schedule a medical check-up and ensure you have all necessary vaccinations.
- Obtain an international certificate of vaccination if required by your host country.

Health Insurance Documentation:

- Confirm that your health insurance covers you while abroad.

- Carry health insurance cards and documents, including policy numbers and emergency contact information for your insurance provider.

Emergency Contact Information:

- Compile a list of emergency contacts, including:
  - Local emergency numbers in your host country
  - Contact information for your host institution
  - Embassy or consulate contact details
  - Family and friends' contact information
- Share this list with your family and friends.

Important Contacts List

Contact Type	Name/ Organization	Phone Number	Email Address	Notes
Emergency Services	Local Police, Fire			
Host Institution	International Office			
Embassy/Consulate				
Health Insurance Provider				
Family/Friends				

Packing Essentials

Clothing and Personal Items:

- Pack clothing suitable for the climate of your host country.
- Include versatile items that can be layered and are appropriate for both casual and formal settings.
- Remember essential accessories such as hats, gloves, and scarves if needed.

Electronics and Chargers:

- Bring essential electronics, such as a laptop, mobile phone, and chargers.
- Pack plug adapters and voltage converters compatible with your host country's electrical outlets.

Medications and Toiletries:

- Bring a sufficient supply of prescription medications along with a doctor's letter.
- Pack a basic first-aid kit and over-the-counter medications you might need.
- Include personal hygiene products and toiletries.

Packing Checklist

Item Category	Items to Pack	Notes
Travel Documents	Passport, visa, copies of important documents	
Clothing	Weather-appropriate clothing, versatile items	
Electronics	Laptop, phone, chargers, plug adapters, converters	
Medications	Prescription meds, first-aid kit, toiletries	
Academic Materials	Syllabi, textbooks, notebooks, stationery	
Personal Items	Photos, mementos, day bag, reusable water bottle	

Accommodation and Transportation

Securing Housing:

- Confirm your housing arrangements with your host institution or landlord.
- Keep copies of rental agreements and housing contracts.

Booking Flights and Transportation Arrangements:

- Book flights well in advance to secure the best rates.
- Arrange transportation from the airport to your accommodation (consider airport shuttles, taxis, or public transit).
- Familiarize yourself with local transportation options.

Academic Preparation

Course Registration and Academic Documents:

- Complete course registration and ensure you meet all prerequisites.
- Obtain syllabi and required textbooks or materials for your courses.

Contacting Host Institution Advisors:

- Reach out to your academic advisors and the international office at your host institution.
- Schedule an introductory meeting to discuss your academic plan and any support services available.

Appendix B: Important Contacts and Resources

Emergency Contacts

Local Emergency Numbers:

- **Police:** Dial the local emergency number for police services (e.g., 911 in the US, 112 in Europe).
- **Ambulance:** Dial the local emergency number for medical emergencies.
- **Fire Department:** Dial the local emergency number for fire emergencies.
- **Country-Specific Emergency Numbers:**
  - **United States:** 911
  - **United Kingdom:** 999 or 112
  - **Australia:** 000
  - **Canada:** 911
  - **Germany:** 112 (general emergency), 110 (police)
  - **Japan:** 119 (fire/ambulance), 110 (police)

Embassy and Consulate Contact Information:

- **Embassy:** Locate the contact information for your country's embassy in your host country. They can assist with various issues, including lost passports, legal problems, and emergencies.
- **Consulate:** Find the nearest consulate offices, which provide similar services as embassies but may be located in different cities.

Institutional Contacts

Host Institution International Office:

- **Primary Contact:** Include the phone number, email address, and office location of the international office.
- **Office Hours:** Note the operating hours for in-person visits or phone calls.
- **Services Offered:** Detail the services provided, such as orientation, housing assistance, cultural events, and academic support.

Academic Advisors and Mentors:

- **Advisor Contact Information:** Provide the name, phone number, email address, and office location of your academic advisor.
- **Mentor Contact Information:** Include the name, phone number, email address, and office location of your assigned mentor or any peer support contacts.

Healthcare Providers

Local Hospitals and Clinics:

- **Hospital Contact Information:** List the names, addresses, phone numbers, and websites of nearby hospitals.
  - Example: **City Hospital:** 123 Main Street, City, Country. Phone: +123-456-7890. Website: www.cityhospital.com
- **Clinic Contact Information:** Include similar details for local clinics that provide non-emergency medical care.

Mental Health Support Services:

- **University Counseling Center:** Provide contact information, including phone number, email, and location.
- **Local Mental Health Providers:** List nearby therapists, psychologists, and counseling services with contact details.
- **Emergency Mental Health Services:** Include hotline numbers and emergency contacts for mental health crises.
  - Example: **National Suicide Prevention Lifeline (USA):** 1-800-273-TALK (8255)

Legal and Regulatory Contacts

Visa and Immigration Offices:

- **Local Immigration Office:** Provide the address, phone number, email, and website for the nearest immigration office.
  - Example: **City Immigration Office:** 456 Government Building, City, Country. Phone: +123-456-7891. Website: www.cityimmigration.com
- **Host Institution Visa Support:** Include contact information for the university office that assists with visa issues.

Local Legal Aid and Support Services:

- **Legal Aid Services:** List local organizations that provide legal assistance, including contact information and types of services offered.

- Example: **City Legal Aid:** 789 Justice Lane, City, Country. Phone: +123-456-7892. Website: www.citylegalaid.com
- **Support Services for International Students:** Include details of organizations that offer support and advocacy for international students.
  - Example: **International Student Support Network:** Phone: +123-456-7893. Email: support@studentsupport.org

Emergency Contact List Template

Contact Type	Name/ Organization	Phone Number	Email Address	Address	Notes
Local Police					
Ambulance					
Fire Department					
Embassy					
Consulate					
Host Institution Intl Office					
Academic Advisor					
Primary Hospital					
Nearest Clinic					
University Counseling Center					
Local Mental Health Hotline					
Local Immigration Office					
Legal Aid Service					

Institutional Contact Information Template

International Office Contact Information:

- **Phone Number:** [Insert Phone Number]
- **Email Address:** [Insert Email Address]
- **Office Location:** [Insert Office Location]
- **Office Hours:** [Insert Office Hours]

Academic Advisor Contact Information:

- **Name:** [Insert Name]
- **Phone Number:** [Insert Phone Number]
- **Email Address:** [Insert Email Address]
- **Office Location:** [Insert Office Location]
- **Office Hours:** [Insert Office Hours]

Additional Resources

For further support and detailed information on navigating your exchange experience, refer to the following resources:

B.C. International Education Website: Visit Brilliant Consulting & Advocacy International Education website for additional tips, resources, and digital content to improve your international experience.

Host Institution Website: Visit your university's website for comprehensive information on student services, campus resources, and academic support.

Local Government Websites: Access up-to-date information on local laws, visa regulations, and public services.

Health and Safety Apps: Download apps that provide emergency contacts, health information, and safety tips for international travelers.

Online Student Forums: Join online communities where you can connect with other international students, ask questions, and share experiences.

Appendix C: Cultural Adjustment Tools

Culture Shock Stages

Detailed Descriptions of Each Stage:

Honeymoon Stage:

Description: This initial stage is characterized by excitement and fascination with the new culture. Everything seems fresh and interesting, and the differences are embraced with enthusiasm.

Tips for Coping:

Enjoy the Moment: Take advantage of your enthusiasm to explore and learn as much as you can.

Document Your Experiences: Keep a journal or blog to capture your first impressions and adventures.

Build Connections: Start forming friendships and join activities that interest you.

Frustration Stage:

Description: The initial excitement wears off, and the differences between your home culture and the host culture become more apparent. You may feel confused, frustrated, and homesick.

Tips for Coping:

Learn the Language: Improve your language skills to ease communication barriers.

Seek Support: Talk to fellow international students or a counselor about your feelings.

Stay Patient: Understand that this is a normal part of the adjustment process.

Adjustment Stage:

Description: Gradually, you begin to adjust to the new culture. You develop routines, become more comfortable with the local customs, and start to see the host culture more objectively.

Tips for Coping:

Create a Routine: Establish a daily schedule to create a sense of normalcy.

Stay Active: Engage in activities that make you feel at home, such as hobbies or sports.

Be Open-Minded: Continue to learn and adapt and view challenges as opportunities for growth.

Acceptance Stage:

Description: You fully embrace the new culture and feel comfortable in your host country. You have developed a sense of belonging and can navigate daily life with ease.

Tips for Coping:

Stay Connected: Maintain relationships with both locals and other international students.

Give Back: Volunteer or participate in community activities to deepen your connection to the host culture.

Reflect on Growth: Recognize and appreciate the personal growth and new perspectives you have gained.

General Norms and Etiquette

Overview of Common Cultural Norms in Various Regions:

North America:

- **Common Norms:**
    - Punctuality is highly valued.
    - Direct communication is appreciated.
    - Personal space is important.
- **Dos and Don'ts:**
    - Do be on time for appointments and meetings.
    - Do engage in small talk and be polite.
    - Do not invade personal space or touch others unnecessarily.

Europe:

- **Common Norms:**
    - Formality varies between countries; know your specific region.
    - Table manners are important, especially in Southern Europe.
    - Public transportation etiquette includes quietness and respect for personal space.
- **Dos and Don'ts:**
    - Do greet people with a handshake or appropriate greeting.
    - Do be aware of local dining customs.
    - Do not speak loudly or disruptively in public transport.

Asia:

- **Common Norms:**
    - Respect for elders and authority is paramount.
    - Non-verbal communication, such as bowing, is common.
    - Group harmony is often valued over individual expression.
- **Dos and Don'ts:**
    - Do use both hands when giving or receiving items.
    - Do remove shoes before entering homes.
    - Do not point feet at people or religious objects.

Middle East:

- **Common Norms:**
    - Hospitality is a significant part of the culture.

- Dress modestly and conservatively.
- Gender interactions may be governed by cultural or religious norms.
- **Dos and Don'ts:**
  - Do accept offers of food and drink graciously.
  - Do dress modestly, especially in public places.
  - Do not engage in public displays of affection.

Central and South America:

Social Interactions:

- Warm and friendly interactions are the norm.
- Personal space is less rigid compared to some other cultures; physical touch like hugs and cheek kisses are common.

Family Importance:

- Family ties are very strong and family gatherings are frequent.
- Respect for elders is highly emphasized.
  Time Perception:
- Time is perceived more flexibly; punctuality is less strict, especially for social events.

Dos and Don'ts Central America

Do's:

- **Greet Warmly:** Use a warm handshake or a light hug and cheek kiss for greetings.
- **Show Respect:** Use titles (Señor, Señora) when addressing elders and professionals.
- **Be Polite:** Express gratitude frequently and use polite phrases such as "por favor" (please) and "gracias" (thank you).
- **Share Meals:** Accept offers of food and drink; it is considered rude to refuse hospitality.
- **Engage in Small Talk:** Spend time chatting about non-business matters before getting down to business.

Don'ts:

- **Do not Rush:** Avoid rushing into business discussions without first engaging in social conversation.
- **Do not Be Distant:** Maintain eye contact and be expressive in conversations.
- **Do not Refuse Hospitality:** Refusing food or drink can be seen as disrespectful.
- **Do not Discuss Sensitive Topics:** Avoid sensitive topics such as politics, religion, and personal finances unless you know the person well.

- **Do not Point:** Pointing with your index finger is considered rude; use your whole hand or chin to indicate direction.

Dos and Don'ts South America

Do's:

- **Use Appropriate Greetings:** Greet with a handshake, hug, or kiss on the cheek, depending on the level of familiarity.
- **Dress Well:** Dress smartly for both social and business occasions; appearance is important.
- **Be Punctual for Business:** While social events are more flexible, punctuality is appreciated in business settings.
- **Respect Personal Space in Business:** Maintain a comfortable distance in formal business settings, though this may be closer than in North American or European contexts.
- **Learn Basic Phrases:** Using basic Spanish or Portuguese phrases shows respect and effort to integrate.

Don'ts:

- **Do not Be Impersonal:** Avoid being too formal or distant; warmth and friendliness are valued.
- **Do not Discuss Business Too Early:** Allow social conversation before business topics in meetings.
- **Do not Touch or Pat Heads:** Touching someone's head can be seen as offensive.
- **Do not Ignore Hierarchies:** Respect the hierarchical nature of business and social structures.
- **Do not Rush Through Meals:** Meals are social events; take time to enjoy and converse during dining.

Country-Specific Norms and Etiquette

Brazil:

- **Do's:**
  - Use "bom dia" (good morning), "boa tarde" (good afternoon), and "boa noite" (good night) for greetings.
  - Engage in personal discussions and show interest in family and personal lives.
  - Dress fashionably; Brazilians appreciate style.
- **Don'ts:**
  - Avoid discussing Argentina or comparing Brazil to other countries in a negative light.
  - Do not assume everyone speaks Spanish; Portuguese is the official language.

Argentina:

- **Do's:**
  - Use "usted" instead of "tú" when addressing elders or in formal situations.
  - Kiss on the cheek when greeting friends and acquaintances.
  - Show interest in football (soccer); it is a popular topic.
- **Don'ts:**
  - Do not be offended by direct communication; Argentinians can be very straight-forward.
  - Avoid discussing the Falklands/Malvinas conflict unless you know the person's views.

Mexico:

- **Do's:**
  - Greet with a handshake and a warm smile; friends may hug and kiss on the cheek.
  - Be polite and use titles such as Señor, Señora, and Señorita.
  - Accept offers of food and drink graciously.
- **Don'ts:**
  - Do not refuse invitations to social gatherings; it is important to show respect for hospitality.
  - Avoid being overly punctual for social events; arriving a little late is acceptable.

Colombia:

- **Do's:**
  - Use appropriate greetings such as a handshake or cheek kiss.
  - Show respect by addressing people with their titles.
  - Engage in conversations about family and personal interests.
- **Don'ts:**
  - Do not discuss the country's violent history or drug-related issues unless you know the person well.
  - Avoid being overly formal; Colombians are generally warm and informal.

By understanding and respecting these cultural norms and etiquette, you will be better equipped to navigate social and professional settings in Central and South America, fostering positive interactions and deeper connections.

Cultural Norms and Etiquette for Asia

Overview of Common Cultural Norms

Asia:

Respect for Authority and Elders: Hierarchies are respected, and deference is shown to those in positions of authority or to elders.

Group Harmony: Emphasis on maintaining harmony and avoiding confrontation in social and professional settings.

Non-Verbal Communication: Non-verbal cues, such as gestures and facial expressions, play a significant role in communication.

Dos and Don'ts East Asia

China:

- **Do's:**
  - **Greetings:** Use a handshake and slight nod; greetings are generally formal.
  - **Business Cards:** Present and receive business cards with both hands and take a moment to look at the card before putting it away.
  - **Gifts:** Give and receive gifts with both hands; small, meaningful gifts are appreciated.
  - **Respect:** Show respect for elders and authority figures.
  - **Politeness:** Use polite expressions and avoid confrontational language.
- **Don'ts:**
  - **Pointing:** Avoid pointing with your index finger; use your whole hand instead.
  - **Public Displays of Emotion:** Avoid showing strong emotions in public, such as anger or affection.
  - **Tipping:** Tipping is not customary and can be seen as rude.
  - **Discussing Sensitive Topics:** Avoid sensitive topics such as politics, Taiwan, and Tibet.

Japan:

- **Do's:**
  - **Bowing:** Bow when greeting, thanking, or apologizing; the depth of the bow depends on the formality.
  - **Business Cards:** Present and receive business cards with both hands and treat them with respect.
  - **Shoes:** Remove shoes before entering a home or certain traditional establishments.
  - **Punctuality:** Be punctual for meetings and social events.
  - **Quietness:** Keep noise levels low in public places, especially on public transportation.
- **Don'ts:**
  - **Pointing:** Avoid pointing at people or objects; use your whole hand instead.
  - **Eating in Public:** Avoid eating while walking or on public transportation.
  - **Tipping:** Tipping is not customary and can be considered rude.
  - **Blowing Your Nose:** Avoid blowing your nose in public; it is considered impolite.

South Korea:

- **Do's:**
  - **Bowing:** Bow when greeting, and use a handshake for business settings, often accompanied by a slight bow.
  - **Respect:** Show respect for elders and authority figures by using honorifics and polite language.
  - **Dining Etiquette:** Wait for the eldest person to begin eating before you start.
  - **Gift-Giving:** Offer and receive gifts with both hands.
- **Don'ts:**
  - **Pointing:** Avoid pointing with your index finger; use your whole hand.
  - **Public Displays of Affection:** Avoid excessive displays of affection in public.
  - **Personal Space:** Avoid physical contact beyond a handshake in professional settings.
  - **Writing in Red Ink:** Avoid writing someone's name in red ink, as it symbolizes death.

Dos and Don'ts of Southeast Asia

Thailand:

- **Do's:**
  - **Wai Greeting:** Use the traditional "wai" greeting, pressing palms together in a prayer-like gesture.
  - **Respect for the King:** Show respect for the royal family and refrain from criticizing them.
  - **Shoes:** Remove shoes before entering homes and temples.
  - **Head Respect:** Avoid touching people's heads; the head is considered the most sacred part of the body.
- **Don'ts:**
  - **Pointing:** Avoid pointing with your feet; it is considered disrespectful.
  - **Public Displays of Anger:** Avoid showing anger or frustration in public.
  - **Dress Modestly:** Dress conservatively, especially when visiting temples.
  - **Touching:** Avoid touching monks, especially if you are a woman.

Vietnam:

- **Do's:**
  - **Greetings:** Use both hands to shake hands or a slight bow; greet elders first.
  - **Respect for Elders:** Show respect to older people and authority figures.
  - **Shoes:** Remove shoes before entering homes.
  - **Dining Etiquette:** Wait to be shown your seat and for the eldest person to start eating.
- **Don'ts:**

- **Pointing:** Avoid pointing with your index finger; use your whole hand or chin.
- **Public Displays of Affection:** Avoid public displays of affection.
- **Sensitive Topics:** Avoid discussing the Vietnam War or political issues.
- **Gifts:** Avoid giving handkerchiefs, anything black, or yellow flowers, as these are associated with funerals.

Indonesia:

- **Do's:**
  - **Handshakes:** Use a gentle handshake and sometimes a slight bow; greet with "Selamat."
  - **Respect:** Show respect for elders and use polite forms of address.
  - **Modesty:** Dress modestly, especially in rural areas and religious sites.
  - **Right Hand:** Use your right hand for giving and receiving items.
- **Don'ts:**
  - **Pointing:** Avoid pointing with your index finger; use your right thumb or the whole hand.
  - **Touching:** Avoid touching someone's head, as it is considered impolite.
  - **Left Hand:** Avoid using your left hand for eating or handing things over.
  - **Public Displays of Affection:** Avoid public displays of affection.

Dos and Don'ts of South Asia

India:

- **Do's:**
  - **Namaste:** Use "Namaste" with hands pressed together in a prayer-like gesture as a greeting.
  - **Respect:** Show respect to elders and authority figures.
  - **Shoes:** Remove shoes before entering homes and places of worship.
  - **Right Hand:** Use your right hand for eating and giving/receiving items.
- **Don'ts:**
  - **Pointing:** Avoid pointing with your index finger; use your whole hand.
  - **Public Displays of Affection:** Avoid public displays of affection.
  - **Personal Space:** Maintain a respectful distance in professional settings.
  - **Left Hand:** Avoid using your left hand for eating or handing things over.

Nepal:

- **Do's:**
  - **Namaste:** Use "Namaste" with a slight bow as a greeting.

- **Respect:** Show respect for elders and use polite forms of address.
- **Shoes:** Remove shoes before entering homes and temples.
- **Right Hand:** Use your right hand for giving and receiving items.
- **Don'ts:**
  - **Pointing:** Avoid pointing with your index finger; use your whole hand.
  - **Public Displays of Affection:** Avoid public displays of affection.
  - **Touching:** Avoid touching someone's head.
  - **Left Hand:** Avoid using your left hand for eating or handing things over.

Pakistan:

- **Do's:**
  - **Handshakes:** Use a firm handshake for men; women may greet each other with a handshake or hug.
  - **Respect:** Show respect for elders and use titles and surnames.
  - **Hospitality:** Accept offers of tea or food when visiting someone's home.
  - **Right Hand:** Use your right hand for eating and giving/receiving items.
- **Don'ts:**
  - **Pointing:** Avoid pointing with your index finger; use your whole hand.
  - **Public Displays of Affection:** Avoid public displays of affection.
  - **Left Hand:** Avoid using your left hand for eating or handing things over.
  - **Discussing Religion:** Be cautious when discussing religious topics.

By understanding and respecting these cultural norms and etiquette, you will be better equipped to navigate social and professional settings across Asia, fostering positive interactions and deeper connections.

Cultural Norms and Etiquette for Africa

Overview of Common Cultural Norms

Africa:

Respect for Elders: Elders are highly respected, and their opinions are valued.

Community and Family: Strong emphasis on community and family ties; individuals often identify themselves in relation to their family and community.

Politeness and Courtesy: Politeness is important; greetings are a significant part of social interaction.

Non-Verbal Communication: Non-verbal cues such as gestures, facial expressions, and body language play a crucial role in communication.

Dos and Don'ts of East Africa

Kenya:

- **Do's:**
  - **Greetings:** Shake hands firmly; use both hands for a more respectful gesture.
  - **Politeness:** Use polite language and titles, such as Mr., Mrs., or Miss.
  - **Respect for Elders:** Show respect by using titles and offering seats to elders.
  - **Hospitality:** Accept food and drink when offered; it is considered polite.
  - **Dress Modestly:** Dress conservatively, especially in rural areas.
- **Don'ts:**
  - **Pointing:** Avoid pointing with your index finger; use your whole hand.
  - **Rushing Conversations:** Avoid rushing into business discussions; engage in small talk first.
  - **Public Displays of Affection:** Avoid public displays of affection.
  - **Political Discussions:** Avoid discussing politics, especially tribal politics.

Tanzania:

- **Do's:**
  - **Greetings:** Greet with a handshake and a smile; use the traditional Swahili greeting "Jambo" or "Habari."
  - **Respect:** Show respect to elders and authority figures.
  - **Hospitality:** Accept offers of food and drink; it is a sign of respect.
  - **Dress Modestly:** Especially in Zanzibar and coastal areas, dress conservatively.
  - **Politeness:** Use polite forms of address and show courtesy in conversations.
- **Don'ts:**
  - **Pointing:** Avoid pointing with your index finger; use your whole hand.
  - **Touching:** Avoid touching someone's head; it is considered disrespectful.
  - **Public Displays of Affection:** Avoid public displays of affection.
  - **Taking Photos:** Ask for permission before taking photos of people.

Dos and Don'ts of West Africa

Nigeria:

- **Do's:**
  - **Greetings:** Use a handshake and a smile; address people with titles and surnames.
  - **Respect for Elders:** Show respect by greeting elders first and using polite forms of address.
  - **Hospitality:** Accept food and drink when offered; it is a sign of respect.
  - **Politeness:** Engage in small talk before discussing business.
  - **Dress Smartly:** Dress smartly, especially in business settings.

- **Don'ts:**
  - **Pointing:** Avoid pointing with your index finger; use your whole hand.
  - **Public Displays of Affection:** Avoid public displays of affection.
  - **Touching:** Avoid touching someone's head; it is considered disrespectful.
  - **Rude Gestures:** Avoid using rude gestures, such as the thumbs-up sign.

Ghana:

- **Do's:**
  - **Greetings:** Greet with a handshake and a smile; use polite titles and surnames.
  - **Respect:** Show respect to elders and authority figures.
  - **Hospitality:** Accept food and drink when offered; it is a sign of respect.
  - **Small Talk:** Engage in small talk before discussing business.
  - **Modesty:** Dress modestly, especially in rural areas.
- **Don'ts:**
  - **Pointing:** Avoid pointing with your index finger; use your whole hand.
  - **Public Displays of Affection:** Avoid public displays of affection.
  - **Sensitive Topics:** Avoid discussing politics and religion unless you know the person well.
  - **Rude Gestures:** Avoid using rude gestures, such as the thumbs-up sign.

Dos and Don'ts of North Africa

Egypt:

- **Do's:**
  - **Greetings:** Use a handshake and sometimes a kiss on both cheeks for close friends.
  - **Respect:** Show respect to elders and authority figures.
  - **Hospitality:** Accept food and drink when offered; it is a sign of respect.
  - **Dress Modestly:** Dress conservatively, especially when visiting religious sites.
  - **Politeness:** Use polite forms of address and show courtesy in conversations.
- **Don'ts:**
  - **Pointing:** Avoid pointing with your index finger; use your whole hand.
  - **Public Displays of Affection:** Avoid public displays of affection.
  - **Religious Sensitivity:** Avoid discussing religion unless you know the person well.
  - **Taking Photos:** Ask for permission before taking photos of people or religious sites.

Morocco:

- **Do's:**
  - **Greetings:** Use a handshake and sometimes a kiss on both cheeks for close friends.
  - **Respect:** Show respect to elders and authority figures.

- **Hospitality:** Accept food and drink when offered; it is a sign of respect.
- **Dress Modestly:** Dress conservatively, especially when visiting religious sites.
- **Politeness:** Use polite forms of address and show courtesy in conversations.
- **Don'ts:**
  - **Pointing:** Avoid pointing with your index finger; use your whole hand.
  - **Public Displays of Affection:** Avoid public displays of affection.
  - **Religious Sensitivity:** Avoid discussing religion unless you know the person well.
  - **Taking Photos:** Ask for permission before taking photos of people or religious sites.

Dos and Don'ts of Southern Africa

South Africa:

- **Do's:**
  - **Greetings:** Use a handshake and a smile; greet people with "Hello" or "How are you?"
  - **Respect:** Show respect to elders and authority figures.
  - **Hospitality:** Accept food and drink when offered; it is a sign of respect.
  - **Politeness:** Use polite forms of address and show courtesy in conversations.
  - **Diverse Cultures:** Be aware of and respect the diversity of cultures in South Africa.
- **Don'ts:**
  - **Pointing:** Avoid pointing with your index finger; use your whole hand.
  - **Public Displays of Affection:** Avoid public displays of affection.
  - **Sensitive Topics:** Avoid discussing politics and race unless you know the person well.
  - **Rude Gestures:** Avoid using rude gestures, such as the middle finger.

Zimbabwe:

- **Do's:**
  - **Greetings:** Use a handshake and a smile; greet people with "Hello" or "How are you?"
  - **Respect:** Show respect to elders and authority figures.
  - **Hospitality:** Accept food and drink when offered; it is a sign of respect.
  - **Politeness:** Use polite forms of address and show courtesy in conversations.
  - **Community Spirit:** Embrace the community spirit and participate in community activities.
- **Don'ts:**
  - **Pointing:** Avoid pointing with your index finger; use your whole hand.
  - **Public Displays of Affection:** Avoid public displays of affection.
  - **Sensitive Topics:** Avoid discussing politics and land reforms unless you know the person well.
  - **Rude Gestures:** Avoid using rude gestures, such as the middle finger.

By understanding and respecting these cultural norms and etiquette, you will be better equipped to navigate social and professional settings across Africa, fostering positive interactions and deeper connections.

Cultural Norms and Etiquette for the Middle East

Overview of Common Cultural Norms

Middle East:

Respect for Elders: Elders are highly respected, and their opinions are valued.

Hospitality: Hospitality is a cornerstone of Middle Eastern culture; guests are treated with great respect and generosity.

Politeness and Courtesy: Politeness is essential; greetings are a significant part of social interaction.

Modesty: Modesty in dress and behavior is important, influenced by religious and cultural norms.

Non-Verbal Communication: Non-verbal cues such as gestures, facial expressions, and body language are crucial in communication.

Dos and Don'ts of the Middle East

General Middle Eastern Etiquette

Do's:

- **Greetings:** Use a handshake, often accompanied by a smile and verbal greetings. In some cases, close friends or family may greet with cheek kisses.
- **Respect:** Show respect to elders and authority figures, often by standing when they enter a room.
- **Hospitality:** Accept offers of food and drink; it is considered polite. Compliment the host on their hospitality.
- **Modesty:** Dress conservatively, especially in public places and religious sites. Women should cover their shoulders and knees, and in some countries, hair should be covered.
- **Politeness:** Use polite forms of address and show courtesy in conversations. Engage in small talk before discussing business.
- **Personal Space:** Maintain an appropriate distance during interactions. Same-gender individuals may stand closer together, but opposite-gender interactions are more reserved.

Don'ts:

- **Pointing:** Avoid pointing with your index finger; use your whole hand.

- **Public Displays of Affection:** Avoid public displays of affection, as they are generally frowned upon.
- **Left Hand:** Avoid using the left hand for eating, giving, or receiving items, as it is considered unclean.
- **Sensitive Topics:** Avoid discussing sensitive topics such as politics, religion, and local conflicts unless you know the person well.
- **Shoe Etiquette:** Do not show the soles of your feet or shoes; it is considered disrespectful.

Country-Specific Norms

Saudi Arabia:

- **Do's:**
  - **Greetings:** Use "As-salamu alaykum" (peace be upon you) as a common greeting. Respond with "Wa alaykumu as-salam" (and peace be upon you too).
  - **Respect for Religion:** Show respect for Islamic customs and practices. Be mindful of prayer times and religious holidays.
  - **Modesty:** Women should wear an abaya (long black cloak) and, in some cases, a headscarf. Men should avoid shorts and sleeveless shirts in public.
- **Don'ts:**
  - **Public Interaction:** Avoid public interactions between men and women who are not family members.
  - **Religious Sensitivity:** Do not discuss religious topics critically or question Islamic practices.
  - **Prohibited Items:** Avoid bringing prohibited items such as alcohol, pork products, and non-Islamic religious materials.

United Arab Emirates (UAE):

- **Do's:**
  - **Greetings:** Use "As-salamu alaykum" as a greeting. Shake hands with the right hand.
  - **Respect:** Show respect to local customs and traditions, especially during Ramadan.
  - **Hospitality:** Accept invitations to homes and compliment the host's hospitality.
- **Don'ts:**
  - **Public Displays of Affection:** Avoid public displays of affection, including holding hands and kissing.
  - **Photography:** Do not take photos of people, especially women, without their permission.
  - **Dress Code:** Dress modestly in public places; women should avoid tight or revealing clothing.

Egypt:

- **Do's:**
  - **Greetings:** Use "As-salamu alaykum" and shake hands. Close friends may kiss on the cheek.
  - **Hospitality:** Accept offers of food and drink and compliment the host.
  - **Respect:** Show respect for elders and avoid criticizing the government or politics.
- **Don'ts:**
  - **Public Displays of Affection:** Avoid public displays of affection.
  - **Religious Sensitivity:** Avoid discussing religion critically.
  - **Dress Code:** Dress modestly, especially when visiting religious sites.

Jordan:

- **Do's:**
  - **Greetings:** Use "As-salamu alaykum" and shake hands. Close friends may kiss on the cheek.
  - **Hospitality:** Accept offers of food and drink and compliment the host.
  - **Respect:** Show respect for elders and local customs.
- **Don'ts:**
  - **Public Displays of Affection:** Avoid public displays of affection.
  - **Sensitive Topics:** Avoid discussing politics, religion, and the Israeli-Palestinian conflict.
  - **Dress Code:** Dress modestly, especially in conservative areas and religious sites.

Iran:

- **Do's:**
  - **Greetings:** Use "Salaam" as a common greeting. Shake hands and place the right hand over the heart.
  - **Hospitality:** Accept offers of tea and food and compliment the host.
  - **Modesty:** Women should wear a headscarf and loose-fitting clothing covering arms and legs. Men should avoid shorts and sleeveless shirts.
- **Don'ts:**
  - **Public Interaction:** Avoid public interactions between men and women who are not family members.
  - **Criticism:** Avoid criticizing the government or discussing sensitive political issues.
  - **Dress Code:** Adhere strictly to the dress code, especially in public and religious sites.

By understanding and respecting these cultural norms and etiquette, you will be better equipped to navigate social and professional settings in the Middle East, fostering positive interactions and deeper connections.

Cultural Norms and Etiquette for Europe

Overview of Common Cultural Norms

Europe:

Punctuality: Being on time is highly valued across most European countries.

Formal Greetings: Greetings often include handshakes, and in some regions, kisses on the cheek are common.

Personal Space: Europeans generally respect personal space, but the level of closeness can vary by country.

Politeness and Courtesy: Using polite forms of address and saying "please" and "thank you" are important.

Dining Etiquette: Table manners are important, and dining can be more formal compared to other regions.

Dos and Don'ts of Europe

Do's:

- **Greetings:** Use a firm handshake, make eye contact, and greet with a polite phrase like "Good morning" or "Good afternoon."
- **Dress Code:** Dress appropriately for the occasion; Europeans often dress more formally than in some other cultures.
- **Respect for Privacy:** Respect personal privacy and avoid intrusive questions, especially about income, politics, or religion.
- **Table Manners:** Wait until everyone is served before starting your meal and use utensils properly. Keep your hands visible but not your elbows on the table.
- **Punctuality:** Arrive on time for social and business engagements.

Don'ts:

- **Loudness:** Avoid speaking loudly in public places, as it can be considered rude.
- **Personal Space:** Do not stand too close to others; maintain a respectful distance.
- **Interrupting:** Do not interrupt someone while they are speaking; wait for your turn to talk.
- **Tipping:** Tipping practices vary; know the local custom. In some countries, a service charge is included in the bill.
- **Assumptions:** Avoid making assumptions based on stereotypes; European cultures are diverse and varied.

Country-Specific Norms

France:

- **Do's:**
  - **Greetings:** Use "Bonjour" (Good morning) or "Bonsoir" (Good evening) followed by a handshake. Close friends might greet with cheek kisses (faire la bise).
  - **Politeness:** Use formal titles and polite forms of address, especially with strangers.
  - **Dining Etiquette:** Keep your hands on the table (not in your lap) during meals, and break bread with your hands.
- **Don'ts:**
  - **Personal Topics:** Avoid discussing personal finances, age, and salary.
  - **Interrupting:** Do not interrupt others; wait for a natural pause in the conversation.
  - **Tipping:** Tipping is not obligatory but rounding up the bill or leaving small change is appreciated.

Germany:

- **Do's:**
  - **Punctuality:** Be on time for all appointments and meetings.
  - **Greetings:** Use a firm handshake with direct eye contact. Greet with "Guten Tag" (Good day) or "Guten Abend" (Good evening).
  - **Formal Address:** Use titles and last names until invited to use first names.
- **Don'ts:**
  - **Personal Questions:** Avoid asking personal questions until you know someone well.
  - **Feet on Furniture:** Do not put your feet on furniture, especially not on chairs or tables.
  - **Crossing the Road:** Always use pedestrian crossings; jaywalking is frowned upon.

Italy:

- **Do's:**
  - **Greetings:** Use "Buongiorno" (Good morning) or "Buonasera" (Good evening) with a handshake. Friends may greet with cheek kisses.
  - **Expressiveness:** Italians are expressive and use hand gestures in conversation. Feel free to engage with similar enthusiasm.
  - **Dining Etiquette:** Wait for the host to start eating and use utensils properly. It is common to use both hands while eating.
- **Don'ts:**
  - **Tardiness:** Italians are more flexible with time for social events but be punctual for business meetings.
  - **Dress Code:** Avoid wearing shorts and flip-flops in churches or upscale restaurants.

- **Tipping:** Service is usually included in the bill but leaving a small tip for exceptional service is appreciated.

Spain:

- **Do's:**
  - **Greetings:** Use "Hola" (Hello) or "Buenos días" (Good morning) with a handshake. Friends and family often greet with cheek kisses.
  - **Dining Etiquette:** Lunch is the main meal and can be lengthy. Dinner is typically late, often after 9 PM.
  - **Politeness:** Use formal titles and polite forms of address, especially in business settings.
- **Don'ts:**
  - **Punctuality:** Spaniards have a more relaxed approach to time but being excessively late is still considered rude.
  - **Topics to Avoid:** Avoid discussing politics, especially regional independence issues.
  - **Dress Code:** Dress modestly when visiting churches or religious sites.

United Kingdom:

- **Do's:**
  - **Greetings:** Use "Hello" or "Good morning" with a handshake. First names are used quickly in informal settings.
  - **Queuing:** Always queue in an orderly fashion and wait your turn.
  - **Politeness:** Use "please," "thank you," and "sorry" frequently.
- **Don'ts:**
  - **Personal Space:** Maintain an appropriate distance in social interactions.
  - **Public Behavior:** Avoid being overly loud in public spaces.
  - **Tipping:** Tipping is common but not obligatory. A service charge may be included in the bill in restaurants.

Sweden:

- **Do's:**
  - **Greetings:** Use "Hej" (Hi) or "God dag" (Good day) with a handshake.
  - **Punctuality:** Be punctual for meetings and social events.
  - **Equality:** Treat everyone equally, showing respect regardless of status or gender.
- **Don'ts:**
  - **Personal Boasting:** Avoid boasting about personal achievements.
  - **Interruptions:** Do not interrupt others during conversations.
  - **Tipping:** Tipping is not mandatory; rounding up the bill or leaving small change is sufficient.

By understanding and respecting these cultural norms and etiquette, you will be better equipped to navigate social and professional settings in Europe, fostering positive interactions and deeper connections

Cultural Norms and Etiquette for Russia and Eastern Europe

Overview of Common Cultural Norms

Russia and Eastern Europe:

Formality in Social Interactions: Social interactions tend to be formal, especially in initial meetings.

Hospitality: Guests are treated with great hospitality and generosity.

Respect for Elders and Authority: Elders and authority figures are highly respected.

Direct Communication: People often communicate directly and straightforwardly.

Modesty: Modesty in dress and behavior is valued.

Dos and Don'ts General Russia and Eastern Europe

Do's:

- **Greetings:** Use formal greetings such as a firm handshake, direct eye contact, and appropriate verbal greetings like "Zdravstvuyte" (Hello) in Russia. Close friends may greet with cheek kisses.
- **Respect for Elders:** Show respect to elders by addressing them formally and offering them priority in social settings.
- **Gift-Giving:** Bringing a small gift when visiting someone's home is customary, such as flowers, chocolates, or a bottle of wine.
- **Dress Code:** Dress smartly and modestly, particularly in business and formal settings.
- **Punctuality:** Be punctual for meetings and social events, though some countries in the region may have a more relaxed attitude towards time.
- **Table Manners:** Keep your hands visible while eating but do not rest your elbows on the table. Wait for the host to begin eating before you start.

Don'ts:

- **Public Criticism:** Avoid publicly criticizing others or the government.
- **Personal Space:** Respect personal space and avoid standing too close to others.
- **Sensitive Topics:** Avoid discussing sensitive topics like politics, religion, and historical conflicts unless you know the person well.
- **Footwear:** Remove your shoes when entering someone's home unless the host indicates otherwise.

- **Tipping:** Know the local tipping customs; in some areas, it is expected, while in others, it is not as common.

Country-Specific Norms

Russia:

- **Do's:**
  - **Greetings:** Use a firm handshake and direct eye contact. Greet with "Zdravstvuyte" (Hello). Close friends may use "Privet" (Hi) and kiss on the cheek three times.
  - **Gift-Giving:** Bring a small gift when visiting someone's home. Flowers should be given in odd numbers, as even numbers are for funerals.
  - **Respect for Authority:** Show respect for elders and authority figures. Stand up when an elder enters the room.
- **Don'ts:**
  - **Smiling:** Do not smile at strangers; it can be seen as insincere.
  - **Empty Handshake:** Do not shake hands across a threshold or with gloves on; it is considered bad luck.
  - **Political Criticism:** Avoid criticizing the government or discussing politics in public.

Poland:

- **Do's:**
  - **Greetings:** Use a firm handshake and direct eye contact. Greet with "Dzień dobry" (Good day) or "Cześć" (Hi) for friends.
  - **Gift-Giving:** Bring flowers, chocolates, or wine when visiting someone's home. Flowers should be in odd numbers.
  - **Respect for Elders:** Show respect by addressing elders formally and offering them priority in social settings.
- **Don'ts:**
  - **Personal Space:** Avoid standing too close to others.
  - **Shoes:** Remove your shoes when entering someone's home.
  - **Sensitive Topics:** Avoid discussing politics, religion, and history unless you know the person well.

Hungary:

- **Do's:**
  - **Greetings:** Use a firm handshake with direct eye contact. Greet with "Jó napot" (Good day) or "Szia" (Hi) for friends.
  - **Politeness:** Use formal titles and polite forms of address.

- **Punctuality:** Be on time for meetings and social events.
- **Don'ts:**
    - **Personal Questions:** Avoid asking personal questions until you know someone well.
    - **Interruptions:** Do not interrupt others during conversations.
    - **Tipping:** Tipping is expected in restaurants and for services, usually around 10-15%.

Czech Republic:

- **Do's:**
    - **Greetings:** Use a firm handshake with direct eye contact. Greet with "Dobrý den" (Good day) or "Ahoj" (Hi) for friends.
    - **Politeness:** Use formal titles and polite forms of address.
    - **Respect for Elders:** Show respect for elders by addressing them formally.
- **Don'ts:**
    - **Feet on Furniture:** Do not put your feet on furniture, especially chairs and tables.
    - **Public Criticism:** Avoid criticizing others publicly.
    - **Personal Space:** Maintain an appropriate distance during interactions.

Romania:

- **Do's:**
    - **Greetings:** Use a firm handshake and direct eye contact. Greet with "Bună ziua" (Good day) or "Salut" (Hi) for friends.
    - **Gift-Giving:** Bring a small gift such as flowers, chocolates, or wine when visiting someone's home.
    - **Respect for Elders:** Show respect by addressing elders formally and giving them priority in social settings.
- **Don'ts:**
    - **Political Criticism:** Avoid discussing politics, especially the local government.
    - **Shoes:** Remove your shoes when entering someone's home.
    - **Punctuality:** Be on time for meetings and social events, though social events can have a more relaxed start time.

By understanding and respecting these cultural norms and etiquette, you will be better equipped to navigate social and professional settings in Russia and Eastern Europe, fostering positive interactions and deeper connections.

Appendix D: Language Learning Resources

Recommended Language Learning Apps and Websites:

Duolingo:

- **Description:** A popular app that offers courses in various languages through interactive lessons and gamification.
- **Website:** Duolingo

Babbel:

- **Description:** Provides language courses with a focus on real-life conversation skills. Offers a variety of languages.
- **Website:** Babbel

Rosetta Stone:

- **Description:** Uses immersive techniques to teach new languages. Known for its thorough approach and extensive course offerings.
- **Website:** Rosetta Stone

Memrise:

- **Description:** Focuses on vocabulary building and uses spaced repetition to help users retain new words.
- **Website:** Memrise

Tandem:

- **Description:** A language exchange app where users can practice speaking with native speakers through text, audio, and video.
- **Website:** Tandem

Tips for Practicing Language Skills Daily:

Daily Practice:

- Dedicate a specific time each day to practice language skills.
- Use language learning apps to reinforce vocabulary and grammar.

Language Exchange Partners:

- Pair up with a native speaker who wants to learn your language.
- Engage in regular conversations, focusing on everyday topics.

Immersive Activities:

- Watch movies, listen to music, and read books in the target language.
- Try to think in the language and use it in your daily activities.

Interactive Exercises:

- Join local language classes or conversation groups.
- Participate in online forums or social media groups where the language is spoken.

Real-Life Practice:

- Use the language in real-life situations, such as ordering food, asking for directions, or shopping.
- Do not be afraid to make mistakes; they are part of the learning process.

By utilizing these cultural adjustment tools, you can navigate the challenges of living in a new culture more effectively, develop a deeper understanding of cultural norms and etiquette, and enhance your language skills, all of which will enrich your overall exchange experience.

Appendix E: Academic Success Tools

Study Aids and Resources

Recommended Study Apps and Tools:

Quizlet: Create flashcards and study games to reinforce learning.

Evernote: Organize notes, to-do lists, and research materials in one place.

Grammarly: Enhance writing with grammar and spell-checking tools.

Forest: Improve focus and productivity by setting study timers.

Khan Academy: Access a wide range of free online courses and tutorials.

Anki: Use spaced repetition flashcards to boost memory retention.

Mendeley: Manage and share research papers and collaborate online.

Google Scholar: Find scholarly articles, theses, books, and conference papers.

Online Libraries and Research Databases:

JSTOR: Access academic journals, books, and primary sources.

PubMed: Explore biomedical and life sciences literature.

Google Books: Search the full text of books and access previews.

ERIC: Education Resources Information Center for educational literature and resources.

Project MUSE: Full-text versions of scholarly journals and books in the humanities and social sciences.

WorldCat: A global catalog of library collections.

Library of Congress: Extensive digital collections and research guides.

DOAJ: Directory of Open Access Journals for free, full-text, quality-controlled scientific and scholarly journals.

Academia: A full-text scholarly database featuring scholarly works published directly by the author.

Time Management Templates

Sample Study Schedules:

Weekly Study Schedule Template:

- **Monday to Friday:**
    - 8:00 AM - 9:00 AM: Review previous day's notes

- 9:00 AM - 12:00 PM: Class/Lecture
  - 12:00 PM - 1:00 PM: Lunch Break
  - 1:00 PM - 3:00 PM: Study Session 1 (Focus on specific subject)
  - 3:00 PM - 4:00 PM: Break/Exercise
  - 4:00 PM - 6:00 PM: Study Session 2 (Group study or library)
  - 6:00 PM - 7:00 PM: Dinner Break
  - 7:00 PM - 9:00 PM: Review and complete assignments
- **Saturday:**
  - 10:00 AM - 12:00 PM: Study Session (Review week's materials)
  - 1:00 PM - 3:00 PM: Project work/Research
- **Sunday:**
  - 10:00 AM - 12:00 PM: Study Session (Prepare for the upcoming week)
  - 1:00 PM - 3:00 PM: Rest/Leisure activities
  - **Daily Study Schedule Template:**
- **Morning:**
  - 7:00 AM - 8:00 AM: Breakfast and Planning
  - 8:00 AM - 9:30 AM: Study Session 1
  - 9:30 AM - 10:00 AM: Break
  - 10:00 AM - 12:00 PM: Study Session 2
- **Afternoon:**
  - 12:00 PM - 1:00 PM: Lunch Break
  - 1:00 PM - 3:00 PM: Study Session 3
  - 3:00 PM - 3:30 PM: Break
  - 3:30 PM - 5:00 PM: Study Session 4
- **Evening:**
  - 5:00 PM - 6:00 PM: Dinner Break
  - 6:00 PM - 8:00 PM: Review and complete assignments

Time Management Techniques:

Pomodoro Technique:

- Work for 25 minutes, then take a 5-minute break. After four sessions, take a longer break (15-30 minutes).

Eisenhower Matrix:

- Prioritize tasks by urgency and importance to focus on what truly matters.

SMART Goals:

- Set Specific, Measurable, Achievable, Relevant, and Time-bound goals.

Time Blocking:

- Allocate specific time slots for different activities to maintain focus and productivity.

ABC Method:

- Categorize tasks as A (most important), B (important but not urgent), and C (nice to do if you have time).

Academic Writing Guides

Tips for Writing Essays and Research Papers:

Understand the Assignment:

- Read the prompt carefully and make sure you understand the requirements.

Choose a Topic:

- Select a topic that interests you and meets the assignment criteria.

Research Thoroughly:

- Use credible sources such as academic journals, books, and reputable websites.

Develop a Thesis Statement:

- Create a clear, concise thesis that outlines your main argument.

Create an Outline:

- Organize your thoughts and structure your paper with an introduction, body, and conclusion.

Write a Draft:

- Start with a rough draft to get your ideas down, then refine and polish your writing.

Edit and Proofread:

- Review your work for clarity, coherence, and correctness. Check for grammatical errors and proper formatting.

Cite Your Sources:

• Give credit to the original authors and avoid plagiarism by using proper citation styles.

Citation Styles and Academic Integrity:

APA Style:

• Commonly used in social sciences. Includes in-text citations and a reference list.
• Example: (Smith, 2020)

MLA Style:

• Commonly used in humanities. Includes in-text citations and a works cited page.
• Example: (Smith 45)

Chicago Style:

• Commonly used in history and some other disciplines. Includes footnotes or endnotes and a bibliography.
• Example: ^1John Smith, *Book Title* (Publisher, Year), page number.

Academic Integrity:

• Understand the importance of academic honesty.
• Avoid plagiarism by properly citing all sources.
• Familiarize yourself with your institution's academic integrity policy.

Appendix F: Health and Wellbeing Resources

Physical Health

Recommended Fitness Apps and Workout Routines:

Fitness Apps:

- **MyFitnessPal:** Track your diet and exercise to reach your health goals.
- **Nike Training Club:** Offers a variety of free workouts guided by professional trainers.
- **FitOn:** Provides personalized workout plans and live classes.
- **7 Minute Workout:** Quick, effective workouts that you can do anywhere.
- **Sworkit:** Customizable workouts with videos demonstrating each exercise.

Workout Routines:

Beginner Routine:

- Warm-up: 5 minutes of light jogging or brisk walking
- Circuit (Repeat 3 times):
    - 10 bodyweight squats
    - 10 push-ups
    - 10 sit-ups
    - 10 lunges (each leg)
    - 30-second plank
- Cool-down: 5 minutes of stretching

Intermediate Routine:

- Warm-up: 10 minutes of dynamic stretching
- Circuit (Repeat 3 times):
    - 15 jump squats
    - 15 push-ups
    - 20 mountain climbers
    - 15 tricep dips
    - 1-minute plank
- Cool-down: 10 minutes of stretching

Advanced Routine:

- Warm-up: 15 minutes of cardio (running, cycling, etc.)
- Circuit (Repeat 4 times):
    - 20 burpees
    - 20 push-ups
    - 20 jump lunges (each leg)
    - 20 bicycle crunches (each side)
    - 2-minute plank
- Cool-down: 15 minutes of yoga or deep stretching

Healthy Eating Guides and Meal Planning Tips:

Healthy Eating Guides:

- **ChooseMyPlate.gov:** USDA guidelines for balanced meals, portion control, and nutrition tips.
- **Harvard Healthy Eating Plate:** Recommendations on building a healthy diet.
- **BBC Good Food:** Recipes and tips for nutritious meals.

Meal Planning Tips:

- **Plan Ahead:**
    - Create a weekly meal plan to save time and money.
    - Include a variety of foods to ensure a balanced diet.
- **Grocery Shopping:**
    - Make a shopping list based on your meal plan.
    - Stick to the outer aisles of the grocery store where fresh foods are typically located.
- **Prep in Batches:**
    - Cook larger portions and store leftovers for later.
    - Pre-cut vegetables and prepare ingredients ahead of time.
- **Healthy Snacks:**
    - Keep healthy snacks on hand, such as nuts, fruits, yogurt, and vegetables.
- **Stay Hydrated:**
    - Drink plenty of water throughout the day.
    - Limit sugary drinks and alcohol.

Mental Health

Mindfulness and Relaxation Techniques:

Mindfulness Apps:

- **Headspace:** Guided meditation and mindfulness exercises.
- **Calm:** Meditation, sleep stories, and relaxation techniques.
- **Insight Timer:** Free meditation app with a large library of guided sessions.
- **Simple Habit:** Quick mindfulness practices for busy people.
- **Smiling Mind:** Mindfulness programs for various age groups.

Relaxation Techniques:

- **Deep Breathing:**
  - Find a quiet place and sit comfortably.
  - Inhale deeply through your nose for 4 counts.
  - Hold your breath for 7 counts.
  - Exhale slowly through your mouth for 8 counts.
  - Repeat 4-5 times.
- **Progressive Muscle Relaxation:**
  - Tense each muscle group for 5-10 seconds.
  - Gradually release the tension and notice the relaxation.
  - Start from your toes and work your way up to your head.
- **Guided Imagery:**
  - Close your eyes and imagine a peaceful, calming scene.
  - Focus on the details, such as sounds, smells, and sensations.
  - Spend 5-10 minutes visualizing this scene.
- **Yoga and Tai Chi:**
  - Practice gentle movements and stretches to enhance relaxation.
  - Follow along with online classes or apps.

Online Counseling and Support Services:

Online Counseling Platforms:

- **BetterHelp:** Online therapy with licensed professionals.
- **Talkspace:** Connect with a therapist via text, video, or voice messages.
- **7 Cups:** Free emotional support and counseling.
- **ReGain:** Online relationship counseling.
- **MyTherapist:** Professional therapy for individuals and couples.

Support Services: (US based services):

Crisis Text Line: Text "HELLO" to 741741 for free, confidential crisis counseling.
National Suicide Prevention Lifeline: Call 1-800-273-8255 for 24/7 support.

SAMHSA National Helpline: Call 1-800-662-HELP (4357) for substance abuse and mental health services.

Work-Life Balance

Tips for Balancing Academic, Social, and Personal Life:

Time Management:

- Use a planner or digital calendar to organize your tasks and commitments.
- Prioritize your activities based on urgency and importance.
- Break larger tasks into smaller, manageable steps.

Setting Boundaries:

- Establish clear boundaries between study time and personal time.
- Communicate your limits to friends and family.
- Learn to say no to commitments that overwhelm you.

Self-Care Strategies:

- **Physical Self-Care:**
  - Engage in regular exercise and physical activity.
  - Ensure you get adequate sleep and rest.
  - Eat nutritious meals and stay hydrated.
- **Emotional Self-Care:**
  - Take time for hobbies and activities you enjoy.
  - Connect with loved ones and build a support network.
  - Practice mindfulness and relaxation techniques.
- **Mental Self-Care:**
  - Set realistic goals and celebrate your achievements.
  - Take breaks to avoid burnout and reduce stress.
  - Engage in activities that stimulate your mind, such as reading or puzzles.

Self-Care Strategies and Resources:

Creating a Self-Care Plan:

- Identify activities that recharge and relax you.
- Schedule regular self-care activities into your routine.
- Monitor your well-being and adjust your plan as needed.

Utilizing Self-Care Apps:

- **Shine:** Daily self-care tips, meditations, and motivational messages.
- **Happify:** Science-based activities and games to boost happiness.
- **Sanvello:** Tools for managing stress, anxiety, and depression.
- **Moodfit:** Mental health fitness tracker with customizable self-care plans.

Online Communities:

- **Reddit (r/selfcare):** Community discussions on self-care practices and tips.
- **HealthUnlocked:** Support network for health-related communities.
- **Mighty Networks:** Platform for building and joining online communities focused on well-being.

Appendix G: Career Development Resources

Resume and Cover Letter Templates

Sample Resumes and Cover Letters:

Sample Resumes:

- **Chronological Resume:** Focuses on your work history, starting with the most recent job.
- **Functional Resume:** Emphasizes skills and experiences rather than chronological work history.
- **Combination Resume:** Blends the elements of both chronological and functional resumes.
- **Student Resume:** Highlights education, internships, volunteer work, and part-time jobs.

Sample Cover Letters:

- **Application Cover Letter:** Used when applying for a specific job.
- **Referral Cover Letter:** Mentioning a mutual contact who referred you to the job.
- **Cold Contact Cover Letter:** Inquiring about potential job openings at a company.
- **Internal Position Cover Letter:** Applying for a different position within the same company.

Tips for Tailoring Applications to Specific Jobs:

Customize Your Resume:

- **Match Keywords:** Use keywords from the job description in your resume.
- **Highlight Relevant Experience:** Emphasize work experience and skills that align with the job requirements.
- **Use a Professional Format:** Ensure your resume is easy to read and professionally formatted.

Customize Your Cover Letter:

- **Address the Hiring Manager:** Use the hiring manager's name if possible.
- **Specify the Job Title:** Clearly state the position you are applying for.
- **Connect Your Experience to the Job:** Explain how your skills and experiences make you a good fit for the job.

Interview Preparation

Common Interview Questions and Answers:

General Questions:

- **Tell me about yourself:** Provide a brief summary of your background, education, and experience.
- **Why do you want to work here?** Highlight your knowledge of the company and your enthusiasm for the role.
- **What are your strengths and weaknesses?** Focus on your strengths and discuss how you are working to improve your weaknesses.

Behavioral Questions:

- **Describe a challenging situation and how you handled it:** Use the STAR method (Situation, Task, Action, Result) to structure your answer.
- **Give an example of a time you worked in a team:** Discuss your role and how you contributed to the team's success.
- **Tell me about a time you demonstrated leadership skills:** Provide a specific example and explain the outcome.

Technical Questions:

- **Explain a complex concept to someone unfamiliar with it:** Demonstrate your communication skills and expertise.
- **Describe a project you worked on and the technologies you used:** Highlight your technical skills and problem-solving abilities.
- **How do you stay updated with industry trends?** Discuss your methods for continuous learning and professional development.

Tips for Virtual and In-Person Interviews:

Virtual Interviews:

- **Test Your Technology:** Ensure your internet connection, camera, and microphone are working properly.
- **Choose a Quiet Location:** Find a quiet, well-lit space where you will not be interrupted.
- **Dress Professionally:** Wear professional attire as you would for an in-person interview.

In-Person Interviews:

- **Arrive Early:** Plan to arrive at least 10-15 minutes before the scheduled interview time.
- **Bring Copies of Your Resume:** Have multiple copies of your resume and any other relevant documents.
- **Maintain Good Body Language:** Offer a firm handshake, make eye contact, and sit up straight.

Professional Networking

Networking Strategies and Tips:

Networking Events:

- **Attend Industry Conferences:** Participate in conferences and seminars related to your field.
- **Join Professional Organizations:** Become a member of relevant professional organizations and attend their events.
- **Utilize University Events:** Take advantage of networking events hosted by your university or alumni association.

Online Networking:

- **LinkedIn:** Create a professional LinkedIn profile and connect with industry professionals.
- **Professional Forums:** Participate in online forums and discussion groups related to your field.
- **Webinars and Virtual Meetups:** Join webinars and virtual meetups to expand your network.

Informational Interviews:

- **Request Meetings:** Reach out to professionals in your field to request informational interviews.
- **Prepare Questions:** Prepare thoughtful questions about their career path, industry trends, and advice.
- **Follow Up:** Send a thank-you email after the meeting and keep in touch.

Recommended Professional Organizations and Associations:

General Professional Organizations:

- **American Management Association (AMA):** Offers resources and training for management professionals.
- **National Association of Colleges and Employers (NACE):** Provides career development resources for students and professionals.

Industry-Specific Organizations:

- **Institute of Electrical and Electronics Engineers (IEEE):** For professionals in the technology and engineering fields.
- **American Marketing Association (AMA):** For marketing professionals.
- **Society for Human Resource Management (SHRM):** For HR professionals.
- **Project Management Institute (PMI):** For project management professionals.

Appendix H: Returning Home and Reintegrating

Reverse Culture Shock

Detailed Guide on Managing Reverse Culture Shock:

Understanding Reverse Culture Shock:

- **Definition:** Reverse culture shock refers to the feelings of disorientation and discomfort that can occur when returning to your home country after an extended period abroad.
- **Symptoms:** These may include feelings of isolation, frustration, boredom, or longing for the host country.

Phases of Reverse Culture Shock:

- **Honeymoon Phase:** Initial excitement about being home and reuniting with family and friends.
- **Disenchantment Phase:** Feeling out of place, critical of home culture, or nostalgic for the host country.
- **Readjustment Phase:** Gradual adaptation to home culture, integrating experiences from abroad.
- **Resolution Phase:** Full adjustment, embracing a blend of both home and host country experiences.

Tips for Readjusting to Home Culture:

Stay Connected:

- **Maintain Communication:** Keep in touch with friends and mentors from your host country via social media, email, or messaging apps.
- **Share Your Experiences:** Talk about your exchange experience with family and friends to help them understand your journey and changes.

Stay Active:

- **Join Clubs and Groups:** Engage in activities or organizations that relate to your experiences abroad, such as language clubs, cultural groups, or international student associations.

- **Volunteer:** Get involved in community service or international projects to stay connected with global issues.

Reflect and Integrate:

- **Journal:** Write about your experiences, challenges, and achievements during your time abroad to process your emotions and thoughts.
- **Set Goals:** Use the skills and knowledge gained from your exchange to set new personal, academic, or professional goals.

Reflective Practices

Journaling Prompts for Reflecting on the Exchange Experience:

Personal Growth:

- What are the most significant changes you have noticed in yourself since your exchange experience?
- Describe a moment when you felt most challenged during your exchange and how you overcame it.

Cultural Insights:

- What cultural differences did you find most intriguing, and how did you adapt to them?
- Write about a memorable cultural experience that had a lasting impact on you.

Skills and Knowledge:

- How have the skills and knowledge you gained abroad influenced your academic or career goals?
- Reflect on a time when you applied something you learned during your exchange to a situation back home.

Activities for Integrating New Skills and Knowledge:

Cultural Sharing:

- **Host a Cultural Night:** Share food, music, and traditions from your host country with friends and family.
- **Presentations:** Give a presentation at your school or community center about your exchange experience and its impact on you.

Continuous Learning:

- **Language Practice:** Continue practicing the language spoken in your host country through classes, language exchange partners, or apps.
- **Global News:** Stay informed about current events in your host country to maintain a connection and understanding of its culture.

Maintaining Connections

Tips for Staying in Touch with Friends and Mentors:

Regular Communication:

- **Schedule Calls:** Set regular times for video or phone calls with friends and mentors from your host country.
- **Social Media:** Use social media to share updates and stay connected with your international network.

Collaborative Projects:

- **Joint Initiatives:** Work on collaborative projects with your international contacts, such as research, volunteering, or cultural exchanges.
- **Pen Pals:** Engage in traditional letter writing or email exchanges to maintain a personal connection.

Planning Future International Opportunities:

Further Education:

- **Study Abroad Programs:** Research opportunities for further studies in your host country or other international locations.
- **Scholarships and Grants:** Apply for scholarships and grants that support international education and research.
-

Career Development:

- **International Internships:** Look for internships with multinational companies or organizations with a global presence.
- **Networking Events:** Attend international conferences and networking events to expand your professional connections.

Volunteering and Travel:

- **Global Volunteer Programs:** Participate in international volunteer programs to gain new experiences and make a positive impact.
- **Travel Planning:** Plan future trips to visit friends and mentors abroad and explore new cultures and countries.

Glossary of Terms

Key Terms and Definitions

Common Terms Related to International Exchange and Cultural Adjustment

- **Acculturation:** The process of cultural change and psychological adaptation that occurs when individuals from different cultures come into contact.
- **Culture Shock:** The feelings of confusion, disorientation, and anxiety that individuals may experience when exposed to a new and unfamiliar cultural environment.
- **Cultural Assimilation:** The process by which individuals adopt the cultural norms and values of the host country, often leading to the loss of aspects of their original culture.
- **Cultural Competence:** The ability to understand, communicate with, and effectively interact with people across cultures.
- **Exchange Program:** A program in which students from one institution study at another institution, often in a different country, for a set period.
- **Global Citizenship:** Recognizing and acting upon one's responsibilities towards the global community and understanding the interconnectivity of the world's people and cultures.
- **Intercultural Communication:** The exchange of information between individuals from different cultures, involving both verbal and non-verbal communication.
- **Reverse Culture Shock:** The feelings of confusion, disorientation, and anxiety that individuals may experience when returning to their home culture after an extended period abroad.

Academic Terminology and Concepts

- **Academic Advisor:** A faculty or staff member who provides guidance on course selection, academic planning, and other educational concerns.
- **Academic Integrity:** The commitment to honesty, trust, fairness, respect, and responsibility in academic work, avoiding cheating, plagiarism, and other forms of academic dishonesty.
- **Credit Transfer:** The process by which academic credits earned at one institution are recognized and accepted by another institution.
- **Curriculum:** The set of courses and their content offered at a school or university.
- **GPA (Grade Point Average):** A standard way of measuring academic achievement in the U.S., calculated as an average of grades received in courses.

- **Plagiarism:** The act of using someone else's work or ideas without giving proper credit, considered a serious academic offense.
- **Prerequisite:** A course or requirement that must be completed before enrolling in a more advanced course.
- **Syllabus:** An outline of the topics, assignments, exams, and policies for a particular course, provided by the instructor at the beginning of the term.

Health and Wellbeing Vocabulary

- **Counseling Services:** Professional services provided by trained counselors to help individuals manage mental health issues, stress, and personal challenges.
- **Health Insurance:** A type of insurance coverage that pays for medical and surgical expenses incurred by the insured.
- **Mental Health:** A state of well-being in which an individual realizes their abilities, can cope with normal stresses, work productively, and contribute to their community.
- **Preventive Health Measures:** Actions taken to prevent disease or injury, rather than treating them once they occur. This includes vaccinations, regular health check-ups, and healthy lifestyle choices.
- **Resilience:** The capacity to recover quickly from difficulties and adapt well in the face of adversity, trauma, or significant stress.
- **Stress Management:** Techniques and strategies used to control a person's level of stress, including relaxation techniques, exercise, and time management.
- **Telehealth:** The use of electronic information and telecommunications technologies to provide health care services remotely.
- **Wellbeing:** A state of being comfortable, healthy, and happy, encompassing both physical and mental health.

Additional Resources

Recommended Reading List

Books on Cultural Adjustment, International Education, and Personal Growth:

"The Art of Crossing Cultures" by Craig Storti:

- A comprehensive guide on managing cultural transitions and navigating cross-cultural encounters effectively.

"Third Culture Kids: Growing Up Among Worlds" by David C. Pollock and Ruth E. Van Reken:

- An insightful book exploring the experiences and challenges faced by individuals growing up in multiple cultures.

"Cultural Intelligence: Living and Working Globally" by David C. Thomas and Kerr Inkson:

- Provides strategies and tools for developing cultural intelligence and enhancing global interactions.

"Global Dexterity: How to Adapt Your Behavior Across Cultures without Losing Yourself in the Process" by Andy Molinsky:

- Offers practical advice on adapting behavior to different cultural contexts while maintaining authenticity.

"The Lonely Planet Guide to the World" by Lonely Planet:

- An extensive travel guide that provides information on destinations, cultural tips, and travel advice.

Academic Texts Related to Various Fields of Study:

"The Craft of Research" by Wayne C. Booth, Gregory G. Colomb, and Joseph M. Williams:

- A valuable resource for conducting academic research and writing research papers effectively.

"Writing for Academic Success" by Gail Craswell and Megan Poore:

- Offers guidance on developing strong academic writing skills and producing high-quality academic work.

"International Business: Competing in the Global Marketplace" by Charles W. L. Hill:

- A comprehensive textbook on international business, covering global strategies, management, and cultural considerations.

"Introduction to International Relations: Theories and Approaches" by Robert Jackson and Georg Sørensen:

- An essential text for understanding the key theories and approaches in international relations.

"Psychology: An Introduction" by Benjamin B. Lahey:

- A foundational textbook for psychology students, covering various aspects of psychological theories and practices.

Useful Websites and Online Platforms

Travel Planning and Safety Websites:

Travel.state.gov:

- The U.S. Department of State's website providing travel advisories, passport and visa information, and safety tips.

Centers for Disease Control and Prevention (CDC) - Traveler's Health:

- Offers health and safety recommendations for international travelers, including vaccination requirements and travel notices.

Lonely Planet:

- A popular travel guide website offering destination information, travel tips, and itineraries.

TripAdvisor:

- A comprehensive travel platform with reviews, recommendations, and forums for planning trips.

Academic and Research Databases:

Google Scholar:

- A freely accessible web search engine for scholarly articles, theses, books, and conference papers across various disciplines.

JSTOR:

- A digital library providing access to academic journals, books, and primary sources in multiple fields of study.

PubMed:

- A database of biomedical literature, including research articles, clinical studies, and reviews, maintained by the National Center for Biotechnology Information (NCBI).

ERIC (Education Resources Information Center):

- An online library of education research and information, sponsored by the U.S. Department of Education.

Career Development and Job Search Platforms:

LinkedIn:

- A professional networking site for building connections, searching for jobs, and showcasing professional accomplishments.

Indeed:

- A job search engine that aggregates job postings from various sources, including company career pages and job boards.

Glassdoor:

- A platform that provides company reviews, salary information, and job listings, helping job seekers make informed career decisions.

Handshake:

- A career services platform connecting students and recent graduates with employers and career opportunities.

Mobile Apps

Travel and Navigation Apps:

Google Maps:

- An essential app for navigation, providing directions, traffic updates, and information on local businesses and attractions.

TripIt:

- A travel planning app that organizes travel itineraries, reservations, and confirmations in one place.

Skyscanner:

- A travel search engine app for finding flights, hotels, and car rentals at competitive prices.

Grab:

- An essential app for finding rideshares (the app searches multiple rideshare providers at once), food, grocery, and general delivery. This app also includes features for bill pay and additional discount services across SE Asia.

Bolt:

- A rideshare app generally used across SE Asia and Europe.

Language Learning and Translation Apps:

Duolingo:

- A popular language learning app offering interactive lessons in multiple languages.

Babbel:

- A language learning app with courses designed by language experts, focusing on practical conversation skills.

Google Translate:

- An app providing instant translations of text, speech, images, and real-time conversations in various languages.

Health and Fitness Apps:

MyFitnessPal:

- A fitness app for tracking diet, exercise, and nutrition, helping users achieve their health and fitness goals.

Headspace:

- A mindfulness and meditation app offering guided meditation sessions, sleep aids, and relaxation techniques.

Nike Training Club:

- A fitness app providing workout routines, training plans, and expert advice for various fitness levels and goals.

References

American Psychological Association. (2020). *Publication manual of the American Psychological Association* (7th ed.). American Psychological Association.

American Psychological Association. (n.d.). *About APA*. Retrieved from https://www.apa.org/about/

Babbel. (n.d.). *Language learning app*. Retrieved from https://www.babbel.com/

BetterHelp. (n.d.). *Online counseling*. Retrieved from https://www.betterhelp.com/

Booth, W. C., Colomb, G. G., & Williams, J. M. (2016). *The craft of research* (4th ed.). University of Chicago Press.

Calm. (n.d.). *Meditation and relaxation app*. Retrieved from https://www.calm.com/

Centers for Disease Control and Prevention. (n.d.). *Traveler's health*. Retrieved from https://wwwnc.cdc.gov/travel

Craswell, G., & Poore, M. (2011). *Writing for academic success* (2nd ed.). Sage.

College Board. (n.d.). *Education resources*. Retrieved from https://www.collegeboard.org/

Duolingo. (n.d.). *Language learning app*. Retrieved from https://www.duolingo.com/

ERIC (Education Resources Information Center). (n.d.). *ERIC - Institute of Education Sciences*. Retrieved from https://eric.ed.gov/

European Commission. (n.d.). *Erasmus+ Programme*. Retrieved from https://ec.europa.eu/programmes/erasmus-plus/

Glassdoor. (n.d.). *Company reviews and job search*. Retrieved from https://www.glassdoor.com/

Google Maps. (n.d.). *Navigation app*. Retrieved from https://www.google.com/maps

Google Scholar. (n.d.). *Google Scholar*. Retrieved from https://scholar.google.com/

Handshake. (n.d.). *Career services platform*. Retrieved from https://www.joinhandshake.com/

Headspace. (n.d.). *Mindfulness and meditation app*. Retrieved from https://www.headspace.com/

Hill, C. W. L. (2021). *International business: Competing in the global marketplace* (13th ed.). McGraw-Hill Education.

IAESTE (International Association for the Exchange of Students for Technical Experience). (n.d.). *IAESTE International*. Retrieved from https://iaeste.org/

Indeed. (n.d.). *Job search engine*. Retrieved from https://www.indeed.com/

Jackson, R., & Sørensen, G. (2016). *Introduction to international relations: Theories and approaches* (6th ed.). Oxford University Press.

JSTOR. (n.d.). *JSTOR digital library*. Retrieved from https://www.jstor.org/

LinkedIn. (n.d.). *Professional networking site*. Retrieved from https://www.linkedin.com/

Lonely Planet. (2021). *The Lonely Planet guide to the world* (13th ed.). Lonely Planet.

Lonely Planet. (n.d.). *Travel guide*. Retrieved from https://www.lonelyplanet.com/

Molinsky, A. (2013). *Global dexterity: How to adapt your behavior across cultures without losing yourself in the process*. Harvard Business Review Press.

MyFitnessPal. (n.d.). *Fitness app*. Retrieved from https://www.myfitnesspal.com/

NAFSA (National Association of Foreign Student Advisers). (n.d.). *NAFSA: Association of International Educators*. Retrieved from https://www.nafsa.org/

National Center for Biotechnology Information. (n.d.). *PubMed*. Retrieved from https://pubmed.ncbi.nlm.nih.gov/

Nike Training Club. (n.d.). *Fitness app*. Retrieved from https://www.nike.com/ntc-app

Pollock, D. C., & Van Reken, R. E. (2009). *Third culture kids: Growing up among worlds* (3rd ed.). Nicholas Brealey Publishing.

Skyscanner. (n.d.). *Travel search engine*. Retrieved from https://www.skyscanner.com/

Storti, C. (2001). *The art of crossing cultures* (2nd ed.). Nicholas Brealey Publishing.

Thomas, D. C., & Inkson, K. (2017). *Cultural intelligence: Living and working globally* (3rd ed.). Berrett-Koehler Publishers.

TripAdvisor. (n.d.). *Travel platform.* Retrieved from https://www.tripadvisor.com/

TripIt. (n.d.). *Travel planning app.* Retrieved from https://www.tripit.com/

U.S. Department of State. (n.d.). *Travel.state.gov.* Retrieved from https://travel.state.gov/

Brandon Arroues, M.Ed.

Brandon Arroues is an accomplished educator and consultant with a master's degree in Instructional Design. He has earned numerous scholarships and excellence awards, including the Excellence Award in Research Writing and the Excellence Award in Classroom Management, Engagement, and Motivation. As a member of Kappa Delta Pi, the International Honor Society in Education, Brandon has demonstrated a commitment to academic excellence and professional growth.

Brandon's educational journey is marked by continuous learning and research. He is actively engaged in research in educational psychology, counseling, and phenomenology, and is currently pursuing a Ph.D. in Industrial and Organizational Psychology with a focus on Evidence-based Coaching.

Brandon began his career in international education in 2013 with his first role in Shandong, China. Since then, he has had the privilege of living and working across the United States, Europe, Eastern Asia, and Southeast Asia. His extensive experience includes roles in general education, special education, administration, and counseling within the international education sector.

In 2018, Brandon founded Brilliant Consulting & Advocacy, a consultancy dedicated to supporting individuals and institutions in navigating the complexities of education and mental wellness. His work focuses on enhancing outcomes through innovative strategies and personalized support.

Brandon's passion for international education and mental wellness is driven by his belief in the transformative power of cross-cultural experiences. Through his work, he aims to empower others to embrace new challenges and grow personally, academically, and professionally.

When he is not working, Brandon enjoys traveling, exploring new cultures, engaging in research, arts and crafting, and spending time with loved ones. He is always eager to connect with readers and fellow educators to share insights and foster a global community of learning.